CHRISTIAN ETHICS FOR TODAY

CONTEMPORARY COLLEGE THEOLOGY SERIES

GENERAL EDITORS: J. FRANK DEVINE, S.J.

BOSTON COLLEGE

RICHARD W. ROUSSEAU, S.J.

FAIRFIELD UNIVERSITY

CHRISTIAN ETHICS FOR TODAY is one of the volumes in the Christian Living section of the Series.

CHRISTIAN
ETHICS
for TODAY

THOMAS A. WASSMER, S.J.

THE BRUCE PUBLISHING COMPANY / *Milwaukee*

*TO MY INCOMPARABLE MOTHER AND FATHER
WHO TRAINED ME IN BOTH AN ETHIC OF CONVICTION
AND AN ETHIC OF RESPONSIBILITY
AND WHO ALLOWED ME TO RESOLVE THE DIALECTICAL
TENSION BETWEEN THESE TWO ETHICS*

Library of Congress Catalog Card Number: 69-17477
Copyright © 1969 The Bruce Publishing Company
Made in the United States of America

EDITORS' INTRODUCTION
THE CONTEMPORARY COLLEGE THEOLOGY SERIES

This series begins with the presupposition that theology is necessary. It is necessary if Christian intelligence is to search for meaning in its dialogue with God, man, and the world. Since Christian intelligence is not the exclusive possession of the theological specialist or the cleric, the search must be carried on in all those areas of life, secular as well as religious, including the college situation, where meaning is to be found.

This search is a peaceful one, for in some mysterious way it has already achieved its goal: the vision of faith and the fullness of love. Still it remain a relentless and universal search. Its inner certainty must radiate out not only to the edges of the mind but also into the farthest recesses of the world. We could call it "lay" theology, but this word seems too pale a description for such an exciting enterprise of the Christian life.

In view of this, the editors of this series are convinced that new questions had to be asked, new structures created, and new books written. These books would be neither catechetical nor apologetic. They would be purely and simply theological. The primary audience would be believers, but all thinking men would find them useful. In scope they would be broad enough to ensure perspective. They would be scholarly enough to be intellectually relevant. They would avoid pedantry. In short, they would try to present a rich and deep understanding of Christian revelation in such a way that today's college students would be able to respond with a Christian faith and life that are both culturally mature and scientifically precise. Finally, the authors of these books would be, for the most part, teachers in colleges and universities where much of the contemporary theological dialogue is now going on.

The series falls into four parts: biblical, historical, ecclesial, and ethical. The divisions were not predetermined by the editors. They follow the shape of the most vigorous theological work now being done.

The books in the biblical section are intended to go beyond the traditional treatment of Bible history and the now familiar perspectives of salvation history. They concentrate on various books of the Bible. Their method has been especially designed for college work. Tentatively it might be called "exegetical theology." Every verse is not considered after the fashion of a commentary, nor are narratives developed as a biography, nor is there any attempt to create large theological syntheses. Rather the individual books are studied in chronological sequence; key passages are treated in detail and the rest are summarized. At the same time some attention is paid to the growing theological synthesis.

Since scholastic theology already is represented by individual works and sets of textbooks, the books in our historical section study dogmatic questions from a developmental point of view. In this way the editors hope to make the college students more aware of the great wealth of theological thinking that recent historico-theological studies have uncovered. This method, which is more inductive than deductive, should happily coincide with the thought processes of the college student. The three basic poles for synthesis are: God, Christ, and Man. In each area the historical development will be studied and a significant number of basic source texts presented. The problems raised in these studies will range all the way from Augustinian pessimism to Teilhardian optimism.

The textbooks for the third part of the series will deal with issues of great contemporary importance. They will examine questions discussed by the Second Vatican Council. As the name implies, ecclesial theology must first concern itself with Church, what the Church knows herself to be, as expressed in the insights of the new *Constitution on the Church* and with the more significant of the Church's allied concerns: other world religions, American Protestantism, its history, its motivating forces and spirit, and finally the new sacramental theology so enriched by the many magnificent liturgical advances. All of this growth has brought a wider and deeper appreciation of the nature of the Roman Catholic Church and her relationship, rooted in understanding and love, with the whole world.

The fourth and final section of the series is devoted explicitly to Christian moral response. The editors subscribe to the position that the proper place for the Catholic college or university to examine ethical questions is in a revelational rather than in a purely philosophical context. In addition to the "virtue" divisions of the *Summa* or the classic moral theology text, designed primarily for confessors, there is a need and a place for a "Christian ethics" that reflects the new insights which both biblical and dogmatic theology can provide. These books will strive to be openly Christian in spirit, eclectic in approach, up to date in scholarship, and will address themselves to those ethical problems which are most real to the modern American mind.

Finally, the editors would like to express their thanks to all those whose interest, advice, and cooperation have made this series possible. They are especially grateful to Dr. William May of The Bruce Publishing Company, who not only initiated the project and sustained it through the inevitable disappointments and complications, but contributed so much of his editorial skill to its final shape. To the individual authors who so graciously added to their heavy burden of academic responsibility by undertaking these books, we can only express the hope that their share in the shaping and influencing of the American Catholic community of today and of tomorrow will be far more meaningful to them than any meager thanks of ours.

> The Editors,
> REV. J. FRANK DEVINE, S.J., Boston College
> REV. RICHARD W. ROUSSEAU, S.J., Fairfield University

Acknowledgments

We are grateful to the following for graciously giving us permission to reprint copyrighted material in CHRISTIAN ETHICS FOR TODAY:

The America Press, New York, for excerpts from Richard McCormick's "Aspects of the Moral Question" (*America*, December 9, 1967):

The Ave Maria Press, Notre Dame, Indiana, for excerpts from R. Tinnes' review of Josef Fuch's *Natural Law* (*Ave Maria*, January 1, 1966);

The *Catholic Lawyer*, Brooklyn, for excerpts from George Regan's "Natural Law in the Church Today" (*The Catholic Lawyer*, January, 1967);

The *Commonweal*, New York, for excerpts from Brian Wicker's "Law, Love and Politics" (*Commonweal*, November 25, 1966);

The Critic, Chicago, for excerpts from Gregory Baum's "The Christian Adventure: Risk and Renewal" (*The Critic*, 33, 1965);

Helicon Press, Baltimore, for excerpts from Louis Dupre's *Contraception and Catholics* and from Iltyd Evans' *Light on the Natural Law;*

Herder and Herder, New York, for excerpts from Justus George Lawler's "On Discovering the Natural Law," in *Contraception and Holiness*; and for excerpts from Karl Rahner's *The Christian of the Future;*

The Heythrop Journal, Oxon, England, for excerpts from an article by Frederick Copleston in the April, 1967 issue of *The Heythrop Journal;*

Holt, Rinehart, and Winston, Inc., New York, for excerpts from William F. May's *A Catalogue of Sins;*

ix

International Philosophical Quarterly, New York, for excerpts from Charles Fay's "Human Evolution: A Challenge to Thomistic Ethics" (*International Philosophical Quarterly*, Vol. II, 1962);

Little, Brown & Company, Boston, for excerpts from David W. Louisell's "Transplantation: Existing Legal Constraints," from the Ciba Foundation Symposium *Ethics in Medical Progress: With Special Reference to Transplantation*;

The Living Church, Milwaukee, for excerpts from an article by Wilford O. Cross in the May 22, 1966 issue of *The Living Church*;

Louvain Studies, Louvain, for excerpts from Francis W. Swift's "An Analysis of the American Theological Reaction to Janssens and "The Pill'" (*Louvain Studies*, Fall, 1966);

John J. Lynch, S.J., and *Theological Studies*, for excerpts from John J. Lynch's "Notes on Moral Theology" (*Theological Studies*, June, 1964, and June, 1965);

Dr. Richard L. Means and *The Saturday Review*, for excerpts from Dr. Means' "Why Worry About Nature?" (*The Saturday Review*, December 2, 1967);

Frank J. Ayd, Jr., M.D., for excerpts from Dr. Ayd's "Is Brain Death Legal Death?" in the January, 1968 issue of *The Medical-Moral Newsletter*;

John G. Milhaven, S.J., and *Theological Studies*, for excerpts from John G. Milhaven's review of Joseph Fletcher's *Situation Ethics* (*Theological Studies*, September, 1966);

The Paulist-Newman Press, New York, for excerpts from Volumes 5 and 26 of *Concilium*, and for excerpts from Joseph Arntz' "Natural Law and History," from *Moral Problems and Christian Personalism*;

Presbyterian Life, Philadelphia, for excerpts from Norman F. Langford's "Ethics in Cold Blood" (*Presbyterian Life*, April 15, 1966);

The Saturday Review, New York, for excerpts from the article "On Heart Transplants," which originally appeared in the Science and Humanity Supplement of the *Saturday Review*, April 6, 1968;

Sheed & Ward, New York, for excerpts from *Sex, Love and the Person* by Peter A. Bertocci, © Sheed and Ward, Inc., 1967, from *Law and Conscience* by Franz Böckle, © Sheed and Ward, Inc., 1966, from *Sin, Liberty and Law* by Louis Monden, S.J., © Sheed and Ward, Inc., 1965, from *Natural Law* by Joseph Fuchs, © translation M. H. Gill and Son, Ltd., 1965, published by Sheed & Ward, Inc., New York;

The Sign, Union City, for excerpts from an interview with Dr. Robert White and Charles Curran ("The Morality of Human Transplants") which appeared in the March, 1968 issue of *The Sign*;

The Westminster Press, Philadelphia, for excerpts from Joseph Fletcher's *Situation Ethics* and *Moral Responsibility*;

The World Medical Journal, for excerpts from Jorgen Voight, M.D., "The Criteria of Death" from F. H. Muller's "Legal Medicine and the Delimitation of Death," and from Gunnar Biörck "On the Definitions of Death," all from the Sept.-Oct. 1967 issue of *World Medical Journal*.

We are also grateful to the editors and publishers of the following journals in which some of the material included in these pages appeared in slightly different form:

Chicago Studies, "Is Intrinsic Evil a Viable Term?" (Vol. V, No. 3, Fall, 1966, pp. 307–314);

The Catholic World, "The Crucial Question About Abortion," (Vol. 206, No. 1232, Nov. 1967, pp. 57–61);

Villanova Law Review, "Between Life and Death," in the special issue entitled *The Medical, Moral, and Legal Implications of Recent Medical Advances* (Vol. 13, Summer, 1968, No. 4, pp. 759–783);

New Catholic Encyclopedia, article "Categorical Imperative" (New York: McGraw-Hill, 1967).

INTRODUCTION

One of the most intellectually stimulating areas of human inquiry at the present time centers on man's moral life. Men, precisely because they are men, have always been concerned with the meaning of their actions, inasmuch as these shape their lives, deeply affect their relationships with other men, and give tone and life to the society of which they are a part. Because of many interrelated factors—scientific, theological, cultural—contemporary Christians have been deeply rethinking the meaning of the ethical maxims and moral codes which have, in the past, contributed to the shape of "Western civilization,"[1] and in recent years some very

---

[1] On this see, for instance, W. H. van de Pol, *The End of Conventional Christianity* (New York: Newman, 1968), Bishop John Robinson, *Christian Morals Today* (Philadelphia: Westminster, 1964), Charles Curran (ed.), *Absolutes in Moral Theology?* (Washington: Corpus Books, 1968).

perceptive and significant work has been carried out by moralists, Catholic, Protestant, and humanist, which demands intelligent investigation by anyone who is serious about forming his own conscience on the meaning of human life and the significance of acting in a human way. It is the purpose of this book to help provide some lines of thought which are, I believe, of importance in carrying out this crucial work.

As the reader will discover, throughout the text there runs the theme that a truly authentic Christian morality must be an ethic of dynamic tension, drawing upon both the ethic of conviction or of principles and the ethic of responsibility. Such an ethic, naturally, must be personally incorporated if it is to be a viable force in one's life, a force guarding against simplistic solutions to the complex questions of human conduct, whether formulated by a pure ethic of conviction (illustrated by many moral textbooks and manuals of the past) or by a pure ethic of responsibility (typified today by the "Playboy" mentality).

Much of the book is concerned with a critical appraisal of situational morality, particularly as set forth so persuasively by Joseph Fletcher. I think that we owe a special debt to those moralists, such as Dr. Fletcher, who have so ably highlighted the role which empirically verifiable consequences, responsibly envisaged, must play in making moral decisions. Yet, as will be shown at more length later on, a situational morality true to itself must, in my view, be absolutely serious about *all* the values found in the situation. For it is only in this way that the ethic of responsibility can be complemented by the ethic of conviction and that a morality open to all the existential values of lived situations can be developed.

As will be discovered, recent literature dealing with the role of the natural law in determining moral conduct calls attention to the fact that an authentic natural law must respect the existential, concrete situation of man and that it must allow room for the dynamism of the human person, who must act responsibly within the situation in which he is placed. Consequently this too is an issue discussed at length within these pages. It might be added here that the hostile reception accorded Paul VI's recent encyclical, *Humanae vitae*, stems from the conviction, on the part of reputable theologians, that the natural law theory reflected in his encyclical is simply unrealistic in the light of contemporary philosophy and science.

Finally, attention turns to some critical practical questions facing contemporary man. In the light of Gordon Rattray Taylor's *The Biological Time Bomb*,[2] the questions taken up in the final chapters of this book assume larger proportions.

---

[2] Cleveland: World Publishing Co., 1968. Cf. also Charles Kindregan, *The Quality of Life: Reflections on the Moral Values of American Law* (Milwaukee: The Bruce Publishing Company, 1969).

CONTENTS

CHAPTER ONE

AN ETHIC OF DIALECTICAL TENSION

There is little doubt that in American colleges the course in ethics has undergone enormous changes in the last several years. This is certainly due to the changes that have taken place elsewhere in our culture. Students coming into philosophy and learning for the first time the speculative side of questions which they have already been experiencing in their lives for some years stubbornly resist any presentation that proceeds deductively from an examination of rational human nature regarded as a universal essence. In other words, students are aware of the contemporary mind and find themselves more and more sympathetic with the way it operates. This contemporary mind has four major characteristics: (1) a sense of historical evolution; (2) a keen awareness of personal subjectivity; (3) a scientific attitude suspicious of any position that is

1

not empirically verifiable; (4) an appreciation of the human situation as described in existential theology and existential phenomenology. These four characteristics seriously confront anyone who attempts to teach college students ethics; to succeed to any extent he must be aware of the role these four characteristics play in the thinking and acting of the students that he faces. It is futile for him to propose an ethic that is only a plausible theory but not operative in their own lives. In fact, it is idle to propose an ethic which is not operative in his own.

The great challenge for the ethician is to show that his values are not alien to the scientific attitude and that they can in some way be empirically verified. Most students are attracted by intrinsic values but they raise questions whether these intrinsic values are always so patent and so demonstrable. Is it possible for a student to accept the intrinsic values of physical life, promise-keeping, fidelity, etc. when he is convinced that in the present existential situation they are destructive of certain other values with which they are in conflict? Values in themselves are easily appreciated and admired; it is when they are found in a constellation of other competing values that the student begins asking embarrassing questions about which values should survive in the encounter. In other words, anyone who attempts to propose a relevant and significant ethic today must take into account the type of ethical thinking that is going on. It is found in many circles within Protestant and Catholic groups, and the students are experiencing this kind of thinking although they may be hearing a different kind of ethical analysis in the classroom. For this reason, efforts have to be made to bring together in living contact the best features of situational morality with the traditional morality of the past.

I. The Ethic of Responsibility and The Ethic of Conviction

Possibly the best way to begin this development of a contemporary ethic is to state and defend a few propositions of my own. It seems to me that an authentic morality is one resulting from the dialectical tension of two ethics, *the ethic of responsibility* and *the ethic of conviction*. The past has been more interested in the ethic of conviction than in the ethic of responsibility. Let me explain the root meaning of both of these terms. The *ethic of responsibility* is one whose ultimate concern is personal consequences, the empirically verifiable results that eventuate from an act. It is in terms of these consequences that the act is characterized as good or bad. On the other hand, the *ethic of conviction* is one whose ultimate concern is principle, with more or less indifference to consequences. Situational morality tends to polarize and absolutize the *ethic of responsibility*, whereas traditional morality tends to absolutize and polarize the second. My position is that a person cannot consistently live on either ethic but must live on both in dynamic dialectical tension.

Contemporary ethical thinking is more in the direction of an *ethic of responsibility* than in the direction of an *ethic of conviction*. Nevertheless, much of the criticism of leaders in civil society or in the Church is raised by persons who use only one of these ethics as the norm for criticism. Let me illustrate. Hochhuth criticizes the Holy Father for not speaking out against the Nazis because he seems to think that the Pope is obliged primarily if not solely by an *ethic of conviction*. He contends that Pope Pius XII should have been directed by principle to speak out boldly and to disregard the consequences that might have followed. He should not have calculated; others may do this but not a Holy Father. Even if the worst results would have befallen the Christian Churches, the voice of the Pope should never have remained silent. The Pope, in other words, should be a man of conviction, directed by the ethic of conviction and not by the ethic of responsibility. Is this reasonable or unreasonable? To live on one ethic rather than on both in dynamic tension strikes me as most unreasonable and unrealistic.

A striking illustration of criticism directed primarily on the basis of an *ethic of responsibility* is provided by the reactions to Paul VI's encyclical on family life and the regulation of births, *Humanae vitae*. Many reputable journals and over 500 American Catholic theologians, among others, have strongly criticized the position of the Pope on the question of contraception. Basically the argument against his stance is supported by an evaluation of the personal consequences that work to the destruction of marital harmony if rhythm is the sole means for achieving responsible parenthood. Opponents also argue that the empirically verifiable consequences resulting from contraception work to the harmony of marriage and to the mutual personal satisfaction of the married parties. The principle operative in this mode of argument is that the Pope is obliged to recognize these personal, empirical good consequences which result from the responsible use of contraception within the framework of family life. Implicit in this criticism is the idea that the *ethic of responsibility* should exercise priority in determining the morality of contraception, and that the Pope, in formulating the teaching of the Church on this subject, should recognize the value of these personal, empirical good consequences. Here again, the criticism proceeds from the adoption of one polar ethical position rather than from the recognition that the Pope finds himself in the ambiguous position of trying to reconcile in the dynamic tension of his own thinking the two ethics of responsibility and conviction. (One of the crucially important factors in formulating a stance on the morality of contraception is the role of the natural law in this area of human conduct; more will be said on this in our chapter on the natural law.)

A final example is taken from an experience which is quite current today. Let us consider the case of the conscientious objector who is opposed to a specific war, such as that in Vietnam. Conscientious objection to a specific war is not legally recognized at present, and therefore, faced with a conflict between his conscience and military service laws, the individual has two basic alternatives. He can be directed by the *ethic of conviction* and accept the consequences that will probably be painful to him. These consequences primarily befall *him* and not *others* as the result of his decision. Nonetheless, if he were directed by both ethics, he would realize in his moral choice, by reason of the *ethic of responsibility*, that harsh consequences, empirically verifiable, to others would result. A man's genuine love of freedom is shown by his willingness to accept not only the consequences that follow from his own right not to participate but also the consequences of his decision on others, whether they choose to participate or not. The *ethic of conviction* without the *ethic of responsibility* can be a cold and mindless ethic. The ethic of responsibility opens a person to all the consequences which will affect himself and others as a result of his moral decisions. The ethic of conviction is the encounter of a *person* with *law*, while the ethic of responsibility is the encounter of a person with the *Person* who is incarnate in all other persons. Just consider how difficult the situation becomes for the man who is struggling to become more and more responsible. Consider the young man who, instead of immediately deciding because of an *ethic of conviction* that he should not enter a war that is immoral and unjust, proceeds to re-examine the notion of participation in an unjust and illegal war and in illegal and immoral wartime practices. If he looks to the Nuremberg precedent for guidance, it seems to me that he will *not* take the view that *any* participation in the armed forces is necessarily immoral. If he participates, as marginally as possible, and manages with good fortune to stay out of positions and situations wherein immoral behavior is almost unavoidable, it seems to me that he has not necessarily betrayed his conscience. After all, if people did not act ethically in this way they could never have German friends who served in the German armed forces during the second World War and whose participation was remote and marginal.

No one questions that these difficult situational decisions should be left up to the individual and no one else. Criticism can be made of the man who thinks that he is more ethical if he is guided only by the ethic of conviction and not by the ethic of responsibility as well in dynamic tension with the ethic of conviction. *The Man For All Seasons* (St. Thomas More) was quite the calculator—in fact, most of his life seemed to be controlled by this ethic. The consequences to his family, his country, himself—he had no taste for death—these empirically verifiable personal consequences were most operational in his thinking. Only toward the very end did the resolution of the tension become manifest when principle and conviction were in deadly combat with these consequences.

Let us apply some of this tension between the two ethics to the painful decision which must be made by the young man who is convinced of the unethical and immoral nature of a specific war or a specific war practice. As he makes these difficult situational decisions I would suggest that he re-examine the apparently prevalent idea that, while service necessarily means participation in war and a sharing of all the moral consequences that flow from the character of the war, refusal to serve means effectively *non-participation*. Then where does this non-participation stop? If the conscientious objector is really serious about non-participation in an unjust war (on an *ethic of conviction*) a suggestion might be made that he ponder the writings of Walter Stein and his English Catholic pacifist colleagues. Perhaps non-participation should mean boycotting political elections. For some it may mean refusing to pay taxes. Many times, however, these will not be the most important means of protest and disaffiliation possible. What about the universities that are government-supported; what about government-subsidized scholarships, grants, and loans? Where will non-participation stop? These questions have been legitimately raised by others. Is a draftee who folds blankets for a year in a supply room in Fort Dix participating in an unjust war to a decisively greater degree than a student attending a university heavily subsidized by the Federal government and engaged in all manner of projects related to the effective functioning of the United States war effort? *Is participation mainly a question of a uniform?* Whoever expects an easy and generally acceptable answer to these questions in terms of legal—as opposed to moral—rights of conscientious objection is *indeed* indulging in fantasy.

The more responsible the individual the more is he aware of all the consequences involved not only in participation but also in non-participation. He is bound to ask eventually in the case of his objection to a specific war—where shall our non-participation stop? We have come to the real existential agony of the whole problem of evil and how we contribute to it. Unavoidably, ineluctably we contribute to the quantity of evil in the world. What does this ultimately mean? We might illustrate this by considering a French motion picture which had as its theme the unavoidability of evil, the fact that possibly we should measure the success of our lives both by the amount of evil that we have been able to avoid rather than only by the quantity of good that we have done. If there is some ambiguity in our moral decisions because of the attempt to reconcile the two ethics of responsibility and conviction, it is only because we are in a world of enormous good, and enormous evil, and it is foolish for us to deny that in the ambivalence of our own moral and ethical lives we are contributing to the unintended delinquency of one another. While we pride ourselves for our rational existence in which nonetheless so much rationalization is being done, we should not overlook this truth. While we continue to satanize the opposition and to deify ourselves, we are in a fundamental sense only adding to the evil in existence. It is in the light of this ambivalence that we should approach the most profound and agonizing decisions of war, painful decisions regarding participation in what we are convinced is evil, decisions regarding the proximity and avoidability of this participation, decisions regarding our freedom and the limitations on our freedom in a wounded society of man. It is only in this light that the responsibility as well as the conviction of the person will grow. In other words, it is only by living the dynamic tension of these two ethics of responsibility and conviction and in experiencing the ambivalence and ambiguity of moral and ethical decisions that we will come to an appreciation of the genuine ethic that will be the personal, autonomous, and authentic ethic.

Therefore this is the first proposition that appears to me to be theoretically and practically defensible: *A person cannot consistently, constantly and uniformly live on just one of these two ethics; he must live on both in dynamic tension, in dynamic dialectical tension.* Let me now advance to my second proposition.

II. ABSOLUTES (?) IN MORAL THEORY

In the ethic of responsibility empirically verifiable evidence is of great importance, and it is this evidence which is sought to demonstrate the value in the existential moral act here and now. The empirical data may not bear out the practical wisdom of the universal affirmative principles and the universal negative prohibitions that we have associated with the ethic of conviction. Nevertheless, this empirically verifiable evidence is needed more and more in the methodological and systematic presentation of any contemporary and meaningful ethic. The moral absolutes that we associate with the ethic of conviction should be supported by this empirical evidence, because to show the intrinsic validity of these absolutes is not at all simple. In addition, students are asking more and more why the values implicit in the moral absolutes appear more and more to be stripped of supporting evidence in conflicts with other values. Does the empirically verifiable evidence support contraception or rhythm? Does the empirical evidence support the arguments for the absolute indissolubility of marriage? Does the evidence support the position for absolutizing and polarizing the value of physical life? In other words, are the few moral absolutes that seem to remain in the ethic of conviction supported by empirically verifiable evidence? It is in the order of sexuality and direct killing that the ethic of conviction for the Catholic moralist seems to be still standing. But is it not true that some erosion has even taken place among these moral imperatives? Is the concept of intrinsic evil viable any more, or do so many qualifiers have to be added to the original moral object that the notion is no longer useful in moral discourse?

I will, in the next chapter, attempt to show that the idea of intrinsic evil applied to a particular act is not viable as a term in moral discourse and that it can operate as an albatross around the neck of the user. It seems to me that this has happened in the treatment of contraception and that now the harsh moral term remains one of the principal difficulties in the discussions that are taking place among moralists. A moral act can still be designated as wrong without bringing out the megaton words of intrinsic evil, evil of its very nature, etc.

It is difficult for anyone to see how some marital practice can be intrinsically evil if this judgment is not supported by the empirically verifiable data in the largest number of ethical and moral married unions. Recently, a Jesuit journal described the difficulties which many married persons are experiencing with the practice of rhythm. This fact seemed to indicate the necessity of some form of contraception for the harmony and happiness of married couples. Does this not seem to be stating that the empirical evidence behind rhythm is open to question and that the evidence seems to be in favor of contraception? If this is true, then the prohibition of contraception is no longer supported in the largest number of marriages by the empirically verifiable evidence that would be expected. The ethic of conviction, in other words, regarding contraception is unsupported by the evidence which persons are seeking in their moral experience. Ethical and moral persons are more and more looking to an ethic that will be reasonable and helpful to them, and the pendulum is swinging more and more to an ethic of responsibility and away from the ethic of conviction that is not borne out by supporting evidence.

To say this is not to claim for the evidence that it necessarily constitutes the ethical or moral nature of the act. However, the empirical evidence does manifest the ethical and moral nature of the act in some way. It does seem strange to the unsophisticated in moral science that moral principles, affirmative and negative, are stated by persons in face of contradictory empirically verifiable evidence. This evidence requires the constant attention of the moral philosopher; he cannot ignore it and insist that his ethical philosophy is relevant and contemporary. For the person of faith the acceptance of the prohibitions against divorce, abortion, and contraception may not occasion the agonies they do for the person without faith. Nevertheless, even the person of faith finds the difficulties mounting when he is told that his faith is eminently reasonable, that "faith builds upon reason" and then looks to the empirically verifiable evidence which does not bear out the moral absolutes of his faith. The person of faith confronts the evidence and he is anxious to discover in the evidence the validation of these absolutes. But does he find the evidence supporting the moral absolutes that remain in the ethic of conviction? To me the few moral absolutes that do remain in the ethic of conviction are in the order of sexuality and direct killing, and it makes one wonder whether these are any longer moral absolutes validated sufficiently by empirically verifiable evidence. Are these values vindicated by evidence? Does the evidence speak for or against these values? For example, does the empirical evidence for contraception in the present historical context outweigh the evidence against it? Does it seem wise, therefore, to designate contraception as intrinsically evil, evil *semper et pro semper* in the face of this evidence? Is it wise to make contraception a prescriptive principle? Any moral imperative, negative or positive, should be first an *ordinance of reason for the common good*. Does this not seem to indicate that its reasonableness should become evident in the empirically verifiable ethical and moral living of persons?

We should make clear that our dissatisfaction is not with characterizing contraception, direct killing, and divorce as unethical under most circumstances. Our complaint is with the qualification that these moral acts are *intrinsically* wrong in the face of contradictory empirical evidence. What we are saying is that while non-contraceptive relations, and absolutely indissoluble marriages might be the ideal, is the ideal always a moral imperative? Are we wise in insisting that moral disvalues are always forbidden and that in the concrete situation they are always unethical and morally wrong to bring about?[1]

Let me summarize, then, my second proposition in the light of every-

---

[1] Cf. my article "Morality and Intrinsic Evil," *The Catholic Lawyer* II (1965), 180–183, and chapter two, below. John G. Milhaven, S.J., has complemented my efforts in showing how we can know which values are absolute. Cf. Millhaven's "Towards an Epistemology of Ethics," *Theological Studies* 27 (1966), 228–241. Also cf. Bishop Simons, "The Catholic Church and the New Morality," *Cross Currents* 16 (Fall, 1966), 429–445, and Dennis Doherty, "Sexual Morality: Absolute or Situational?," *Continuum* 5 (Summer, 1967), 235–253.

thing that has been said to develop it in the last few pages. The ethic of conviction turns principally on the moral absolutes in the order of sexuality and direct killing. With the speculation that has been done in these two areas it can be asked whether these are any longer moral absolutes in the sense that they are validated sufficiently by empirically verifiable data. If they are not, and it seems to me that they are not, is it wise to characterize these acts any longer as intrinsically evil? In another form the question can be placed in this way: If these areas can no longer be classified as intrinsically good areas which must be preserved at any ethical cost, and if contraception, direct killing (apart from the aggressor or capital punishment), and divorce in the case of a sacramental and consummated marriage are no longer to be characterized as intrinsically wrong, then might we not admit that there is some validity to saying that an erosion has set into the last few moral absolutes? Is it reasonable to call these areas moral absolutes when empirically verifiable data are no longer supporting them? Is it so temerarious to say that the moral situation questions the validity of universal affirmative principles and especially the validity of universal negative prohibitions?

III. A Constellation of Values

Let me now consider a third proposition in the structuring of a contemporary relevant moral philosophy. We have already seen the plausibility of considering that a genuinely authentic ethic results from the personal resolution of the two ethics that are in dialectical tension: the ethic of responsibility and the ethic of conviction. In the second place, considering the moral absolutes that are implicit in the ethic of conviction, we raised questions about their validation by the empirical data. We saw that the disvalues were not always supported by negative empirical data to the extent that these disvalues in contraception, direct killing and divorce should be characterized as always wrong. We asked whether it is reasonable to make the moral ideal a moral imperative? Now, let us consider a third proposition, which might be put this way: Any value (life, promise-keeping, fidelity, etc.) should never be seen in isolation but should be viewed in a constellation of other values and disvalues. No value should be so polarized or absolutized that it is viewed essentially and not existentially in concrete experience, where it is surrounded by a multiplicity of other values and disvalues which have to be harmonized and synthesized into a reasonable ethical whole. It seems to me that this isolation of one value apart from a concrete existential consideration of competing values and disvalues has been done too frequently in the past in regard to physical life, procreation, indissoluble marriage, etc. No one doubts that a resolute stand in defense of the value of physical life, procreation, and absolute indissolubility is admirable and often defensible. However, questions are raised with justification whether such a polarization and absolutization of one value is realistic when the human situation is to find this value always in a vortex of values and disvalues which have to be experienced and resolved. For example, is it always reasonable to polarize and absolutize the physical life of the fetus (doubtfully rational at the moment of conception) at the expense of the quality of life of the mother? Is there not some inconsistency in the polarization and absolutization of intra-uterine physical life and in the indifference to the quality of its existence in countries suffering from evident population problems? Life would be simple and uncomplicated if only one value had to be protected, but life is never that simple.

Values compete with one another in the human situation, and existential experience is never the mere observation of intrinsic good and intrinsic evil. Other values press in on ethical experience and make themselves present; disvalues assert themselves and narrow the area of the ethical and the moral. The situational and contextual analysis of any moral case in business or in medicine will make it evident to the ethically naive that moral imperatives must await in the wings until all the values and disvalues are heard. Responsibility is not the immediate application of a single universal affirmative or a universal negative principle. It is the slow, torturing analysis which softens the affirmative command and alters the negative prescription. To enter into a situational contextual discussion of a moral case with persons of different ethical and moral backgrounds is to listen quietly to all the voices and claims that assert themselves, all the values and disvalues that are seen more by others than ourselves and then to offer humbly, tentatively, hesitatingly, stammeringly the final resolution of the conflicting claims on conscience.

Such an experience can sophisticate the most naive. It may lead to longer examinations of conscience and to longer professional relationships with a confessor. It certainly will generate a respect for the depth of conscience, for the intrinsic worth of the person. It is not extraordinary that this period of our history is characterized by a refined conception of the person and a real appreciation of the inviolability of conscience. If the person has dignity it is because of his conscience. It is in conscience that one person meets the person and before Him he resolves all the claims that are set up by the values and disvalues that operate with himself in the center of the vortex. Conscience is not a person before law; it is a person before the *Person* and before Him he makes the prismatic analysis of the conflict of values and disvalues. It is here where real responsibility is manifest, and where more and more existential experience produces the person of maturity and real growth. It is a paradox, but true, that the harder ethic to live is the ethic of responsibility and not the ethic of conviction. The hardest morality of all is to live on both ethics in dialectical tension and to resolve personally the claims and counter-claims that are set up by all the values and disvalues in the moral experience. It is the hardest morality of all but it is the only morality that will be true to the metaphysics of conscience.

IV. The Importance of Evidence for Contemporary Ethics

In order to clarify the precise difference between the two ethics that have to be confronted in moral experience and in order to aid in the resolution of the tension that exists between the two of them, let us consider the importance of the role of empirically verifiable data. Traditional morality, placing much emphasis upon the ethic of conviction and on the notions of intrinsic good and intrinsic evil, argues that no amount of evidence can invalidate absolute intrinsic values. Any evidence which can be brought in favor of the intrinsic value is something additional; any evidence that will be adduced from consequences to show the wrongness of lying will only be an extrinsic argument against the real intrinsic wrongness of a lie. In other words, evidence in the ethic of conviction plays a minor role if it plays any role at all. Circumstances, or other evidence that may be found, will be employed possibly to show that there are great difficulties in applying the ethic of conviction immediately. The evidence may help to reduce the responsibility of the person and to indicate that the place of prudence in all of this is of much importance. Nevertheless, empirical evidence is extrinsic to the consideration of absolute values. By very definition the intrinsic good or the notion of intrinsic value arises from a relationship with the idea of rational human nature looked at adequately. Conversely, intrinsic evil is predicated of the act, which, prescinding from motive and circumstances, is always in disagreement with rational human nature looked at adequately. In this consideration of intrinsic good and intrinsic evil contrary evidence plays a minimal role. An ethic of conviction that accepts the concepts of intrinsic good and intrinsic evil will minimize the importance of the role of evidence in the structuring of the act itself. At the most evidence may point out or manifest the goodness or the wrongness of the act but it does not constitute the goodness or the wrongness of the act. This goodness or badness is already there in the moral value or disvalue by the essential relationship that exists between the act and the adequate consideration of rational human nature.

It must be evident that these notions of intrinsic good and intrinsic evil are philosophically wedded to an essentialistic consideration of human nature. Evidence in such a systematic presentation plays an *epistemological* role but never the *ontological* role of structuring the very values or disvalues themselves. It is here that the issue is really placed between the *ethic of responsibility* and the *ethic of conviction*. For the ethic of responsibility, evidence plays both an ontological and an epistemological role. Empirically verifiable data not only *show* the rightness and the wrongness of an act but they *constitute* the rightness and the wrongness of the act. We can now see why these two ethics are in dialectical tension and that this tension enters into the resolution of the two ethics in a genuine decision of conscience. To put the question into sharpest relief: Is evidence, empirically verifiable evidence to play merely an epistemological role in making the quality of the moral act manifest or is it to play in addition an ontoiogical role in the very structure of the moral act? My own thinking at present is the result of several papers on the non-viability of the concept of intrinsic evil and proceeds from the admitted scarcity of acts which are intrinsically evil to the tentative conclusion that we must re-evaluate the role of evidence more and more. Empirical evidence seems to be required not only for epistemological purposes but for ontological ones as well. In other words, the ethic of responsibility at the present historical moment is assuming a more important role in a genuine ethic. Indeed, as we shall see in Chapter II, the very concept of intrinsic evil has become non-viable and almost impossible to employ in moral discourse.

Daniel Callahan placed his finger on the nerve-ends of these two ethics in their stance toward the importance of empirical data.[2] For example, in the case of divorce the moral philosopher who considers the practice of divorce to be morally wrong and never permitted will argue that in the generality of cases divorce is socially harmful. In other words, the moral absolute against divorce is supported by empirical data. Nevertheless, the empirical evidence is hardly so decisive as to establish its necessary evil in every case. As a matter of fact, almost everyone can find within his own circle of friends or relatives instances where divorce and re-marriage seem to have promoted some notable social goods (children restored to normal life, an end to parental fighting, and so on). The generality of cases is sufficient for the ethicist who defends the ethic of conviction with its notion of intrinsic good and intrinsic evil. This raises some very interesting questions about the interplay of evidence and the ethic of conviction. On the hypothesis that a moral absolute would not

[2] Daniel Callahan, "Ethics and Evidence," *Commonweal* (October, 21, 1966), 76–78.

be borne out by the evidence in the generality of cases, would the ethic of conviction undergo a change in the notion of intrinsic value? To illustrate, suppose it could be shown that in the generality of cases the empirical evidence for successful marriages was in favor of the adoption of contraception as opposed to the practice of rhythm, would the ethicist who has held to the intrinsic disvalue of contraception allow his position to undergo a change? It is conceivable at least that the generality of cases could be adduced in favor of the change in what was originally a moral absolute. Would the original moral absolute then have to yield as an absolute?

It seems that there are additional problems for anyone who takes empirical data seriously. For many ethicists the generality of cases is sufficient to show that the moral absolute has been vindicated and supported by the evidence. The exceptional cases where the moral absolute is not supported by evidence are counterbalanced by the evidence in the generality of cases. But does this attitude take seriously enough the role of evidence? Where there is almost a parity of evidence for and against the moral absolute, is the ethicist willing to adapt and "tailor" (the word is Callahan's) the principle in order to give full play to the range of evidence? In this way the moral absolute would forbid a practice like divorce, where the empirical evidence shows it would probably be harmful to individuals and society, and allow it where no evil or only slight evil would result. Callahan does not think that the moralist is really considering the evidence with great seriousness if he is unwilling to adapt his moral principles in this way. When the issue is placed in this way the die is cast and the nerve ends of the ethicist are exposed. What are his presuppositions? In a conflict between an ethics wherein evidence plays a serious role and one wherein it plays only an epistemological role where does the ethicist stand? Is his priority in favor of the *ethic of responsibility* or in favor of the *ethic of conviction*? If my own position that a man must live on both in real dialectical tension and that he cannot live consistently just on one or the other is valid, then this agonizing ambivalance has to be faced by every man, and no one will know the outcome but God and the individual conscience. Tension and agony are here, but they must be honestly faced.

Callahan and others have shown how James Gustafson of the Yale Department of Religious Studies has helped to explain the nature of moral principles by his plausible distinction between a "prescriptive" and an "illuminative" use of principles.[3] In the first, "the center of gravity

---

[3] James Gustafson, "Context Versus Principles: A Misplaced Debate in Christian Ethics," *Harvard Theological Review*, Vol. 58, April 1965. Also available in Martin E. Marty and Dean G. Peerman, (eds.), *The New Theology*, No. 3 (London: Collier-Macmillan; New York: Macmillan, 1966).

is on the reliability of traditional moral propositions." They are considered to be the "most important or sole authority for the governing of action." In the second, the principles are used "to *interpret* what is morally wrong and morally right about a particular occasion." The center of gravity here is on "the newness, the openness, the freedom that is present . . ." Gustafson with this distinction contends that the discussion over context versus principles is "misplaced": it is, according to him, not a question of ethicists choosing one or the other, but of the use they assign to principles. Gustafson's distinction appears to be in agreement with my own that the evidence for some will play at the most an epistemological role, while for others, much more contextual and situational, it will play in addition an ontological role. More and more, it appears to me that ethicists are giving the evidence the center of gravity and expecting that the principle should be open to corrigibility if the evidence is against it.

Gustafson's contributions in this general discussion are by now accepted by almost all moralists. He shows how contemporary moralists usually start from one of four places: (1) some begin with "as accurate and perceptive social or situational analysis as possible"; (2) some "begin with fundamental theological affirmations"; (3) "still others locate moral principles as the center point for discussion"; (4) for some finally, "it is the nature of the Christian's life in Christ and its proper expression in moral conduct." Regardless of the starting point the direction is always toward a consideration of the relationship of this starting point to the other three. If #2 and #4 are considered with real seriousness we will have to say that the role of evidence will be assuming more and more importance in ethical discussions and that moral absolutes will have to be re-evaluated again and again.

Earlier in this chapter we characterized the contemporary mind in four ways, one of which was the scientific attitude which is suspicious of any position not empirically verifiable. More and more is this true of moral positions that would want to be considered seriously by contemporary man. Empirical data have had an enormous impact upon contemporary Catholic consciousness. Witness the role it is playing in the justified arguments for a change in Church attitudes toward contraception. As Callahan has remarked in *Commonweal:* "Whether moralists like it or not, Catholics today are influenced by empirical evidence and by their own experience. The sudden collapse of opposition in many quarters to the use of contraceptives reflects the impact of evidence that their use does not necessarily harm the husband-wife relationship (but may even do the couple and their children much good). The debate on private property, the incipient struggle on divorce, homosexuality, masturbation and suicide likewise show the cumulative impact of new evidence. To use Gustafson's phrase, there are many signs in the Church of an implicit shift from a 'prescriptive' to an 'illuminative' use of principles. Contributing to this shift also, of course, has been a re-examination of theological principles and a fresh look at the requirements of the Christian life."[4]

It seems to me that the role of empirical evidence is now forcing a re-examination of the principles that have remained in the ethic of conviction. Evidence is now pointing not only to a support for the principle but for a possible change of the principle and to a re-thinking of the few moral absolutes that remain. Moral absolutes, in other words, are having hard days and are undergoing the same searching reappraisal as the doctrinal absolutes in religion. Evidence is making life hard for the continued survival of both. We should not think that this has not always been so. The evidence might have had to ask for equal time with the absolute, either doctrinal or moral, but eventually the evidence has been heard and accomodations have been brought about. The evidence has been heard in cases of justified killing, in legitimate taking of someone's else's property, in the articulation of the notion of a just war, in what way precisely parents are dishonored, etc. Intrinsic values have been altered by a whole series of cases which were gradually permitted to coexist and were no longer considered exceptions to the intrinsic value. Will it be more so in the future development of ethics? It appears to me that the notion of intrinsic evil or intrinsic disvalue has had harder days than the notion of intrinsic good. In fact, serious re-examination of the concept of intrinsic evil will show that it is no longer a viable concept in contemporary ethical discourse. I would like to show that this is so in the next chapter. If the concept can be shown to be non-viable, then this in itself is an additional threat to its existence in addition to the evidence that can be adduced against characterizing specific acts as intrinsically evil when the empirically verifiable data compel us to re-examine these very acts.

Let us now turn to the point that I first made—that the very concept of intrinsic evil is for me non-viable and no longer operational in moral discourse.

---

[4] art. cit.

CHAPTER TWO

Is Intrinsic Evil a Viable Term?

Most students of ethics soon realize why the concept of sin is not introduced into a course of philosophical ethics. They know that sin is a theological term referring to a state of separation from God by an inordinate turning to a creature. The dual formality of an aversion from God (*aversio a Deo*) and a conversion or inordinate turning to a creature (*conversio ad creaturam*) is recognized as present in every sin. The students easily understand how wrongdoing is a turning away from good and, in some way, a turning away from ultimate Good or God; but they raise many objections to the inclusion within this notion of turning away from God any reference to offending him, displeasing him, or injuring him. They have problems in reconciling wrongdoing with injury to God. They accept this theologically, but seem to urge the detachment of the

16

God of Deism when they reflect on the possible consequences of their evil acts in relation to the divine. What possible harm to God can be done by our wrongdoing?

They see early in philosophical ethics that sin is a difficult term to introduce into the course and they accept in its place the concept of moral evil. But here, precisely, is the rub. If traditional Thomistic texts in philosophical ethics omit the term sin and readily adopt the term moral evil, non-Thomistic texts seem to give slight attention even to moral evil, employ it infrequently and, in many cases, ignore it altogether. Why is the term moral evil not used more often and considered more profoundly than it is in philosophical ethics?

Professor A. E. Taylor puts his finger on this inadequate treatment of the problem of moral evil and says that it is the outstanding defect of philosophical treatises on ethics. He points out that most writers on the subject seem to think that they have done all that is expected of them when they have tried to tell us what the good for man is, and what virtue, or the moral law, demands of us. Their concern is with a theory of good and little more; writers may set before us a "theory of good *and* evil" but the student will have to be satisfied with the perfunctory consideration given to moral evil. The influential *Principia Ethica* of G. E. Moore barely mentions the term. It might not be going too far to say that, of the principal philosophers who have dealt expressly and at length with the moral life of man (independent of a theological tradition), there are only two, Plato and Kant, whose language reveals an acute and constant sense of human evil. Professor Taylor denies that interest in the problem of moral evil can be found in Aristotle, Descartes, Spinoza, Leibniz, or Hegel. He finds that it is not prominent even in such vigorous supporters of an "eternal and immutable" morality as Cudworth, Clarke, and Price. Throughout the history of moral philosophy there is the paradox that most thinkers have been preoccupied with the problem of good and have reduced almost to relative unimportance the agonizing problem of moral evil.

To illustrate this, let us consider briefly once again G. E. Moore, for whom the basic problem in ethics is the meaning of good in its intrinsic sense. The intrinsic sense of good is realized if a thing is good in the sense that "it would be a good thing that the thing in question should exist, even if it existed quite alone" without any further accompaniments or effects whatsoever. What, then, does intrinsic good mean? The fact is that intrinsic good cannot be defined; it is a simple, unique, irreducible characteristic, it can be known only immediately or intuitively. The knowledge of the goodness of a thing is directly apprehended when the thing is known, if it is apprehended at all. This does not mean that there is a special faculty by which good is known, and it does not mean that one cannot be mistaken in judgments of value; but it does mean that such questions as whether or not, and to what extent, a thing is good are in no sense subject to argument or capable of being clarified by reasoning. Propositions to the effect that something is intrinsically good are not debatable: "No relevant evidence can be adduced: from no other truth, except from themselves, can it be inferred that they are either true or false."[1]

This is just a capsule summary of Moore's notion of intrinsic good. He barely mentions evil in his *Principia Ethica*, but there is more than a mere mention of evil in the traditional texts on ethics. In fact, where Moore was primarily interested in intrinsic good, Thomistic ethicians lead many students to believe that their primary interest is in moral evil and frequently in intrinsic evil. It is here that I come to the heart of my reflections on philosophical ethics and moral evil. Let me put it this way. The Thomistic moral philosopher finds it easier, it appears, to define intrinsic evil than to discover satisfactory examples to illustrate the definition. This should make the moralist reflect whether it is not unwise to denominate some moral act intrinsically evil without fearing that he may possibly have painted himself into a corner. To retreat from this position requires some delicate footwork.

This calls for some elaboration. Let me explain why it appears to me that the term "intrinsic evil" is not viable in moral philosophy and why it causes more problems than it attempts to solve or even to explain adequately. I shall try to defend this position by considering the meaning of "intrinsically evil" and then by examining the representative acts which are usually designated as intrinsically evil.

An act is considered to be intrinsically evil if, viewed just from its moral object, prescinding from circumstances and motive, it is always in difformity with the proximate norm of moral actions, namely rational human nature. The moral object of an act is that relationship which it bears to the norm of morality. The object of an act is the *whatness* of the act. For example, homicide has a different moral object from that of murder; fornication has a different moral object from adultery. If the act is regarded solely from its objects and is found to be repugnant to rational human nature (adequately considered), then such an act is characterized as intrinsically evil. The object of most acts, or to phrase it more precisely, most acts, viewed from their objects, prescinding from circumstances and motive, are morally indifferent. Walking, smoking, even killing are morally indifferent acts considered just from their objects. It is only when walk-

---

[1] G. E. Moore, *Principia Ethica* (Cambridge: Cambridge University Press, 1903). Reprinted New York: Cambridge University Press, 1959.

ing is done under certain circumstances and with this or that motive that it acquires the moral dimension of being either morally good or morally bad. Likewise, it is only when smoking is done in excess by some-one whose health may become endangered that the act assumes a moral dimension of good or bad. Incidentally, this latter example provides a rash of problems because, while smoking in excess may involve conse-quences upon physical health, there is no doubt that it provides psycho-logically good consequences which may well be intended to counter-balance the possible harmful consequences to physical health.

The last example cited above, of homicide, is a more interesting one to consider. Homicide, the killing of a man—just this act, viewed from its object—is morally indifferent. It requires the addition of several factors to become an act morally evil. Not every homicide is the same. Which circumstances have to be added to homicide to constitute an act of mur-der? These are circumstances that are required even to constitute the physical integrity of the act of murder, but what is interesting is that these very circumstances that change a mere act of homicide into an act of murder also are the circumstances that change the moral object of in-difference to a moral object of evil. What is added to homicide to make a case of murder? Here the moral philosopher becomes even more techni-cal and begins to add elements that almost inflate the original moral object of mere homicide. What is murder for the moralist?

Murder for many moralists is the unjust killing of another man. What does this really mean? When spelled out it becomes this expanded defini-tion, which, as John Hospers says, dilutes the original moral rule "do not kill" almost into a tautology. The articulated meaning for unjust killing or murder is: *the direct killing of another man on one's own authority outside a case of legitimate self-defense. Direct* killing refers to the act of killing intended as an end or as a means to an end; *on one's own authority* means that one is exercising a right over another person's life which he does not have. By the inclusion of *self-defense* within the defini-tion, the definer surely wants to exclude from murder the act of killing an assailant. But what happens if someone considers it just for a society to exercise capital punishment? In order to exclude capital punishment as an act of murder when the criminal is killed, does this not compel the advocate of the above definition to include this exception? Murder then assumes this definition: the direct killing of another man on one's own authority outside a case of legitimate self-defense *and capital punishment.* If anyone wants to designate this moral act with its expanded, articulated object, an act morally wrong, he will receive wide acceptance in western society. However, suppose this definition is offered to the pacifist who takes the moral rule not to kill literally; suppose it is submitted to the

Hindu who extends the prohibition against taking life to all forms of life; suppose it is submitted to Dr. Schweitzer?

I do not quarrel with the fact that there is general acceptance in many quarters of this definition of murder. What I do suggest is that murder has been so defined that it excludes everything that we regard as not exercises of murder and it is here that some moralists with one constellation of values will add or subtract cases and other moralists with a different constellation of values will add or subtract other cases. If then, for us, murder is defined as it was above—direct killing of another man on one's own authority outside a case of legitimate self-defense and capital punishment—and if this act of murder is then considered to be evil merely from its object, just how viable has this notion of intrinsic evil become? Viable for all who accept, but not viable for those who dissent from, our own constellation of values, our own value system.

This speculation on the problems that arise from any designation of an act as intrinsically evil can be extended to include a consideration of similar problems in the cases of suicide, lying, and sterilization. It seems to lead to the conclusion that the moral philosopher must struggle to develop the most authentic meaning for murder, suicide, lying and sterilization, but after he has constructed such a moral act, he should be very hesitant to designate it as intrinsically evil. Why is this so? Because by characterizing this act with all of its qualifications as intrinsically evil, he has little ground on which to move unless he is willing to re-examine each of the qualifications and admit that the definition is malleable. The problem with the person who readily designates an act to be intrinsically evil is that he will tolerate very little modification within the definition of the moral act as he proposes it. In fact, does not the very term *intrinsic* evil seem to imply that modifications are not in order? However, any student of the history of ethics knows well that modifications arising from a more penetrating knowledge of human nature and the complexities of the human act are very much in order.

An examination of most texts in ethics will reveal a general reluctance to refer to any act as intrinsically evil. Most books mention blasphemy and stop there; others, dishonesty, infidelity and dishonor, but these latter are really dodging the issue because they do not specify the very moral act which *is* an act of dishonesty, infidelity or dishonor. Any moral act can be built up into something approaching the notion of intrinsic evil if we construct upon the simple moral object of the act a variety of circumstances and motives which will alter its moral species from moral indifference to moral evil. But how far does this construction have to go before we are sure that the moral act is intrinsically evil?

Take sterilization as a further example. Sterilization in itself is morally indifferent; indirect therapeutic sterilization in the presence of a pathological disorder is morally good; direct punitive sterilization would be acceptable to anyone who accepts the DeLugo position on the lawfulness of direct killing of an aggressor in the case of legitimate self-defense. If the DeLugo position warrants direct killing of a criminal in these circumstances, then, a fortiori, direct sterilization of a criminal can be allowed because to intend directly the death of the man himself is something more serious than to intend directly the mutilation of his generative system. The further problem with the moral dimension of sterilization is the formidable question involved in the controversy over the anovulants: if the anovulants result in temporary sterilization may such a sterilization be *directly* intended in the absence of a pathological condition such as menorrhagia, dysmenorrhea, or an irregular menstrual cycle? In other words, may this kind of sterilization be intended as a means for the further good of marital intimacy and in the presence of serious psychological reasons? To say that direct sterilization is always wrong, to say that indirect sterilization is licit only in the presence of a *physical* pathological condition, is to narrow the area of moral dialogue.

More can and should be said about the non-viability of the concept of intrinsic evil. It is hoped that these reflections will stimulate some further discussion on the problem of moral evil in general and on the prudent unwillingness to characterize any moral act as intrinsically evil. "Intrinsically evil," applied too freely, can place an albatross around the neck of the user.

CHAPTER THREE

THE PHENOMENOLOGY OF GUILT AND MORAL EVIL

If our analysis of the concept of intrinsic evil is valid, then it would seem that it is a difficult one to employ in moral philosophy as soon as we apply it to specific acts rather than to basic disvalues. What I am insisting upon is that no one will deny that dishonesty, infidelity, meaningless killing are basic disvalues; what starts the disagreement is the definition that one assigns to these fundamental disvalues. We showed this above in regard to the problems associated with a simple notion such as murder when we articulated its meaning into *Direct killing of another man on one's own authority outside a case of legitimate self-defense.* More and more qualifications have to be added to this basic moral object in order to render it more and more precise. When finally we have done this we have only succeeded in constructing a tautological proposition that certainly has become so awkward that it convinces no one of the validity of our definition. It would appear then that the converse of G. E. Moore's position is applicable to *evil* even more than it is to the concept of *good*. Just as everyone knows what *good* is but it is really indefinable, so it seems to me that everyone knows what *evil* is but it is really undefinable. All definitions are synthetic and merely approach the notion of the basic disvalue or evil of which everyone is aware. No one denies that meaningless killing is an evil; dissent begins only when meaningless killing is defined in terms of a specific act. Likewise a lie is an evil, but how to tell what a lie is becomes the wonderful land of definition for the speculative moralist. Which definition really gives the essence of the lie—is it the definition of Thomas, Augustine, Grotius or that of Dorzynski?

In other words, we seem to know what evil is, just as Augustine knew what time is, but do not ask us or him to define either. For G. E. Moore good is intuitively known but it is indefinable; here it would seem that evil is known (in what way I am still struggling to say) but it is indefinable. Some might want to say that *evil* is *hatred* just as the situationalist considers only love as intrinsically good. But this only puts off the difficulty for a spell. What constitutes the real malice of hatred in a specific act? If the epistemology of love is a problem for the situationalist (that is, can he ever be sure that he is exercising agapaic love for the person), is it not true that the identification of hatred with evil contains even more serious epistemological problems?

It seems to me, then, that the converse of G. E. Moore's position is defensible. If, according to Moore, good is known by everyone but is ultimately indefinable, I would think that evil is known by everyone but it is ultimately indefinable in certain specific acts which are intrinsically evil. We seem—all of us—to know basic disvalues. Do not ask us to define these fundamental disvalues because we shall finally have to throw up our arms in despair. This would lead us inevitably to come to terms with the phenomenology of moral evil, with the experience each one of us has with moral evil. What, however, is this phenomenological experience? Can we find any common features in the experience which will initiate for us the beginnings of a more personalistic and concrete moral philosophy? The experience of moral evil is identified with an authentic experience of guilt, and there is little doubt that a sense of guilt about some behavioral acts exists in the consciousness of most persons. Much of the time of psychoanalysts is spent on the psychological problems of their clients and on tracing these problems back to irrational guilt experiences. No one can deny that this guilt-experience exists as a fact to be confronted. It is something that exists in the consciousness of each one of us, and with its phenomenology I would like to deal here.

Guilt is more than an equivocal term and calls for many precise quali-fications. Guilt is theological, psychologico-moral, purely psychological or even psychiatric. Our interest here is in a phenomenological examination of the data in a guilt experience in an attempt to find in that experience criteria which distinguish it from every other psychological experience. The sense of guilt depends clearly on a sense of right and wrong. One feels guilty about the things one is convinced are wrong. Lord Devlin has shown the relevance of a sense of guilt as an instrument of law and order. For the sense of guilt to have any value or any relevance in the maintenance of order in society there must be a common sense of right and wrong. Individual ideas of right and wrong would produce disorder rather than order. A common sense of right and wrong about a number of activities produces a law, which is referred to as the moral law. He maintains that for a sense of guilt to be effective in the maintenance of order there must be a moral law which covers a part, at least, of the same range of activities as the criminal law. Our moral reaction of guilt to the violation of 'some law or to the wrong that we have done some person is a genuine ethical reaction. It has characteristics which are proper and specific to this experience and to no other. It may be caused by re-actions to different conceptions of what is right and what is wrong, but when the experience occurs it shows common features that interest the phenomenologist.

I.   THE CHARACTERISTICS OF THE GUILT EXPERIENCE

The first quality that strikes us in an experience of guilt is the self-condemnation that it always involves. This is completely different from any discontent or dissatisfaction that we might find from an ordinary experience in which the personality is expressed but is in no way responsi-ble. Butler in his "Sermons on Human Nature" made much of this psychological fact of self-condemnation and associated it with the distinc-tion between the *actus humanus* and the *actus hominis*. From this psycho-logical feature Butler insisted upon the supreme principle of conscience, which for him had two aspects, a purely cognitive and an authoritative aspect. He merely reiterated the experience of everyone else when he said that the peculiarity of conscience is that it reflects on actions from the point of view of their rightness or wrongness. The very fact that we use words like "right," "wrong," "duty," etc., shows that there is an intellec-tual faculty within us which recognizes the realities denoted by these names. Otherwise such words would be as meaningless to us as the words "black" and "white" are to a man born blind. We clearly distinguish between a wrong action and one that happened to turn out unfortunately.

Again, we distinguish between mere unintentional hurt and deliberate injury. Conscience is indifferent to the former but condemns the latter. Finally, conscience recognizes a certain appropriateness between wrong-doing and pain and between right-doing and happiness; i.e., it recognizes the fact of merit or demerit. If we see a man being hurt we judge the situation quite differently according to whether we think that he is innocent or that he is being punished for some wrong act. We always make the familiar explicit distinction between unmerited "hard luck" and deserved unhappiness. How often do we hear men appealing to our sense of pity for their misfortunes by insisting that their misfortunes are due "to no fault of their own." How often do we distinguish even in language between a stupid mistake that we have made and a moral wrong of which we are guilty?

Why this distinction between real self-condemnation and mere discontent and dissatisfaction? Why do we smile when we read of the example cited by the famous idealist, F. H. Bradley, who in a passage of *Appearance and Reality* suggests that something analogous and continuous with moral self-condemnation is to be found in the sulky brooding of a beast of prey which has missed its "kill?"[1] Certainly Bradley would not have concluded from this observation to a naturalistic interpretation by saying that a man, so overwhelmed by a sense of moral guilt, is nothing more than a sulky and discontented brute. He would not have used the example to lower the psychology of man but to elevate the sulkiness of the brute. Bradley himself saw the deepest reaches of the personality expressed in the psychological state of self-condemnation. If personality reveals itself transparently in any situation it is in that experience of guilt. It is there that the existentialists study the enigma of personality and whether they depart from the definition of Boethius ("*naturae rationalis individua substantia*") or remain close to it they are all impressed by the fact of self-condemnation implied in every responsible moral act. Why this self-condemnation? Is it an admission that from the very testimony of personality itself a disvalue, a stain is present in this very act that we have performed or failed to perform?

Professor Pierre-Henri Simon, who is both a novelist and a poet, has shown how during periods of crisis when cultural values and the very principles of the structure of society are questioned it is natural that feelings of personal responsibility, attended by anxiety, frustration and remorse, should lead to uneasy consciences and then to feelings of guilt. There is even the danger that an obsession of general guilt tends to follow. The

---

[1] F. H. Bradley, *Appearance and Reality* (London, 1893; 2nd. ed., ninth impression, Oxford: Clarendon Press, 1930), p. 431n.

individual feels that he is immersed in it and seeks to escape in order to save his interior balance. Nevertheless, if he should yield to the impulse of some psychic disorder or moral weakness, he finally acquiesces in that guilt. Of this state of mind many symptoms could be mentioned, but Simon limits himself to those observable in present-day literature. Rarely, according to him, has the field of letters been more serious in its themes, graver in tone, more preoccupied by the problems of the human conscience than it is today. There is good reason for regarding those works of art as human and social documents.

Let us illustrate how Simon finds this first feature of self-condemnation in the guilt experience described by Anouilh in *La Sauvage*: "One theme which occurs frequently is the refusal of individual happiness"— a rejection inspired by the intense pity for the suffering and misery of others. In *La Sauvage* the heroine is confronted by a love which is pure and genuinely reciprocated, one that would miraculously deliver her from the humiliation of a life of squalor and shame. But in the end, she cannot bring herself to pass over into the camp of those fortunate ones who, through their material wealth, are able to keep up their self-respect. She refuses to give up her solidarity with the unfortunate and the oppressed and runs away, her little valise in hand: "There will always be a lost dog somewhere who will keep me from being happy." It is the valuable function of existentialism to show us that man always acts in concrete situations, that his freedom is exercised not in abstract space and time defined by some rarefied intellect but within the actual confines of an historical context and destiny. We would do well to study literature, the cinema, and the theater to understand the concern of all three with the self-condemnatory feature of the guilt experience. Traditional philosophy used to refer to the *consequent conscience* and then proceeded to ignore it while building a whole structure of law to confront the *antecedent conscience*. And it is this *consequent conscience* which tantalizes the artist more than the legalist in moral philosophy. It strikes one interested in a contemporary ethical philosophy of personalism and genuine subjectivity that the *consequent conscience* should be reevaluated and assigned its proper importance. If Kant was impressed by the presence in moral experience of the categorical imperative, it might be the insight of contemporary moral philosophy to re-instate the immediacy of the testimony of the *consequent conscience*.

Let us look at the second feature of the guilt experience. Moralists would say that this is the expression of the *consequent conscience* and it manifests itself in the indelibility, the apparent indestructibility, of the sense of guilt. Confessors well know of the situations of some penitents in which such a condition can approach the state of questioning the forgiveness of moral evil by God. Guilt seems to have the terrifying property of asserting itself despite the lapse of time and of geographical position. Even the imposition of a sanction by civil society or by nature itself and accepted in its finality by the person himself as containing remarkable therapeutic effects, does not eliminate this terrifying consciousness of guilt. Why this permanency, why the continuation of such poignant suffering long after the offense has been committed? Why is it felt by someone when he is immoderately indignant or impatient? Why does it continue to remain in the consciousness of a woman who has lost an unborn child although the doctor advises her that it was not her responsibility? Surely the man who has repented for his offense and has made restitution ought to be free from all reproach. Why, then, this constant self-criticism? Society may have lost all right to punish this man but self-condemnation continues. Think of the remorse of a Peter or a Magdalene! A real penitent who regards sin to have a theological dimension and who is forgiven by a priest's absolution never seems to forgive himself or to condone his fault. Paul referred to himself as "the greatest of all sinners" and it requires no great imagination to conjure up the picture of the converted Apostle constantly bringing before the tribunal of his conscience the horrible scene of the martyrdom of Stephen. Psychologists tell us of the patient afflicted with a fixed idea and on the suffering that such an obsessive notion can have on the harmony of a person's life. It seems that in every guilt experience these two elements are always present: the element of stain which continually plagues the person with repugnance and horror, and the undoubted fact of the centrality of the person that is reached in every act of guilt. Any explanation of the phenomena of the *consequent conscience* is bound to superficial if it minimizes or omits these two important elements.

A personalistic phenomenology interprets these two factors well and relates them to the observed psychology of ourselves and others in terms of value and disvalue in concrete existential experience. We can begin to get some understanding of the profound reasons why even the most ethical individuals testify that the self-condemnation in their experience is not a temporary concomitant of their sense of guilt but a continuous and permanent feature of it. We cannot help seeing some plausibility in the explanation of certain philosophers who hold that the metaphysical essence of personality resides in the element of "incommunicability," because the experience of an individual who is stirred by thoughts and preoccupations of guilt cannot be appreciated by someone who stands outside his experience. The ultimate reason why this self-condemnation belongs to the guilty party even after his exoneration by the state and by society is that in this situation the personality is reached and touched at its metaphysical core—the very area of incommunicability which is his and no one else's. Possibly in guilt the person is closest to the Person of God because God touches his soul, his personality, at the incommunicable core of his being. It would seem that just as personality is incommunicable, so is guilt, and no one can be held for the personal moral wrong of another save the person who committed it. We can see this clearly if we apply the metaphysical theory of personality which radicates its deepest roots in the incommunicability of the self. There does not seem to be any other theory or explanation of personality which so perfectly reproduces or rather exposes the incommunicability of guilt. We might say that guilt touches personality more intimately than any other experience because it partakes so much of the very nature of the thing it touches—the very incommunicability of personality.

It would be interesting to develop these notions into a much longer study of the metaphysical relationships that seem to exist between personality on the one hand and moral evil and guilt experiences on the other. However, we might make two tentative statements about these inter-relationships: (1) Since *person* should be equated or identified with the intellectual or conscious nature of someone, and since guilt is the product of deliberation and freedom exercised in what a person has considered to be wrong, it follows that guilt should be ascribed more immediately and more properly to person than to nature. (2) Since the root of personality seems to reside in incommunicability we might plausibly conclude that since guilt touches the personality and appears to partake of its nature in a very profound sense, the root explanation of the phenomena of the permanency of guilt is found precisely here. Guilt touches personality, partakes of its nature, and in its incommunicability it is and remains just as incommunicable as personality itself.

Some critics of the constancy of the experience of guilt would lay it at the door of some morbid preoccupation with the ego. But if this be true then we would have to say that this morbid experience is universal. It is hard to see how any experience which can be described as something felt "always, everywhere, and by all" is an experience that is morbid and unhealthy. The indelibility, the indestructibility of the guilt experience demands a more realistic explanation than locating it in the sick and morbid preoccupations of a "too severe super-ego." We should admit that while it is true that memory often accentuates those guilt experiences that are associated with the least wicked of our offenses this same memory never succeeds in making of the guilt experience itself a mere delusion. While we may in a similar fashion testify that something is more beautiful than it really is, there is no denial of the fact that something aesthetic has been experienced by us regardless of how much we have exaggerated the evidence. Any person who attempts to make the sense of guilt and the sense of discomfort felt by a blunder equivalent is simply testifying that he has the experience, although in the concrete he may be attaching the guilt feeling to the wrong objects. Implicitly therefore he is testifying to the presence of a moral wrong in his conscience and to the permanency and incommunicability of something which touches his personality at its most central core. Just as a person cannot strip himself of his own metaphysical personality so he cannot divest himself of this constant and poignant experience of guilt.

Gilbert Murray in his *Rise of the Greek Epic* has demonstrated very conclusively that this sense of guilt to which we have been paying so much attention is not due in any way to certain superstitious impressions from some primitive belief. He maintains that the concept of guilt existed first in the ethical field and only then was transferred to the theological. The example that Murray uses is the horror that the Greeks had for putting poison on arrows and the sense of real guilt that would be experienced by anyone who was responsible for this offense. This proves for him and for ourselves that such a crime was believed to be unpardonable because the Greeks always looked upon it as a crime that *ought not* to be pardoned. In other words, they themselves in their instinctive repugnance to this offense give eloquent testimony of the defilement that they felt was done the soul by anyone guilty of placing poison on arrows. Homer also cites other offenses which he treats as unforgivable in some special or peculiar way. In the Old Testament as well we see the same phenomenon in which emphasis is placed upon the consideration that should be paid the orphan and the poor. There appears to be present in these examples an ethical and moral judgment on the evil of those offenses that are directed to the unfortunate of God. It is useless to say that social convention played the constitutive part in the formation of this impression because certainly we could well conceive of cases where poisoned arrows would be of much help to the common good. We should not find primitive morality expressing itself in defense of the widow and the poor but in defense of the more important members of the tribal society. No extenuation of this behavior that is granted by everyone can eliminate the distinct indelibility of guilt that is so much a part of our own psychological awareness. Some social psychologists attempt to explain this reaction of guilt by stating that animals betray the same expressions of regret when they have done something unclean in their masters' homes. These psychologists overlook the fact that these animals are the least convincing proofs to allege because they themselves have been domesticated by their masters and whatever poor and inadequate equivalent of the guilt-experience they manifest has been something projected upon them by the very individuals who are supposed to be so dependent upon the animals they train.

Therefore, we can say with some assurance that in our experience and in the experience of the generality of men there is a guilt-phenomenon which has the characteristics of the self-condemnatory and the permanent. This abiding presence of the guilt experience, this continuous living with the past, this brooding over the effects of our responsible acts, all this seems to point to a disorder in our lives, to a stain or *macula* which has often been associated with guilt. The permanency of this guilt experience for an Augustine is evident to anyone who has read his *Confessions*. The presence of this permanent reminder of something unethical or immoral in our past seems to imply that this irresponsible act was unworthy of us and constantly recurs to let us know just who we are.

Let us advance to another feature of the guilt experience which will, from a different vantage point, reinforce the same conclusion as above. Independent of the conviction that religious persons have from their faith that moral evil should be punished, it appears to be true from our own psychological experience that we recognize that a sanction of punishment is a concomitant of this sense of guilt. In other words, the feeling of punishment is a genuine ethical accompaniment of the guilt experience. This reaction is readily understood in an ethic of personalism where the relations between persons set up an entire series of claims and counter claims. In a genuine ethic of responsibility the ultimate concern is the recognition of the consequences that follow upon the performance of a moral act. These consequences are principally those that effect persons and personal relations. Moral evil that expresses itself so sharply in the reaction of the guilt experience is not simply the disobedience to some law but it is primarily infidelity to another person. William F. May offers several reasons why legalism is inadequate on the subject of moral evil, which he calls in its proper theological context *sin*. In his challenging book, *A Catalogue of Sins*, he points out how the legalist usually assumes that the law is man's only serious point of contact with God. Only through the law does God communicate himself to creatures. "He is like a much-absent father, distant and remote from his children, who comes alive for them only at one point—when he clears his throat, deepens his voice, and commands them to obey. Such legalism offers an impoverished understanding of man's participation in the life of God. It implicitly denies that man has been created to enjoy the Presence of God in a way that a son might enjoy the presence of a good and undistracted father, a wife the life of her husband, or a citizen the common good of his country."[2] It seems that

---

[2] William F. May, *A Catalogue of Sins* (New York: Holt, Rinehart and Winston, 1966), p. 10.

the legalist has contact only with the solemnity that imposes on him a set of commands and a few hints at punishment; his God is reduced to a specter who hovers elusively on the other side of the law that fences him in. It is difficult (as May asserts) to take seriously a violation of one's life in God if participation in his life has been reduced to mere legality.

The qualities of the guilt experience that we have developed thus far —indelibility, permanency, self-condemnation, acceptance of the notion of concomitant punishment—all these receive additional confirmation and validation in a theological ethic and a philosophical personalism. O. Hobart Mowrer in his significant work *The Crisis in Psychiatry and Religion* has little difficulty identifying moral evil with the notion of sin and contends that sin is very much with us and is not an antiquated and absurd notion. *Sin*, like hell, has conveniently dropped out of most religious as well as secular thought, but Mowrer insists that hell is "still very much with us in those states of mind and being which we call neurosis and psychosis; and I have come increasingly, at least in my own mind, to identify anything that carries us toward these forms of perdition as *sin*. Irresponsibility, wrongdoing, immorality, sin: what do these terms matter if we can thus understand more accurately the nature of psychopathology and gain greater practical control over its ramified forms and manifestations?"[3]

The phenomenology of the guilt-experience seems to bear out the basic insights of the psychologist who does not close his mind to a possible theological dimension in the guilt experience and also the fundamental philosophical and theological explanation of sin. No account of the phenomenology of guilt will be adequate which is confined to the most obvious and certain features of this unique psychological experience. For that reason, since most of my readers will not rule out the plausibility of a theological dimension of the guilt experience it seems wise to summarize briefly the theology of moral guilt and to allow the reader to decide whether this explanation serves to confirm and clarify what are the most general characteristics of guilt.

II. The Theology of Moral Guilt

Moral guilt is more or less the state or condition of accountability incurred as a consequence of sinful acts. The term is used in different but analogous senses, and hence calls for many precise qualifications as it is found in theological, psychologico-moral, purely psychological, or even psychiatric contexts. In our consideration of guilt here we shall examine

---

[3] P. H. Mowrer, *The Crisis in Psychiatry and Religion* (Princeton, N.J.: D. Van Nostrand, Co., 1961).

it theologically, and specifically as it is used by the moral theologian. The theologian is not primarily concerned with a phenomenological examination of the guilt experience (such as we have done up to the present), nor is he interested in distinguishing guilt from other forms of psychological experience, although it is obvious that phenomenological considerations are valuable in the effort to clarify the components of guilt as understood by the moral theologians. There is a mutual help that passes between theology and phenomenology and no adequate study of the guilt experience can be attained without the contributions of each. However, we are here concerned with the *theology* of guilt. Guilt, for the moral theologian, results from the deliberate and wilful violation of the law of God. This conception of sin has to be supplemented by the notion of sin as *infidelity*. The Protestant theologian, William F. May, whose book we referred to before, shows how even the prophets of the Old Testament sought to avoid this reduction of sin to legal abstraction. *Disobedience to law* is one aspect of sin; *infidelity of one person to the Person* is a far richer aspect of the meaning of sin. May shows how sin was described so often in the Old Testament as an act of adultery. "For the Prophets, God is not a remote employer who hedges in his employee with rules, while he busies himself with other projects. He is husband to Israel. He found her in the field when she was nothing to look at, and washed her, and told her to live; and he took her to his own. He promised himself to her and made love to her, adorned her as his bride, lavishing upon her the riches of his love and life. Israel grew and prospered under the hand of God, but she went whoring after other gods. Her sin, therefore, is adultery, which is not simply the breaking of a rule (although it is that) but the violation of the very substance of one's life in the life of another. *Sin is not simply disobedience—it is infidelity.*"[4] According to May D. R. Davies in *Down Peacock's Feathers* provided a helpful analogy when he observed that sin is more like that act of a traitor than the act of a criminal. The rebellion of a criminal against the laws of his country can be seen to be quite limited. "No matter how spectacular his crimes, he breaks only certain specific laws. A traitor, by comparison, commits the far more serious offense of contesting altogether the sovereignty of his country. Analogously, the sinner is distinguished, not so much by the particular laws that he has broken but by the fact that he denies altogether the right of God to rule."[5] The two analogies of sexual betrayal and political treason are shown by May to converge in the word that Calvin chose for his

---

[4] May, *op. cit.*, p. 12.

[5] D. R. Davies, *Down Peacock's Feathers* (New York: Macmillan, 1946), p. 49; as cited by Bernhard Anderson, *Rediscovering the Bible* (New York: Association Press, 1951), p. 75.

primary definition of sin: infidelity. "Each of these analogies for God's relationship to his people presupposes the imparting of life and blessing from one side to another and the subsequent violation of its reception. The wife receives her well-being from her husband, the citizen his substance from the wealth and might and favor of his kind. In both cases, sin is infidelity."[6]

Even other identifications of sin are not as meaningful as infidelity—such other inadequate representations of sin as rejection, rebellion, disobedience, unbelief, corruption. Granting that these conceptions of sin are incomplete let us re-examine the understanding of the theology of sin as it is revealed in the two elements of the violation of the law of God. There is the formal element of turning away from God, our last end (*aversio a Deo*), and the material element of turning inordinately to a finite created good (*conversio ad creaturam*). We can see how the notion of infidelity is contained implicitly in these two elements. All guilt that includes the dual element of an aversion from God and a disordered adherence to a creature is theological guilt. The distinction drawn by some moralists between theological guilt, which includes a knowledge of God and of the fact that one is violating his command, and philosophical guilt, which is the consequence of a morally evil act performed by one who is without knowledge of God or of his law, has been condemned by the Church. Purely philosophical sin cannot exist, because every deliberate and wilful sinful action contains, at least implicitly, a knowledge of the supreme legislator. All guilt, therefore, is theological guilt when it arises from a deliberate and wilful transgression of the law of God, whether the knowledge of God and of his law be explicit or implicit.

Theological guilt is personal to the extent that the deliberation and volition are the deliberation and volition of the transgressor. It is individual guilt, incommunicable to any one else, the responsibility of the person himself who violated God's law by an act of infidelity. This concept of personal individual guilt distinguishes personal from original sin, which pertains to the human race. Although guilt is often identified with the notion of sin, it is more exact to see it as a state or condition following upon the commission of sin, and traditionally moral theologians have recognized this in differentiating personal from habitual sin. It is really in connection with habitual sin, which is the consequence of personal sin, that the theological meaning of guilt becomes clear. In habitual sin there are two aspects or formalities: the *reatus culpae*, which is the state or condition of being "guilty" or at fault; and the *reatus poenae*, which is the state or condition of being rightfully liable to whatever penalty is

---

[6] May, *op. cit.*, p. 11.

due in punishment for the fault. The *reatus culpae* in the present econ-
omy always coincides with the privation of sanctifying grace and this
privation is referred to in a positive way as the *macula peccati* (the stain
of sin).

Personal sin is not adequately understood as a privation of sanctifying
grace and the loss of divine life unless it is also seen as a defilement, a
profanation, a stain that endures until removed. As May puts it so well:
"*My Sin* is not the name of a perfume that supplements my personality
in its allure. It stands for whatever I do that mars, mauls, inflates, depresses, disrupts, distorts, or abandons humanity."[7] This is a striking explanation of what sin does to *others*; what sin does to the personality of
the sinner is what is contained in the term *stain* (macula). A. E. Taylor
shows that there is abundant witness in the universal language of mankind to the recognition of the peculiarly polluting quality of moral guilt.
The vocabularies of all languages show how spontaneously men use the
same terminology when referring to what most offends their consciences
and what is repugnant to sight, touch or smell. In all languages grave
moral offenses violative of the consciences of men are spoken of as things
"filthy," "dirty," "stinking." In addition, this notion of defilement and
stain is revealed in the ritualistic practices of all ages, which treat various
forms of moral guilt as so many physical pollutions or infections, as things
to be washed off by ablutions, or dispelled by fumigations in the same
way that objects infected by noxious germs are fumigated or destroyed
by fire. Edwyn Bevan in *Hellenism and Christianity*, specifically in his
most suggestive essay "Dirt," observes that philosophers have tended to
consider the moral sense in too exclusive a fashion, as a sense of obligation, and to regard the mental disquiet caused by moral evil as only an
uneasy consciousness of violated or neglected obligation. Bevan is critical
of such moral philosophers for not attempting to fathom the real significance of the continuous association in popular language between "sin,"
"guilt," and "uncleanness." He concludes: "the man who is sorry for having done wrong does not only feel that he has violated an obligation;
he feels unclean."[8]

This notion of the *macula*, or stain, associated with guilt, seems to be
borne out in the languages that communicate terminologically the phenomenological experiences of moral guilt. The terms used to describe the
consequences of moral evil bear striking resemblances to what the moral
theologian refers to as the *macula*, the positive resultant of the privation
of sanctifying grace, or the loss of the life of God. At the root of this
sense of moral stain Bevan finds a "primitive and universal" conviction

---

[7] *Ibid.*, p. 7.
[8] Edwyn Bevan, *Hellenism and Christianity* (London: Cambridge U. Press), p. 152.

about the sanctity of the rational soul. Nothing can be morally dirty or stained but an *anima rationalis*, and this consciousness of what the theologian testifies to as the *macula*, or stain, associated with the privation of sanctifying grace, is never adequately explained away as a mere "unsuitable response" or as a "subjective illusion." In other words, phenomenology attests to some suggestive parallels between the evidence of the moral theologian and the consistent reactions of persons manifested in their different vocabularies.

The *reatus poenae* was referred to as one of the two formalities of the notion of habitual sin. A genuinely ethical attitude toward the commission of moral evil seems to be the recognition of the plausibility, if not the necessity, for punishment. Once a person has turned inordinately to the finite creature, and used the finite creature inordinately, justice seems to demand the restoration of order. Punishment in this strictly ethical meaning is not *vindictive* but *vindicative* of the juridical order that prevailed before the commission of the moral evil. Contemporary value theory confirms this notion of the disvalue in moral evil, this disequilibrium that has been set up in nature and that almost demands restoration. It may be unfashionable to imply that moral evil, deliberately and wilfully consented to, demands punishment, and that the notion of *reatus poenae* is also phenomenologically sound. Nevertheless, our affirmation is prompted by a genuinely ethical conviction and contains a most important truth, although it might be open to unethical distortions.

Guilt for the moral theologian in its dual formality of *reatus culpae* and *reatus poenae* and in its emphasis on the *macula peccati* (the stain of sin) can be and should be studied for its striking phenomenological parallels in literature, art, music and sculpture. Obviously the term *moral evil* does not contain the plenitude of meaning contained in the term *sin* and psychologists are opening themselves to an understanding of this important distinction. The terms "sin" and "guilt" can have very formidable meanings for some psychotherapists. It is understandable that the effects of these concepts of guilt and sin are seen in very unpleasant forms in the many ways in which they have affected the lives of emotionally disturbed persons. From this point of view it is frequently difficult for these same persons, daily involved with the problems of disturbed people, to appreciate that these same concepts of sin and guilt might have a positive and constructive value. On the other hand when one views these same concepts in the framework of their philosophical and theological setting as the privation of the goodness that one should have and as a means to spur the person on to more serious efforts to attain that goodness one is not likely to find difficulties in understanding the real disturbance that can be set up in other persons' lives.

Charles Curran in "The Concept of Sin and Guilt in Psychotherapy" has considered both aspects of this question. St. Thomas proposed the notion of sin as we developed it above as the turning away from God and the turning to a creature. Virtue for Thomas was the consistent capacity to turn to others, not as rejecting or opposing oneself but as giving oneself in an act of love to others. In other words, sin is best defined in personalistic terms as a *failure to love*. Christ summarized all the commandments when he said: "Love God above all and your neighbor as yourself." Aquinas said that the sinner does not love himself enough. Because he does not love and respect himself adequately he cannot give himself as something worthwhile to others in love or to God and he does evil to himself in place of good. The central notion of the Judaeo-Christian tradition is the positive notion of love and not sin. Nevertheless, sin and guilt can be appreciated in a positive way even if they are not the principal point of the Judaeo-Christian theological tradition. To quote Curran:

> Sin and guilt warn us of the dangers to ourselves, they alert us to the issues that we must face at the time when we wish to avoid facing them. We would be seriously handicapped without some warning and alerting signals in our psychical, spiritual life. This does not mean that we seek guilt and sin any more than we seek to increase pain. Yet we have only done ultimate harm to a patient if by drugs or neuro-surgery we have removed his feeling of pain without in any way removing the causes of this pain. He is all the more gravely handicapped and his cure can be all the more difficult for him because he has been led to think that feeling no pain, he is actually well.[9]

Curran therefore argues that since sin and guilt have this function of alerting man psychologically and spiritually, nothing would be gained by changing the names of sin and guilt to something more bland. "A rose— and sin—by any other name" would both come out to be the same thing after all. Rank pointed out how sin and guilt are bound up with both man's freedom and his responsibility. He put it this way:

> Free will belongs to the idea of guilt or sin as inevitably as day to night and even if there were none of the numerous proofs for the inner freedom of the conscious will, the fact of human consciousness of guilt alone would be sufficient to prove the freedom of the will as we understand it psychologically beyond a doubt. We say a man reacts *as if* he were guilty but if he reacts so it is because he is guilty psychologically but feels himself *responsible*, consequently no psychoanalysis can relieve him of this guilt feeling by any reference to complexes however archaic.[10]

---

[9] Charles A. Curran, "The Concept of Sin and Guilt in Psychotherapy," *Journal of Counseling Psychology*, Vol. 7, No. 3, 1960, p. 194.
[10] O. Rank, *Truth and Reality* (New York: Knopf, 1936), p. 62.

It is impossible therefore to separate feelings of guilt and sin from the whole psychological process of personal and social reasoned responsibility. To try to do otherwise would only weaken the person psychologically.

III. CONSCIENCE, SIN, AND MORALITY

It is being seen more and more, especially in psychotherapy, that moral responsibility should not be separated from reasoned self-understanding and awareness. It has been the influence of Cartesianism, Rousseauianism and especially Kantianism that has tended to separate these interrelated personal elements. From Kantianism came the interpretation of the categorical imperatives that asserted themselves apodictically and that had their origins from the relations to one's parents, family and the state. In opposition to these influences it is becoming increasingly evident (according to Curran) that "the therapy process itself—no matter how it is brought about—is a process of rational self awareness and personal responsibility. It is a movement from a negative irresponsibility for oneself to an acceptance of responsibility for one's actions toward self and others."[11] Rogers also sees this type of awareness of the central source of responsibility:

> If we take the remaining proposition that the self, under proper conditions, is capable of recognizing, to some extent, its own perceptual field, and of thus altering behaviour, this too seems to raise disturbing questions. . . . We discover within the person, under certain conditions, a capacity for the restructuring and the reorganization of the self, and consequently the reorganization of behaviour, which has profound social implications. We see these observations, and the theoretical formulations which they inspire, as a fruitful new approach for study and research in various fields of psychology.[12]

In the Judaeo-Christian tradition the notion of guilt is associated with the idea of the *consequent conscience*. Sin itself is considered to be present in the violation of the *antecedent conscience* that has demanded something from the conscience. The conscience that we study at work in the behavior of David, Paul and Augustine is completely different from the conception of the Kantian conscience and the autonomous morality expressed in the categorical imperatives that are seemingly blind and unreasonable. It might be well to clarify the Kantian categorical imperative from the non-autonomous (heteronomous) morality we find more compatible with moral experience.

The Kantian categorical imperative follows from his conception of a

---

[11] Curran, *op. cit.*, p. 19.

[12] Carl R. Rogers, Presidential Address, *The American Psychologist*, Vol. 2, No. 9, 1947.

rational morality which is valid and binding for all rational minds. In his *Critique of Pure Reason* Kant considered rational science as knowledge valid and binding for all rational minds. In his *Critique of Practical Reason* Kant addresses himself to the second kind of rationality. Morality is comparable to science in this regard that it is true necessarily and universally without qualification. The categorical imperative is categorical not because of a divine command, nor because of a conformity with nature, nor because of any consensus however large. Just as rational knowledge has universality, objectivity and necessity, i.e., the knowledge is *a priori*, so does rational morality have the category of the *a priori*. Once rational knowledge and rational morality are agreed to according to Kant's reasoning, their universality and validity give evidence of their *a priori* character.

The principle of Kantian rational morality which is found in all moral acts is that an act is moral if and only if the principle in the act is capable of universalization without an internal contradiction. However, even more fundamental for Kant, is the deontological primary principle that "there is nothing in the world or even out of it that can be called good without qualification except a good will." The principle on which the good will wills its acts must not contain any implication of circumstances or pragmatic consequences because these would introduce contingencies that Kant wished to avoid. The right act would be determined by the principle that would be the same for every individual regardless of circumstances. To admit contingent circumstances would destroy the purely rational and categorical nature of the imperative. This led Kant to the first formulation of his categorical imperative: "act only on that maxim which you can at the same time will to become a universal law."[13] This categorical imperative is present in every moral act which is obligatory in itself without reference to any other end. In this way the categorical imperative is distinguished from the hypothetical, which represents the practical necessity of a possible act as a means to something else that is willed or might be willed. An act that is good only as a means to something else is commanded by a hypothetical ought or imperative but an act that is conceived to be good in itself without any ordination to a further end is commanded by a categorical ought or imperative. The hypothetical imperative only asserts that an act is good for some purpose, actual or possible. The categorical imperative declares an act to be binding and exacting in itself without reference to any purpose or end beyond itself.

---

[13] Cf. Kant's *The Fundamental Principles of the Metaphysic of Ethics*. Translated by Otto Mantley-Zorn (New York: Appleton Century-Crofts), pp. 2–4, 8–19, 29–33, 37–51.

If nothing can be called good without qualification except a good will, the good will is good in itself and not because of what it accomplishes or the uses to which it is put. Even if a good will achieves nothing, for Kant it is comparable to a jewel that would shine by its own light as something with intrinsic value. This good will operates solely from the motive of duty, not because God commands the act but because it is good in itself. This deontological strain in Kant leads him to consider the good will as the will to do what ought to be done on the presupposition that man is free. Freedom and duty are reciprocal terms for Kant, although he admits that morality requires us only to be able to think freedom without contradiction, not to understand it. Freedom is postulated by the moral law but human intelligence will never fully uncover how freedom is possible.

Kant stated the categorical imperative in two other forms in addition to the one enunciated about. The second form was "treat every rational being including yourself always as an end, and never as a mere means."[14] The third form asserted that "a principle of moral conduct is morally binding on me *if* and only if I can regard it as a law which I impose on myself."[15] This latter form stresses the autonomous morality of Kant, which denies that the moral law is something imposed upon us *ab extra*. All three formulations of the Kantian categorical imperative have been criticized on the grounds of their *formalism*, which would in application lead to conclusions opposed to established moral judgments. The example of repaying borrowed money does not seem to involve a contradiction which is purely logical or formal; rather it is dependent upon social and economic conditions in which people would not lend money if there were no assurance of repayment. Kantian formulations of the categorical imperative are to be criticized on the ground that they cannot be validly applied rather than on the grounds of their formalism. In addition there is a rigidity, an inflexibility and a harshness in the application of these principles because morally good acts seem to be confined to those which are done out of respect for the moral law. It is good to help others from motives of compassion and love where duty and obligation are not clearly present. These motives have independent moral value according to most moralists, but for Kant there seems to be not only a strong tendency to consider all inclinations other than the inclination to duty as morally irrelevant but also a confusion between the goodness of an act and the merit in performing it. Furthermore, a good will seems to require definition in terms of content as well as form, and Kant concentrated only upon form. There are limitations to a formal principle or categorical

---

14 *Ibid.*
15 *Ibid.*

imperative which consists in obeying laws that are universal and necessary. It leaves out of the moral sphere the performance of unique acts in particular existential circumstances and it implies a consistency and uniformity in good acts which is not borne out in practice, where the moral life is so rich in diversity.

The philosopher with theistic presuppositions will be critical of the autonomous rather than the heteronomous nature of Kantian morality. According to some moralists human reason does not create morality, but merely articulates it in the practical prudential judgments of conscience. This activity might be termed the "prismatic analysis" through which the law of God is transmitted. Obligation is not self-imposed but heteronomously imposed through the mediation of law or the confrontation with God in the individual conscience of man. Circumstances and motives are required for the existential consideration of the moral act, and the moral act is good if motivated by charity as well as by duty. Kant's dissatisfaction with a theistic ethics arose both from his own moral philosophy and his epistemology. For him a theistic ethics would imply a theological voluntarism because the divine perfection in such an ethics would be God's will considered independently of his goodness and wisdom. However one may criticize theological voluntarism, even Kant would not conclude that in such an ethic every moral law would depend exclusively upon God's will alone. Kant's fundamental objection to a theistic ethics arose from his epistemological position that God is accessible neither by intuition nor by demonstrative knowledge. It is clear that a critique of the Kantian categorical imperative reductively leads to a critique of his philosophical position on the respectability of speculative knowledge with respect to God and the nature of the moral ought.

The fundamental criticism of Kantian morality turns on his reduction of freedom to the noumenal order. Freedom is so essentially involved in the testimony of the guilt experience, in its self-condemnatory character, that past unreasonable conduct is looked upon as deserving of the disapproval by the *consequent conscience*. In the data of the guilt experience the *consequent conscience* bears witness to certain claims and counterclaims that were placed upon the *antecedent conscience* of the person, whether this was the encounter of obedience to law or the encounter of the exigencies of love for another. It is obvious that to do away with genuine guilt in the *consequent conscience* is to do away with what is involved in the data of that conscience—the data of an *antecedent conscience* in which the person has made reasonable judgments of the quality of his conduct. To do away with guilt is to do away with one of the principal instruments for therapy. It seems equally true that to do away with an adequate examination of the role of the *consequent conscience* in structuring a relevant contemporary ethic is to do away with one of the principal blueprints. There may be some legitimate questioning of the relation of guilt and sin in general to the theological notion of sin as implying an offense against God or a loss of His love. It should be more easily seen that sin in general (apart from its theological referrent) is a disordered relationship between ourselves and our neighbors, that it attests to enormous disorders in ourselves. Here it can be seen that sin and the guilt which arises from a recognition of these disorders cannot be separated from the failure to love. By the introduction of the theological referrent the insufficiency of the notion of *philosophical sin* becomes evident. John the Evangelist says that "God is Love" and "he who dwells in love, dwells in God and God dwells in him." Sin is therefore in some way an obstacle to this love between God and man in much the same way as the insensitive, inconsiderate and selfish person withdraws and cuts himself off from the love of others that is reaching out to him. As a result the sinner because of his sin essentially injures himself in his love relationship with God. The Psalms say this pointedly: "He who commits sin is the enemy of his own soul."

Existentially considered, sin exists only as theological sin, but even without admission of its theological dimension by persons who are unwilling to do so because of a more deistic conception of God, the notion should be liberally used in a contemporary ethic. In contemporary America it should not be difficult to show that sin stands for whatever "I do that mars, mauls, inflates, depresses, disrupts, distorts or abandons humanity."[16] It should be easy to show that the person who hates does more damage to himself than the person he hates. Hans Morgenthau describes the ailment of America as follows: "Contemplating the American scene today—the disarray of foreign and domestic policies, the violence from above and below, the decline of the public institutions, the disengagement of the citizens from the purposes of government—one is reminded of the other two great crises which similarly put into question the very identity of America: The crisis of the 1860's and that of the 1930's. However, a comparison among these three crises puts the peculiar gravity of the present one into stark relief."[17] In a period such as this when morality and ethics are being challenged and new responses are being made in terms of what roles are men playing in civil rights, in justice and in charity, in real existential situations, in the nitty-gritty, daily living with one another, there should be no insuperable burden to show the presence and absence of real love. If anything characterizes

---

[16] May, *op. cit.*, p. 7.
[17] Hans J. Morgenthau, "What Ails America?" *The New Republic*, Vol. 157, No. 18, docu. 2761, Oct. 28, 1967, pp. 17–21.

contemporary morality it is the centrality of love in person to person relations and the minimization of the role of law trying to lay down precisely what must be done. Love shows its face, and the evidence of love is clear and unmistakable in the crucial areas of war, race, poverty, concern for the sufferings of others. The absence of love is just as demonstrable and all the rationalizations that we make ourselves in order to explain the absence of love and the presence of hatred and bigotry cannot eliminate the gnawing still whisper of the *consequent conscience*. To sin and to know it is a sin, and face it as a sin is one thing—to sin and refuse to call it sin, and insist by endless rationalization on calling it virtue, is calamitous. We wonder just how long in a country that is open to the new ethic of concern and love for others, the refusal to love and the renunciation of concern for others can be experienced by the *consequent conscience*. A critical analysis of the moral climate of any academic campus points up the great difference in the views of the older and the younger generation. It has been evident that there is not only a new radicalism but also a new *privatism* that interprets morality in strictly personal terms. Moral decisions are resolved in terms of the individual's demand for freedom and authenticity, the unique situation calling for decision, the culture with its own proper ethos, universal ethical principles, and the theological doctrines of some particular form of religion. In his remarkable little study *Personal Ethics In an Impersonal World* C. Eugene Conover shows how our society is making us increasingly dependent upon other persons and how this requires the continuing need for a personal morality. There are new relationships intermediate to those which are fully personal and those which are "open" and impersonal. On the other hand, there is a sense of social responsibility that marks today's theological ethics, and both the scientific resources for overcoming ignorance and prejudice and the universal obligations our moral philosophers formulate, point to a coming social morality that will transcend class, racial, cultural, and religious barriers. In a world that is so technological and so impersonal, it is becoming more and more clear that a personal ethics is indispensable. In the genuine ethics that I have proposed which is the resolution of the tension between the two ethics of *responsibility* and *conviction* there is real need for relating the notions of *guilt, moral evil*, and *sin*. It seems to me that if the notion of conscience has been so exhaustively treated in traditional morality, in an essentialistic ethic, the notion of the *consequent conscience* should be of primary interest in an ethic that is *personalistic, existential, phenomenological*. Guilt is an empirical datum that should be properly evaluated in the articulation of a contemporary personal ethic.

CHAPTER FOUR

NATURAL LAW AND THEOLOGY

I. FUNDAMENTAL PRESUPPOSITIONS

At the very outset of any treatment of natural law and theology several distinctions are indispensable. The pressing questions are at once: "Whose natural law?" and "Whose theology?" Even the justification and the validity of the first question are very much in order. No one who studies the relation of natural law to Roman Catholic theology can be indifferent to the relation of natural law to other theologies. The distinction between the ontology or existence of natural law and the epistemology or the known principles derivable from natural law is the most important. It would seem from the dissent that takes place in any discussion of natural law that the disagreement is more on the epistemological side than on the ontological. For example, Professor Samuel Enoch Stumpf[1] implies this when he asserts that contemporary Protestant thought is fundamentally critical of natural law theory, although it would not repudiate the theory completely. A major reason for Protestant objection to natural law is that Protestants are unwilling to grant the ability of human rational powers to "know" human nature. For him "Catholic" natural law is associated with the Thomistic notion of the analogy of being, according to which the natural law is defined in terms of the eternal law which exists in God. This means that the promulgation of this law is made in the rational nature of man, and that the application of the principles of this law, whether primary, secondary, or tertiary, to contingent situations is made by the consciences of men in their practical prudential judgments.

For many Protestants this explanation places too much importance upon stable natures, rational powers, and not enough upon the ambiguity in every moral situation. Reinhold Niebuhr's[2] criticism of what he calls "classical, catholic, and modern natural law concepts" proceeds along these very lines. He insists that these concepts do not allow for the historical character of human existence because they are radicated in a classical rationalism which did not understand history. Therefore, for Niebuhr these concepts do not appreciate the uniqueness of the historical situation or the accretions which came into the definition of natural law through history. The general principles are too inflexible and the definitions of these general principles are too historically conditioned. Niebuhr does not deny an "essential" nature of man, but the profoundest problem for him is the historical elaboration of man's essential human nature on the one hand, and the historical biases which have insinuated themselves into the definition of that essential human nature on the other.

Secondly, Niebuhr criticizes the tendency in the classical theory to make the law of love an addition to the law of obligation with the result that we have one dealing with the determinate possibilities and the other the indeterminate possibilities of good. Clear lines between determinate and indeterminate possibilities cannot and should not be drawn, and Niebuhr illustrates this by saying that justice is an application of the law of love for which the rules are not absolute but relative. All such rules are applications of the law of love and are dependent on it. They would be autonomous only if they were based upon an "essential" social

---

[1] Samuel Enoch Stumpf, "Natural Law," Handbook of Christian Theology (New York: Meridian Books, 1958), pp. 246–248.

[2] Reinhold Niebuhr, The Nature and the Destiny of Man: A Christian Interpretation, Vol. I, Human Nature (New York: Charles Scribner's Sons, 1941), pp. 286, 293.

structure, and there is no definition of such an essential structure of community except the law of love. Professor Stumpf makes this the cardinal point of criticism between the Protestant and Catholic conceptions of natural law. The ground of ethics is love even for the natural man, and such love is the fulfillment and completion of the law. Love and grace are not dimensions of the supernatural order only, but justice is infused and transfigured by love. The Protestant conception, then, is fundamentally the confrontation of man with the God of judgment and love, commanding him not through the mediation of abstract primary, secondary, and tertiary principles but subjecting him to the single imperative of love. No law mediates between man and God, only love, and this love is the natural law for the very reason that love is the law of man's essential human nature.

Most Catholic and many Protestant theologians would admit to an essential human nature but even then the word *essential* demands precise refinements of meaning. The Catholic stresses reason which is *Aristotelian, classical, ordered, universal*. The Protestant emphasizes reason which is *individualistic, inquiring, experimental*. Dr. Fitch,[3] Dean of the Pacific School of Religion, says that both are needed, and no one will question that conclusion. The combination of the two stresses might be assisted by the suggestive use of the term *"prismatic analysis"* in connection with the formation of the practical prudential judgments of the individual conscience. It can readily be seen how the most general principles of law pass through this individual human prism and receive all the nuances, ambiguities, obstacles and helps from the particular existential historical moment of their passage. For the person who would lean toward a rather complete situationalism no law save that of love passes through the human prism; anything else that he might designate as law would not be obligatory but merely guiding and tentative, provisional and contingent. The position of the moderate situationalist would appreciate both the imperative of obligation and the imperative of love while giving full validity to all the contingent factors in the ambiguous ethical situation.

Between the divine transcendence and the ever-changing human situation Dr. John C. Bennett[4] places the "middle axioms" which seem to be employed to mediate between more general norms and the unique structural situation. Reinhold Niebuhr speaks of "enduring structures of meaning and value" which must be assured a valid role in the ethical

---

[3] Robert E. Fitch as cited by A. R. Jonsen, S.J., in "Arguing Ethics," *Homiletic and Pastoral Review* (January, 1964), 302.

[4] John C. Bennett, *Christian Ethics and Social Policy* (New York: Scribner's, 1946), pp. 76 f.

choice.[5] Will Herberg[6] finds some clarification of Niebuhr's concept of the "enduring structures of meaning and value" and Bennett's "middle axioms" by citing Edmund Burke who has this to say about natural rights: "these metaphysical rights, entering into common life, like rays of light which pierce into a dense medium, are . . . refracted from a straight line . . . [and] undergo such a variety of refractions and reflections that it becomes absurd to speak of them as if they continued in the simplicity of their original direction."[7]

The fundamental disagreement on natural law theory, therefore, is rooted in philosophical and theological presuppositions on the nature of law, on the nature of man, on the very meaning of *natural*. For the Roman Catholic, the Protestant, and the secular humanist the meaning of a theory of natural law will be conditioned from the very start by these philosophical presuppositions. In fact, almost all theological disagreements find their ultimate sources of division in philosophical premises. Those who are inclined to consider metaphysical knowledge as less valuable than that given by empirical sciences, will view skeptically the intelligibility of nature, of man, of law, and of God. All these profoundly philosophical obstacles will make it difficult to accept the existence of natural law at its barest minimum. When to differences in philosophical presuppositions are added the classical differences concerning the nature of original sin and its consequences for the nature of man, we can see even more clearly why a Catholic can use natural law as a dialectical tool only if he constantly appreciates these philosophical and theological differences. Even within Catholic circles where there is basic agreement on philosophical and theological premises, the area of disagreement may have been narrowed or even removed completely on the ontology of natural law but the ground of disagreement on its epistemology may be considerably wide. It is important to distinguish at the outset between the ontology and the epistemology of natural law, for it is less difficult to proceed in a discussion with a person who accepts at least the existence of natural law on whatever philosophical and theological premises than to carry on such a discussion where even its existence is denied. For the Catholic in his domestic exchanges with others of his own faith, the disagreements will arise more frequently on epistemological grounds. Outside these groups in his exchanges with philosophers of

[5] Reinhold Niebuhr, *Faith and History: A Comparison of Christian and Modern Views of History* (New York: Scribner's, 1949), p. 174.

[6] Will Herberg, *Judaism and Modern Man* (New York: Farrar, Straus & Young, 1951), pp. 145–156.

[7] Herberg, "Conservatives, Liberals and the Natural Law II," *National Review* (June 19, 1962), p. 438.

all schools and theologians of all creeds, the disagreements may well arise on both ontological and epistemological grounds.

Natural law, therefore, has influenced the Catholic theologian who has always interested himself in the mutual relation of reason and faith and in his conviction that God operates in history through the natures of things and especially through the nature of man than in Protestant theologians. Presuming that man's nature has not been so deordinated by original sin and that his intellect and will are capable of constructing a natural theology and a moral philosophy that will be valid and complemented by supernatural theology and a moral theology, the Catholic theologian has not hesitated to study essential human nature and to discover certain conformities and difformities with that essential human nature. It is unfortunate that the principal obstacle to the acceptance of natural law in modern times is the mistaken notion that it belongs to the Catholic Church and no other. The Catholic Church has always been a vigorous defender of natural law theory in areas ranging from property rights to contraception and from the problems of medical ethics to those of nuclear warfare. This is only reasonable for a Church whose theology maintains that grace builds upon nature and that nature has not been so deformed by original sin that man's intellect and will are not subtantially the same as they would have been before Adam's fall.

Since the gradual descent of moral standards the Church has given more of her magisterial attention to the claims of *nature* and *justice*. J. Fuchs[8] shows that only since the reign of Pius IX has the term *natural law* been employed with more and more frequency in the documents of the Church. It is constantly mentioned in the allocutions and discourses of Pius XII on the issues of peace and war, on political organizations and on the obligations of the many professions, especially medicine and the law. Simply because the Church has been concerned with the defense of the natural and to relate it to the supernatural does not make the natural something supernatural. The natural law is the basis and foundation for the supernatural code of ethics found in moral theology where the additional evidence for certain forms of ethical conduct is the evidence from biblical sources and tradition. At times papal documents will refer to elevated human nature, to human nature supernaturalized by grace, but where this is done the texts are clear and such citations do not permit a reader to conclude that the argument from reason has been so substantially undermined that only faith provides a valid and cogent ground for ethical conduct. The interrelation between faith and reason on this precise question of the probative value of evi-

---

[8] Joseph Fuchs, *Natural Law* (New York: Sheed & Ward, 1965), pp. 3–13.

dence from natural law is most certainly a fertile one for discussion among Catholic theologians, but no one of them would deny completely all probative value and all cogency to a natural law argument.

The fundamental criticism, especially from circles outside the Church, usually points to the difficulties in the presentation of a natural law that seems to be so indeterminate and unsatisfactory in the ways in which its defenders formulate it. The evidence which the defenders of natural law find may be so infirm in the light of the great difference in moral beliefs and practices at different times and places that it fails to be very convincing. N. Bobbio[9] suggests this criticism when he remarks that philosophers incline to deny that the natural law *is natural* while legal scholars tend to deny that it *is a law*. The response for the Thomistic supporters of natural law is that it is both natural and genuinely a law, that it is verifiable as *natural* and *valid* in an authentic meaning of law.

Robert Gordis[10] points up the fundamental dilemma of those who stand outside the dominant tradition of natural law but are sympathetic to its value. He refers to Robert Hutchins' observation that natural law appears to many to be "a body of doctrine that is so vague as to be useless or so biased as to be menacing."[11] For such persons the vagueness and ambiguity of terms like *nature* and *natural* have been always a part of the history of ideas and for them the opinion of Leslie Stephens may not be the cynical exaggeration that it is for others: "nature is a word contrived in order to introduce as many equivocations as possible into all theories, political, legal, artistic or literary, into which it enters."[12] Critics of natural law are ready to add to the catalogue of meanings given to "nature."[13]

II. CULTURAL ANTHROPOLOGY AND NATURAL LAW

This testimony to the vagueness and ambiguity of the term *nature* was not unknown to the proponents of natural law from their examina-

---

[9] N. Bobbio, "Quelques arguments contre le droit naturel," *Le droit naturel.* Institut International de Philosophie Politique, *Annales de la philosophie politique,* n. 3 (Paris: Presses Universitaires de France, 1959), pp. 175–190.

[10] Robert Gordis, "Natural Law and Religion," *Natural Law and Modern Society* (New York: Meridian Books, 1966), pp. 240–276.

[11] Robert Hutchins, "Natural Law and Jurisprudence," *Natural Law and Modern Society* (New York: Meridian Books, 1966), pp. 29–47; also p. 246.

[12] Leslie Stephen, *English Thought in the 18th Century* (London, 1881), II, pp. 225–226. See also pp. 106, 253, and 280.

[13] Cf. D. G. Ritchie, *Natural Rights* (London: Sonnensschein, 2nd ed., 1903), pp. 20–47; Erik, Wolf, *Das Problem der Naturrechtslehre* (Karlsruhe: Müller, 1955); Philippe Delhaye, *Permanence du droit naturel* (Louvain: Nauwelaerts, 1960), pp. 9–21. Wolf gives nine meanings for "nature" in the context of natural law alone, whereas Delhaye offers at least twenty meanings for "nature."

tions of its meaning for the Stoics, John Duns Scotus, Bishop Butler, David Hume and Jean Jacques Rousseau. Despite the plural meanings for *nature* and *natural*, Hastings *Encyclopedia of Religion and Ethics* does refer to natural law, placing the principal emphasis on the physical laws of nature and some emphasis on the natural *moral* law. The proponent of natural law insists that *nature*, with or without the premise of a God, does manifest design and order whether reference is to the nature of physical bodies or to the rational nature of man. In man there is a determinate nature that has not changed in essentials in this twentieth century. Aristotle's affirmation of the invariability of natural law that goes with nature as contrasted with the variability of civil law that goes with man's free will is just as strongly made by the modern proponent of natural moral law. From the study of human nature, the ordered structure of its parts, the relation and co-relation of its tendencies and appetites, the subordination of vegetative and sentient orders to the rational, conclusions are drawn concerning the rightness and wrongness of certain acts. This analysis of human nature is enormously complicated and sophisticated, but it is a possibility for man. Tradition, revelation and authority are more acceptable for some as helps in this analysis than for others, but the traditional elaboration of natural law must certainly be supplemented by the rich materials from cultural anthropology. Thomistic ethicians have an important function to play in incorporating the contributions of cultural anthropology into a meaningful theory of natural law. Professor Fay[14] has shown how some of the changes resulting from man's bio-cultural evolution may so transform the relation between man and nature (e.g. atomic energy, polymer chemistry) that certain acts may receive a different moral evaluation. Professor Richard H. Beis[15] considers the several advantages that a knowledge of anthropology holds for the ethician and discounts the anxiety of those who consider that anthropology supports only ethical relativity. In fact Professor Beis finds contradictions in the position of anthropological ethical relativity when it attempts to assume values of its own.

The philosopher-theologian, interested in a firm foundation for his natural law position, is not unaware of the advances in the contributions of anthropology to ethics. He is encouraged to realize that anthropology does not provide a scientific basis for ethical relativity. However there is more need for introducing into the presentation of the natural law many more of these findings of anthropology which can help by clari-

---

[14] Charles Fay, "Human Evolution: A Challenge to Thomistic Ethics," *International Philosophical Quarterly* 2 (1962), 50–80.
[15] Richard H. Beis, "Some Contributions of Anthropology to Ethics," *The Thomist* (April, 1964), 174–224.

fying the distinction between what is universal and invariable in human nature and what is relative and conditioned by the circumstances of cultural development. Frederick Crowe[16] has shown that St. Thomas affirmed the changeability of human nature when he considered human nature concretely and realistically existing in each individual as it is subjected to bio-cultural evolution as well as individuation. To say that this mutability of human nature is an ontological accident is not to deny its importance. Even *grace* is an ontological accident but it has the effect of changing man in a very significant way. Likewise an ontological accident introduced into concrete, realistically existing human nature may introduce essential differences into morality. For example, the ontological accident of the married status of one party changes a sin from *fornication* to *adultery,* a specifically different sin. These ontological accidents that bring about essential differences in morality are more appreciated by the natural law proponent who has studied the fertile sources of cultural anthropology. Professor Beis adverts to the several values of these sources by observing that anthropological knowledge places human nature in its proper perspective so that the ethician is aware of the fact that while existing human nature is enculturated, there is still something proper to human nature and something derivable from culture.[17] Much criticism of natural law theory could be avoided by the ethician and theologian if they kept in constant contact with the findings of anthropology. Such contact insures a high degree of sensitivity to the ethnocentric nature of many moral judgments. Natural law ethicians and theologians could assist in the development of a consensus in any discussion if they admitted that ethical judgments can only rarely be understood apart from their cultural contexts.

III. MEDICAL SCIENCE AND NATURAL LAW

It might be overoptimistic and naive to consider that there could be more fruitful agreement on natural law by further clarification of the two aspects of human nature, the universal and the invariable, and the relative and the conditioned. If the former has been emphasized in the past, the latter has not been ignored in the present, and this is especially so in contemporary discussions of natural law jurisprudence. The modern ethicians and theologians who introduce references to natural law in medical morality and in sexual ethics do not ignore any scientific facts which are relevant. The discussion of the licit use of anovulants in certain

---

[16] Frederick Crowe, "The Irreplaceable Natural Law," *Studies* (Summer, 1962), 268–285.

[17] Beis, *art. cit.*

pathological conditions raises many questions for which the ethician is ready to accept all the scientific help he can get. Do the anovulants sterilize by the suppression of ovulation or not? If they do (and almost all commercial advertising for the anovulants say as much) what conditions will warrant an indirect sterilization? What conditions are considered to be pathological? What are the limitations on the meaning of pathology? Does pathology confine itself to the physical, somatic, organic side of human nature or should psychological factors be introduced at all? The modern ethician and the theologian of natural law open their eyes and their minds to all relevant scientific data and frequently find the lack of consensus not among ethicians and theologians but among the scientists. For example, with respect to the oral contraceptive pills, there are some doctors who state that the pill does not induce temporary sterility but merely results in ovarian "repose." Other doctors call this bad science and refer to the literature of commercial drug firms describing the pills as "extremely effective in inhibiting ovulation," in "inducing temporary sterilization," etc. Where does this disagreement on the part of science leave the ethician and theologian of natural law? The moralist must wait upon the judgment of competent medical men and there is little wonder why his own judgment must be tentative and hesitant. Little wonder too why there is possible confusion generated in situations such as these among the less informed.

In order to avoid such confusion for the Roman Catholic it has always been maintained that the natural law is an object of the teaching authority of the Church and that the guidance of the Church is necessary for an adequate knowledge of the natural law. Father Kelly[18] refers to the moral (not physical) necessity of revelation in this regard. In other words, in his view the guidance of the Church is a practical or moral necessity for obtaining an adequate knowledge of the natural law. According to its proponents the natural law is sufficiently promulgated if there is promulgation of its primary and secondary precepts in such a way that no one can be invincibly ignorant of these. But if this is the case, then this alone leaves so much to be discovered by man himself that without the assistance of some guide and authority, his search would not be very satisfactory. Father Kelly mentions the position of most theologians regarding the *moral* impossibility of *observing* the natural law without grace and cites a professor of dogmatic theology who once told him that he thought this *moral* impossibility of *observing* the natural law without grace is so unique as to be practically a *physical* impossibility. Father Kelly then remarks that he had come to the same conclu-

---

18 Gerald Kelly, *Contemporary Moral Theology: Vol I: Questions in Fundamental Moral Theology* (Westminster, Md.: Newman, 1958).

sion about the *moral* impossibility of *adequately knowing* the natural law without grace—i.e. that this *moral* impossibility is so unique as to be practically a *physical* impossibility. The reader should be able to agree or disagree with this position, especially regarding tertiary or more remote principles of natural law, from the experience of those around him of all degrees of culture and education.

IV. THE CONTEMPORARY DEBATE OVER THE VALIDITY OF THE NATURAL LAW

In contemporary philosophical and theological circles there is much discussion going on concerning the very validity of the concept of natural law. This is taking place as much among former proponents of natural law as among its consistent opponents. Rabbi Robert Gordis, in a sentence that has become classical, observed: ". . . natural law needs only to be saved from its friends in order to convert its enemies."[19] The treatment of natural law that is seriously going on at present in the books and articles that have recently been published by Böckle, Fuchs, Murray, Lottin, Monden, Simons, Delhaye, and the contributions by others on subjects closely related to the problem of natural law—all these will present evidence for the great ferment in scholarly circles.

A. *The Position of Franz Böckle and Karl Rahner*

In an orderly and disciplined book[20] Franz Böckle offers a tightly reasoned presentation of both the Lutheran and Catholic positions on the law and the Gospel, the validity of the order of nature and the relation of norm and situation in the ethics of Protestants and Catholic moral theology.

Böckle analyzes the common evangelical position of the Lutheran and reformed position in three assertions: (1) The Gospel as the message of redemption by Christ destroys every form of human self-justification; (2) The Gospel does not take away the will of God, but directly preaches of its fulfillment through Christ and our sharing in it; (3) Insofar as the Gospel does lay down demands, these do not mean demands for action that we must accomplish as leading to our salvation, but rather the Gospel demands are a counsel pointing out things we may venture to achieve as a fruit of our salvation. These three assertions are juxtaposed against the Catholic tradition and the Council of Trent and are sum-

---

[19] Rabbi Robert Gordis, "Natural Law and Religion," *Natural Law and Modern Society* (New York: Meridian Books, 1966), p. 250.
[20] Franz Böckle, *Law and Conscience*, translated by M. James Donnelly (New York: Sheed & Ward, 1966).

marized in these propositions concerning the law and the Gospel: (1) Even if it is portrayed as analogous to a law, the Gospel still stands in sharp contrast to every attempt to use any law whatsoever as a means of justification before God. The first chapter of the decree on justification in the Council of Trent expressly declares that nature and the Mosaic Law are completely incapable of justifying man.[21] St. Thomas says that written prescriptions of the New Testament are a dead letter without prevenient grace. Böckle shows that justification, as the gracious judicial pronouncement of God in Jesus Christ, is God's work alone. (2) If the law does not itself justify, it is not taken away for the person made righteous in Christ, but is brought to real status. Trent refers to Christ the Lawmaker[22] and says that Christian freedom would be misunderstood were it to preach freedom from the observance of the commandments.[23] (3) The fruitfulness of the Christian life in obedience to the law does not mean the re-establishment of the law as a principle of conduct. Hans Küng puts it this way: "God causes everything, but from God's causing everything it does not follow that God alone produces all that he causes, but—and this is the most beautiful marvel of God's being the cause of all things—man's co-causality flows from God's causality."[24]

All of this is relevant to the difference in the conceptions of natural law for the Protestant and for the Catholic. Böckle considers the views of individual representatives on the question of the law of nature in the light of the fundamental presuppositions of Protestant theology. These presuppositions are the teaching of the total corruption of human nature after the fall and the teaching of the complementary relation of law and Gospel. The Protestant attitude toward the law of nature is compared with the Catholic view on the essence and the meaning of natural law. Böckle says that for St. Thomas "man possesses an innate tendency through which, without instruction and outside help, he can recognize whatever fundamental demand is made of him for his own self-realization."[25]

The best and most stimulating portion of the Böckle book is the part on the relation of norm and situation in Protestant ethics and in Catholic moral theology. It is pertinent to the structure of a contemporary moral philosophy. Protestant ethics, we are told, has no favorite reply to the crucial question: "Whether and to what extent the formulated law can

---

[21] Denzinger-Schönmetzer, no. 1521 (793 in old Denz.)
[22] *Ibid.*, 1571 (831 old ed.).
[23] *Ibid.*, 1536 (804 old ed.).
[24] Hans Küng, *Rechtfertigung, Die Lehre Karl Barths und eine katholische Bessinung* (Einsiedeln, 1957), p. 257.
[25] Böckle, *op. cit.*, p. 81.

be expressed as having binding force over the demanding will of God and whether God, in His absolute sovereign freedom, does not stand above all laws and in the ethical experience, calling man aside, can override all general norms."[26] In the Protestant tradition there is a type of relative situation-ethics in which universal norms are recognized; nonetheless, they enjoy only a directive function, a role never to be understood as that of a law. These general norms are necessarly human in their formulation and communication and the sovereign free-will of God is never bound by them. God's personal will is in the highest degree concrete and always reveals itself only in a concrete situation to the believer. How does this attitude compare with the Catholic? Catholic moral theology has always accentuated the circumstances and the motive in its consideration of the sources of morality. However in its own ethics of personal responsibility a refining and sharpening has been going on by reason of the fruitful dialogue with Protestant insights into law and situation. Böckle suggests further discussion along these lines: (1) God, as *Ens Concretissimum*, makes demands of man, not in general, but in the concrete existential situation; (2) this unique and personal call of God discloses itself in this positive uniqueness only to an unobjective, properly personal knowledge.

Protestants have found difficulty with reconciling immutable natural law with Christ's preaching of a morality of love in the New Law. Böckle raises the question, which other Catholic writers have picked up, whether the "morality of the New Covenant tolerates the inclusion of, or at least the limiting recourse to, a natural moral law."[27] George M. Regan[28] comments on Böckle's response in which he affirms this possibility by saying that the novelty of Böckle's treatment lies in his asking this fundamental, yet necessary question. Only several years ago, an affrmative reply entered as a supposition into Catholic writings on natural law. Böckle has contributed valuably to the ecumenical dialogue in his comparisons and contrasts between Protestant and Catholic views on natural law.

Rahner has also assisted in the scholarly exchange and has shown how situation ethics has insights for the Catholic that he would be foolish to ignore:

> There does perhaps exist a radical situation ethics which, because it derives from a purely secular existentialism, is rejected by *all* Christians as moral libertinism. We are not concerned with it here. But there also

---

[26] *Ibid.*, p. 90.
[27] *Ibid.*, p. 55.
[28] George M. Regan, "Natural Law in the Church Today," *The Catholic Lawyer* 13.1 (Winter, 1967), 22.

exists perhaps an attitude to general moral norms, universal in scope and specific in content, which will be affirmed by many Protestants as constituting the specifically evangelical freedom of the Christian man, whereas the Catholic will regard it as an unacceptable variety of situation ethics. The names given to the attitude in question by one side or the other do not matter.

The Protestant will regard specific norms, in the moral sphere, even in the form in which they appear in scripture, rather as a sort of signpost pointing out the way to meet and endure the ever new situations of the personal life of faith, with a critical attitude towards oneself and one's hidden sinfulness. He will mistrust or reject, however, specific moral maxims which, by their universality and eternally permanent character, claim to bind men in every situation without exception, on the sole condition that the universal norm, expressing an essence, is relevant to the particular human being in this or that definite situation, precisely because of the presence there of what the maxim in question designates and applies to. The Protestant will not tend to a state in which he is enabled by grace to fulfill the law from within, to accomplish the law by the spirit of love and in that way to be free of it. He will rather tend to a state in which he is freed from the obligation of the content of the various moral norms and precepts themselves because he can grasp the saving forgiveness of God even as a sinner and while remaining one.

The Catholic, on the contrary, will say that there do exist universal moral precepts explicative of an essence, binding in their universality always and everywhere. He will also reject a situation ethics given a Christian interpretation, as being the denial of a genuine philosophy of essential natures and even more as being unbiblical. He will of course recognize an ethics founded on the philosophical analysis of man in his concrete existence, providing it acknowledges calls from God which apply to the individual not merely in a situation presumed each time to be utterly unique, but in a situation to the constitution of which the universal essence also contributes. But he will not admit that the uniqueness of the moral and Christian human being stands outside a structure of specific universal moral principles founded on essences. He will admit and acknowledge that even the sinner can find his way to God through the grace of God. But he will interpret this turning to God as God's gift, in which God gives man the fundamental capacity and unconditional willingness to fulfill God's commandments and does not justify him without regard to an at least inchoatively active will to obey the law.

Of course, Catholic moral theology has always known that there are concrete moral situations in which the application of universal principles leads to no certain, generally accepted and theoretically unambiguous results. This is shown by its treatises on casuistry, its many *Quaestiones disputatae* and the principles it has elaborated for the indirect solution of cases of conscience by Probabilism, etc. Moreover, it is aware that there are also many disputed theoretical questions and opinions, so that not even all general maxims meet with agreement from all moral theologians. This simple fact shows that for Catholic moral theology it cannot cause any difficulty in principle to assert that there are cases of moral decision in which moral theology based on universal essences, and therefore the Church's magisterium, are not in a position to offer the Christian unmistakable precepts in the concrete case.

What is decisive in the present connection, however, is that the number of such cases has increased in a way that we might almost say involved a change in kind. As a result, the scope for freedom and responsibility which the moral principles of the Church and of Catholic moral theology, based on essences, must concede to the moral conscience of the individual (even if they did not in fact wish to do so) has become considerably greater. Even for the Catholic the road from the general principles of Christian ethics to concrete decision has become considerably longer than formerly, even when he is determined unconditionally to respect all those principles; and for a good part of the way, in the last decisive stages of the formation of the concrete moral imperative, he is therefore inevitably left by the Church's teaching and pastoral authority more than formerly to his own conscience, to form the concrete decision independently on his own responsibility. When here and there in draft decrees of the Council stress was laid on this role of conscience as irreplaceable even in practice, anxious voices could be heard in the aula, pointing out in alarm that in earlier days the Church used to lay down clear and unmistakable norms, whereas now even at the Council appeal was being made to the individual conscience, so running the risk of slipping down into an arbitrary subjective situation ethics. Those who gave these anxious warnings obviously could not see that today, even if all genuinely universal principles are preserved and observed, the scope for the solitary conscientious decision has inevitably become greater. They did not realize that this fact cannot be met by attempting an even subtler casuistry, which after all would only supply more complicated *general* norms, but only by forming the conscience. Then the expansion of the field of personal responsibility will be met by a growth of stronger Christian readiness to assume responsibility and greater moral earnestness, even, and especially, where the conscience can receive from the Church and the written Gospel no immediately applicable prescription for the concrete decision.[29]

This is an extraordinary statement by a mind open to the truth and to the contemporary modes of thinking. Especially in the last several sentences it seems to us that Rahner is bearing witness to the fact that more and more the moral principles that we have relied upon in the past are eroding. This might be put in another form: many of the principles which were considered in Thomistic language to be secondary or tertiary principles that admitted variability are now becoming subject to more and more modification. More and more the *ethic of conviction* that is grounded upon the presence of immutable principles is receding into the background of decisions of conscience and the *ethic of responsibility* is assuming greater importance. This latter ethic is concerned with the

---

[29] Karl Rahner, *The Christian of the Future*, Quaestiones Disputatae, Vol. 18 (New York: Herder & Herder, 1967), pp. 18–19.

empirically verifiable consequences upon persons who are affected by my moral act, whether those consequences are beneficial or deleterious. Once again this points up the priority of the empirical data in the determination of the rightness or wrongness of a moral choice. These elements go together—with the apparent erosion of more and more absolutes or principles there goes the priority of the *ethic of conviction* or the philosophical position on conscience that would ground itself solely on an *ethic of conviction*. If we might place the priorities of these ethics in some Hegelian framework we might see how the undisputed role of the *ethic of conviction* has had to yield in our culture to the *ethic of responsibility*.

It is interesting to reread the citation from Rahner and realize that he identifies conscience with the *ethic of responsibility* deriving ultimately from the erosion of the absolutes implicit in the *ethic of conviction*. Let us explain how he finally comes to this conclusion. He maintains this identification in the last few sentences of the long quotation and especially in these words: "then the expansion of the field of *personal responsibility* will be met by a growth of stronger Christian readiness to assume *responsibility* and greater moral earnestness, even, and especially, where the *conscience* can receive from the Church and the written Gospel no immediately applicable prescription for the concrete decision." The individual conscience has now been identified not with *conviction, the ethic of conviction* but with *responsibility, the ethic of responsibility*.

In our own understanding of the roles of these two ethics we see them in a tension which is not only dialectical in the order of ideas but in a practical existential tension in the individual choice of conscience. We are returning to the original position that we took in the first chapter of this work, that the genuine authentic ethic at this moment in our contemporary moral history is the resolution of this tension by each man in his own personal conscience where the two ethics are always present and where the priorities are never tidily laid out for the individual. It is impossible to live consistently, constantly, and uniformly on either the *ethic of conviction* or the *ethic of responsibility*. This is true of all of us and no amount of covering up will disguise the fact that there is a moral schizophrenia in which at one time the *ethic of conviction* comes out on top and at another time the *ethic of responsibility* takes priority. It is our own thinking that more often than not the ethic that assumes the priority is the *ethic of responsibility* in which we have calculated the good and the bad consequences from our moral behavior. There is no reason to be embarrassed by this. A good measure of calculation went on before Thomas More ever made his final choice. Even then I wonder whether a whole catalogue of consequences unknown to More swayed him to make the decision in favor of an *ethic of conviction* which was itself ultimately determined by the empirical data in an *ethic of responsibility*. To present ethical decisions as solely governed by an *ethic of conviction* or by an *ethic of responsibility* is disingenuous. Just a few hours of reflection on one's own phenomenology of moral decision-making will reveal the ambiguity, the paradox, the agony in the resolution of these two ethics. Conscience is no easy matter, and ethics-manuals in the past have almost reduced it to a simpliste priority of an *ethic of conviction* or a simpliste priority of an *ethic of responsibility*.

B.   The Views of Joseph Fuchs

Thus far we have examined the contributions of Franz Böckle and Karl Rahner to a more contemporary understanding of natural law. We would like to consider now the work of Joseph Fuchs on the subject of natural law. Father Fuchs puts his finger on one of the principal causes of the present ferment in Catholic circles on the question of natural law: "From the days of the Fathers and the mediaeval scholastics Christian teaching on natural law has been associated with a certain anthropology. This in turn was based on a theology of Revelation. Such bases were seldom indicated expressly; they were too obvious. Consequently the natural law tended to reappear continually in philosophical dress."[30] Similar to Bernard Häring's *The Law of Christ* the useful book by Father Fuchs helps to make clear that natural law is in most Catholic traditions a theological and not a philosophical theory. For that reason many natural law scholars and moralists, whether Catholic or non-Catholic, have attempted to reestablish the radical relation between natural law and Christian life. It has become increasingly clear that the doctrine of natural law has to be replaced within a theological structure and the life of faith in love. This has become necessary because "natural law is an abstraction from the total reality which is Christian man." The recognition of the abstract quality of natural law makes evident the necessity of pointing up its absolute value and guarding it against relativistic interpretations. If the notion of natural law is considered in its proper theological framework, we can understand that this theory does not mean "ethics based on abstract reason." It refers to the "light thrown upon concrete ethical problems from non-scriptural sources." In such a context doctrines such as the fall and redemption are not forgotten, passed over or prescinded from; they are vitally involved in the very notion of natural law and in the approach to these moral problems. Fuchs refers to the theory of natural law as a concrete "residual" theory

---

[30] Joseph Fuchs, *op. cit.*, p. xi, Preface.

adapted to consider certain residual concrete problems revelation does not settle.

In evaluating the work of Fuchs Michael Novak judges it from the vantage point of its role in dispelling common misunderstandings of the nature and the role of the natural law.[31] In the first place, there never has been and there never will be a merely natural man; naturalism is both an abstraction and unreal. The natural law is not "natural" in the sense that it establishes what men *would* have been like in a state of pure nature without the fall and the redemption. It is concrete and theological, and attempts to illumine what human action is *in fact* like, in areas in which revelation gives little or no guidance. In the second place, the ethic of Aquinas is not a "natural law ethic" but a "charity ethic." In the *Summa* there is only one short question given to natural law, but the entire second volume of the second part is devoted to charity. It was the reaction of philosophers against Descartes, Spinoza and Voltaire which produced the rationalistic interpretations of the nature of natural law as a doctrine concerning what man would be like in a state of pure nature. It might be helpful also to realize that the conception that most Protestants received of Catholic natural law theory came from Ernst Troeltsch. The Protestant interpretation of Catholic theory was to employ the distinction between "absolute" natural law and "relative" natural law but this distinction is neither found in Catholic theory nor is it accurate as a description of that theory. It is in the light of these notions of "nature" and of "fall" as understood by Protestant and Roman Catholic theology that many unnecessary misinterpretations arise.

The natural law of the Catholic theological tradition is not a "law" in the sense of a law of physics or chemistry. It is not a law in the sense of the positive law of the Ten Commandments. Natural law is theonomous because its thrust is complete love of God and neighbor and it is the participation of the eternal law in rational creatures. The life of God is unattainable without the grace of God, but the natural law in the concrete shows man struggling toward an openness to God's operations in history. It is another misunderstanding of the doctrine to look upon natural law as utilitarian, calculating, an expression solely of measurable or reasonable love or, on the other hand, as adherence to an absolute timeless code. Man is the image of God and natural law gives evidence for the intrinsic quality of human morality. Rational human nature is the adequate norm of morality but not in the sense of ancient Greek philosophy where man was autonomous, but in the sense of Judaeo-

---

[31] Michael Novak, review of Fuchs' *Natural Law* in *The Critic* (Dec. 1965–Jan. 1966), p. 62.

Christian culture where human nature is theonomous. The tragedy of the history of natural law is that it became dissociated from its theological framework because of the apologetical reasons for demonstrating the adequacy of the human mind and the potentialities of human nature. This took man out of history and made him an abstraction.

That man is made in the image of God and that this likeness is fundamentally ontological is insisted upon by Fuchs. Protestant conceptions of man are in general terms in his relationship to God which is personal, dynamic and purely actual. This is a departure from the notion of man as the image of God: "His (man's) likeness to God consists only in responsibility and in the fact of being called and in responding." The ontological relationship provides the foundation for a genuine "Theonomy of natural law." Thus the inadequate phrase representing natural law as the promulgation of the eternal law in a rational creature is supplemented by the conception of natural law as fundamentally the revelation of the very being of God. It is not just the expressed will of God but the necessary revelation of being in its ultimate ground which is God. To the listening man all of nature and creation is the manifestation of the being of God. In this light Christ becomes not the great restorer of a nature that has been lost but the perfector of the natural image of man that has always been present. The absolute value to natural law does not seem to be jeopardized in this interpretation nor does there seem to be foreclosed the possibility of a dynamic development of natural law within the structure of man's historically changing nature. The law therefore is not an ethical code to be obeyed, nor a catalogue of ruls for utilitarian morality, nor is it a set of nonhistorical absolutes.

Some moralists have placed qualifications on the work of Fuchs and have raised some penetrating questions that remain unresolved. Novak points out that the book was written in 1955 before the Second Vatican Council and there are portions of the work "that are marked by cautionary phrases, circumlocutions, and a too-pronounced fear of historical relativism which seem quite clearly foreign to the fundamental orientation of Fuchs' thought. . . . Christian ethics is the most backward area of Catholic scholarship, particularly in America. Father Fuchs' profound recovery of some aspects of one authentic Catholic tradition will help us make progress. In proportion as contemporary Protestants move away from merely kerygmatic and scriptural categories in order to deal with the secular problems of the secular city, they too will be increasingly involved in a theological investigation of such problems as are addressed by a theonomous, concrete, historically conditioned natural law theory. The important step is to disengage natural law theory from classical rational philosophy. Father Fuchs takes that step in his context, as we must in ours."[32]

Tinnes raises some irritating questions for a theonomous ethics: How does man in practice come to recognize this theonomy? How does he overcome the feeling that right and wrong are somehow derived at secondhand from God, that is, through the Commandments and "natural law" rather than in personal relationship. The law may be based on being but it is observed in response to persons. It is this side of the problem that Protestant and other authors stress. Tinnes asks the crucial question when he inquires about the epistemology of natural law:

> Just what is the noetic of natural law? Is it exclusively rational, so that all that is reasonable must always be actually rational? Must the finest sensibilities of man always be subjected to rational exposition, must the admitted movement by the Spirit be tested by the rigidly logical? This question is considered by the author. However, the scientific logic of the solution seems to leave little or no room to personal response. Father Fuchs insists that the response is always within the existential context of the individual and thus always unique. Despite these reflections the uniquely individual seems to be caught in the rationally objective.[33]

The reservations that some have over the explanations of Fuchs are understandable. He defines human nature as "the essence of man, either according to his metaphysical Being ('rational animal,' with all the consequences which necessarily flow from this) or according to his physical Being, by which from the Creator's will the metaphysical Being is actually real, together with any additional relations."[34] This definition seems to be compatible with a very static, non-dynamic view of human nature. However, this definition must be evaluated in terms of the historicity of natural law contained in the observation that "natural law is more historical than positive law, even though the latter is made precisely for historical conditions."[35] Man, in other words, must be considered essentially and philosophically and existentially and phenomenologically as revealing himself and his nature in the historical context of all the external adjuncts and internal conditions in which he finds himself. We have pointed out before that what might blandly be said to be a mere accident can alter the very nature of the moral act. In different historical circumstances nature may show itself to be capable of enormous changes. History, culture, and change may show its malleability and its plasticity

---

[32] *Ibid.*, cf. Fuchs, *op. cit.*, p. 41–58, 59–84.
[33] Tinnes, review of Fuchs' *Natural Law* in *Ave Maria* (January 1, 1966), p. 27.
[34] Fuchs, *Theologia Moralis Generalis* (1963), p. 67–69, 77–83; also *Natural Law: A Theological Investigation*, p. 41 sq.
[35] Fuchs, *Natural Law*, p. 111.

without in any way compromising its fundamental essential structure. Fuchs constantly distinguishes between man's metaphysical, absolute and fixed nature, and his physical, existential, accidentally changeable nature. What is philosophically accidental is not necessarily a mere ordinary change in history:

> Human nature and its likeness to God are immutable in their essentials. . . . The Catholic theologian thinks precisely of man's absolute and metaphysical nature. Nature, taken in this sense, is indeed something fixed yet remains open in many respects to an accidental determination and actualization. Insofar as man's nature is something complete and fixed its meaning and corresponding moral and juridical order are naturally laid down permanently.[36]

Contrast this quotation with this further one in which the historicity of man's nature is emphasized. It is this aspect of man's nature which requires repeated consideration by the philosopher, especially the philosopher who tends to the Parmenidean view of the first consideration of human nature. If the student of Fuchs has any misgivings on this aspect of human nature as understood by Fuchs, listen to these words:

> Even within each stage of salvation-history there exist continuous and accidental changes in human nature . . . Human nature is the primary foundation of all norms, differentiated according to the peculiar character of different circumstances which, as a result, influence the normative power to the same extent. . . . Man's nature, being substantially unchangeable, is accidentally in constant movement . . . The natural law must be considered as an internal law comprising the totality of that moral norm which corresponds to the totality of man's being.[37]

Does this juxtaposition of the two paragraphs from Fuchs vindicate for him a more dynamic view of human nature and its possibility of change? The first referred to the invariability of the essential metaphysical human nature; the second showed how circumstances play a most important role when this nature is plunged into the existential, concrete, personalized individual man or woman. The concrete judgment of natural law refers to "the totality of man's being," that is, man's being as it exists here and now in concrete existential reality. There is little wonder that some still have their suspicions about the importance which Fuchs would assign the second view of human nature—human nature in the concrete—but it seems that the criticism and suspicions might arise from the difficulty of penetrating the philosophical term "accidental circumstance." We had occasion previously of showing how, according to one philosophical explanation in which grace is represented as an *ontological*

---

[36] *Ibid.*, p. 85, 90–91.
[37] *Ibid.*, p. 111–113, 118–134.

accident, a clarification may be introduced. Grace may be only an ontological accident, yet it is responsible for the introduction of man into the life of God and for a participation in an inchoative beatific vision. This means that an "ontological accident" has quite important, one is tempted to say, substantial implications. In similar ways what Fuchs is terming an ontological accident will allow for major modifications in the structure of existential man. We have only to consider what possible genetic changes may be introduced into the structure of men improving the quality of his rationality. These changes would alter considerations in ethics and morality, and nevertheless they would have been caused by what Fuchs might say are ontological accidents. With this we would agree. Persons unacquainted with the metaphysics of *substance* and *accident* might tend to identify ordinary and unimportant changes in the nature of man when these are referred to as ontological accidents. If a genetic alteration in man can possibly be termed an ontological accident, we might see more clearly what range this allows for the influence of history and culture upon the variability of man. We might discover that man has a hundred million faces and nevertheless he is still man. Whether this is a legitimate interpretation for a genuine dynamism in Fuchs we shall leave to others to decide from their own reading of this scholar.

C. *Evolutionary Perspectives*

When we turn to the contributions of Charles Fay we discover additional confirmation of the significance of circumstances and history in regard to the dynamics of natural law. These circumstances may be referred to as *ontological accidents,* and Fay is willing to use this terminology. These circumstances or modifications occasioned by bio-cultural evolution are accidental changes in human nature, where *accidental* is taken in the metaphysical or ontological sense. Although they are philosophical accidents they are important in the evolution of man's morality, his nature, and his interpretation of natural law. Fay gives the example of a philosophical accident which changes the specific morality of an act from fornication to adultery: "Accidents make a big difference, as for instance when a man has sexual relations with someone who is accidentally not his wife."[38] Other changes take place in a highly technological culture between various relations, between the advance of speculative knowledge and the influence and power this advance has upon technology; between men organized in society in a whole series of complicated institutional arrangements; between men in society and

---

[38] Fay, *art. cit.,* p. 55.

nature itself. The implications of these changes for morality, natural law and the very nature of man are so substantial that Fay finally says:

> Certain acts which were formerly good become bad, and vice versa. I do not deny that the species of morally significant acts are determined in the light of universal human needs which are stable: lying, stealing, and murder are bad of their very nature, precisely because they frustrate universal human appetites. But I do deny that the species of moral acts is determined exclusively in the light of such needs: the species of good and bad acts are also determined by a constellation of biological and cultural conditions and emergent needs which are both variable and relative.[39]

We shall show in a later chapter how this distinction between the *essential* and *existential* consideration of rational human nature provides for the introduction into the conceptions of nature, natural law and morality all of the alterations of bio-cultural evolution, polymer chemistry, and atomic energy. In the past the universal and unchangeable characteristics of human morality were stressed and not enough importance was assigned to the cultural conditions and historical influences of existential man. A contemporary Thomism concerned with the concrete and existential order of man operating in history will emphasize the variable and the accidental in the human situation. Fay contends that ". . . in a Thomism brought up to date, the variability of human nature will occupy a much more prominent position in ethical theory."[40] To this same general direction pertain the dynamic insights of Teilhard de Chardin, which are brought by Fay into sharper focus:

> Man is now on the verge of exercising human dominion over the bio-cultural modifications of human existence. It belongs to man that he complete, in the light of the finalities or evolutionary tendencies of his nature, his imperfect biocultural structures, his largely potential principles of action. . . . The evolutionary world entails a moral transformation since it bears on man's distinctive nature in relation to God. . . . We are witnessing at present, in our own time, a formally new degree of participation in the eternal law inasmuch as humans are now exercising human providence not merely in the alteration of human institutions for the improved satisfaction of human needs but even with regard to an artificial selection of genes which will create in our descendants a greater capacity for immanent action and a still more adequate image of God.[41]

The question of evolution and its impact upon our changing concept of man, together with the consequences these will have upon the structuring of a contemporary ethics, have been evaluated by Andreas van

---

[39] *Ibid.*, p. 66.
[40] *Ibid.*, p. 57.
[41] *Ibid.*, pp. 77–78.

Melsen. Even the first principles of morality must be scrutinized in the light of evolution and historical change:

> If we apply what has been said about first principles to the moral order, this will mean that in the moral order, too, the first principles are operative implicitly rather than explicitly. Here, too, they contain implicitly far more than man in some period of history is fully conscious of and can express in some explicit formula. Every explicit formulation is branded by the mark of the respective period, of what, at that time, was seen as possible. When new possibilities arise in man's existence, which must be assessed morally, it is therefore very possible that the traditional moral formulation falls short of the reality. But this does not prevent man from seeing in these new developments possibilities for the realization of ethical values that he has always appreciated. This process can best be described as a new *realization*, which is at the same time a *re-cognition*. What is new can occasionally conflict with older formulas, and yet one recognizes there some moral value because one recognizes the new as something that was already implicitly contained in earlier principles, even though at that time the consequences were not understood.[42]

The evolutionary vision of Teilhard is acceptable to contemporary man who thinks of the world and of nature not as something complete and static but as operational and dynamic. Modern man sees around him all the evidence for creativity and invention. Our whole outlook on the world of reality is characterized by technological and scientific progress. The static view of the world has yielded to the evolutionary and there is no surprise in hearing that contemporary man throws aside any consideration of a natural law as reductively the conformity of some practice with the laws of nature. Fay is convinced that "the evolutionary vision of human moral life reveals universal and necessary features which underlie the humanly created value systems and which constitute a continuing framework for further moral progress." His position on the compatibility of a contemporary Thomism with this evolutionary conception of existential man is similar to the attitude of Andreas van Melsen. Fay concludes his article in this way:

> Human nature considered universally and abstractly may be regarded as an immutable standard enduring throughout the variable relations of man to his environment, to his fellow man, to himself, and to God. If, however, we consider human nature as it actually exists in place and time, we discover that human potentialities and inclinations rooted in it vary within limits, and these variations are ethically significant. Furthermore, progress is made with regard to the existence of the natural moral law in man inasmuch as human knowledge and power, considered as a created participation of the eternal law, tend to expand in time with the result

---

[42] Andreas van Melsen, *Natural Law and Evolution*, Vol. 26 of *Concilium* (New York: Paulist Press, 1967), p. 58.

that man enjoys a greater fullness of life, a higher level of immanence on successive evolutionary levels. . . . Even on one cultural plateau . . . variable adjustments are made in view of unique historical, ecological, and social factors. Hence the value orientation of a people is necessarily relative to their culture.[43]

Contemporary moralists concerned with the existential and concrete conception of natural law, nature, and morality do not deny the validity of the metaphysical conceptions of these realities. They are aware that moral philosophy and theology must today take into account all the fruitful discoveries of the empirical sciences, of anthropology and the philosophy and theology of history if they are to accomplish valid and new syntheses. *The Pastoral Constitution on the Church in the Modern World* shows that contemporary thinking in the Church is not unmindful of the very temporality of man, the historicity of man. It is the moment in history when the moral sciences "should leave the ivory tower of timelessness."[44] The discovery and recognition of the importance of man's temporality will become the source of a greater degree of reality and dynamism in the moral life of the Christian. Columba Ryan suggests this same positioning of man in relation to God, to other men and to inanimate nature, and contends that the sources of empirical studies should constantly add to the existential knowledge of man and his natural law. It might also be said that the contributions of existential psychology should be considered in this empirical reassessment of natural law. Man stands not in isolation but is the communicating existent who stands at the convergence of a whole series of relationships with other persons, physical and moral, with nature constantly variable and insistently demanding. Human growth must be measured in terms of the complete realization of the person's potentialities in relation to other persons. Columba Ryan describes it as follows:

. . . human fulfillment is to be judged not simply in biological terms, but in terms of the full realization of a man's personality in relation with other persons against the background of this network of communications. That will be right for him which enables him to fulfill himself in this dimension, and that wrong, which does not. There is a sense in which the existentialist affirmation that man creates his essence by the decisions he takes rather than comes into the world with a ready made essence represents a profound insight. To be forever progressing is a characteristic of man; the world around him is his world, the world-for-him, the world of his own ceaseless making and realization.[45]

---

[43] Fay, *art. cit.*, p. 79.
[44] Ildefons Lobo, "Toward a Morality Based on the Meaning of History," in *Concilium*, Vol. 25 (New York: Paulist Press, 1967), p. 45.
[45] Columba Ryan, "The Traditional Concept of Natural Law: An Interpretation," in *Light on the Natural Law*, edited by Iltud Evans (London: Burns, Oates, 1965), pp. 13–37.

This relational evolutionary conception of man and natural law will help to answer some of the principal philosophical objections that are raised against any theory of natural law. In the *Journal of Religion* Frederick S. Carney[46] lists four criticisms of natural law that are philosophical and theological, but as one studies them he appreciates the validity in the criticism of a natural law which is non-historical, non-dynamic, non-personal. These criticisms are as follows: (1) It is said that anthropological observations fail to support the claim to many of the universal regularities of human nature upon which natural law doctrine is thought to rest; (2) It is said that natural law presupposes that man is merely a structured being whose highest obligations can be defined by law when, on the contrary, he is also characterized by spirit or freedom for which law presents an inadequate or misleading notion of obligation; (3) It is said that, because man cannot rise above his own subjectivity, the so-called universal norms of natural law are not much more than generalization from the partial perspective of a particular class, nation, or culture; (4) It is said that natural law employs a logically permissible deduction of the "ought" of morality from the "is" of nature.

An examination of the roots of these four criticisms will uncover the generalized criticism of natural law which overstresses the immutable and universal features of nature, natural law and the nature of man at the expense of the variable, historical features of the concrete, existential, phenomenological, of these same three. It is in the light of the examination that we are doing of contemporary approaches to natural law that we can see partial answers being made to these criticisms and to the radical criticism of all—the indifference in the past to the temporality and historicity of man in natural law theory. The more contemporary attitudes to morality and theology without question lay great stress upon these indisputable features of concrete existential man. Nevertheless in this insistence upon the historical and the temporal there is an accompanying unwillingness to associate immutability and universality with just one period of history and culture. A dynamic conception of man, reality and knowledge will make it difficult to determine once and for all what belongs to the unchangeable nucleus of man's being. It would seem that only development will be able to reveal to us more and more of this nucleus of man's being and that this development does not only signify a new application of the *same* basic principles but forces us to adapt and revise these principles frequently. This is obvious in the area of science and we are wondering whether ethics should be any exception to this rule. It has been pointed that there is little reason to consider

---

[46] Frederick S. Carney, "Outline of a Natural Law Procedure for Christian Ethics," *Journal of Religion*, Vol. 47, No. 1 (Jan. 1967), 26–38.

that ethics should be excluded. Father Andreas van Melsen is critical of many treatises dealing with natural law that still proceed from the same concept of science as St. Thomas: "This is bound to have disastrous results because it leads to a highly inadequate treatment of new developments and the problems they bring along with them, or to a rejection of the very idea of natural law, and this would open the door to every kind of situation ethics and relativism. Yet, there is a solution, and this demands that we consider the developments of natural law in the light of what scientific development tells us about the first principles of a science."[47] It is in the working out of his being that man realizes more and more who and what he is. Nevertheless this does not mean that there is no validity for the initial insight that there was into his own being. This insight gave birth to the whole process of working out who and what he is. Science can only develop (according to van Melsen) where man has already seen, however imperfectly, something of the true nature of science and of himself orientated to this science. And this is valid in general. Only by reflecting upon himself can man see in which direction human existence should develop. These considerations "can in no way be classified as relativism, even though they refuse to attach absolute significance to a particular phase of the explicitation of man's being, in the sense that this absolute significance presents us with a final and unchangeable statement on man's being. The process of hominization continues forever."[48]

D.   The Contributions of Louis Monden

There is little reason to deny that situational morality has contributed toward this viewpoint, and it might be well to appreciate the insights of situationalism while dissociating one's philosophical position from its excesses. Louis Monden has scrutinized three problems confronting the contemporary Christian: psychologism, sin mysticism, and situationalism. In honestly encountering the insights of situationalism he brings into sharper focus the influence of the empirical, historical and existential upon contemporary natural law re-evaluation. The natural law is an inner law of growth, a dynamically inviting possibility urging man on to a realization of his genuine authentic self. This vision of an evolving natural law finds its source in the works of Teilhard de Chardin and it has been an influence upon many, including Monden. In order to understand the relations between love, freedom and the law, Monden distinguishes three different levels on which these words can be inter-

---

[47] Van Melsen, op. cit., p. 54.
[48] Ibid., p. 57.

preted: the level of *instinct,* the level of the *moral,* and the *Christian-Religious* level.[49] Failure to appreciate these levels invites difficulties for those who appeal to the law and those who oppose the law in the name of "love" and "freedom."

On the level of instinct, where the law is experienced as a form of coercion directed upon the will from without, there is always a conflict between mature freedom and external law. It is on the *moral* level only that the genuine relation arises between law and freedom, and Monden concentrates on this moral level of law. For Christianity freedom cannot be merely creative arbitrariness because in the faith the most radical roots of man's being are in relation to God, and this relation affects all of his growth and self-realization. Therefore the freedom of a Christian is never just a freedom *from* but a dynamic freedom *toward* Another in a continuous and fulfilling self-realization. Instead of merely looking upon law as the promulgation of the eternal law of God in a rational creature Monden looks upon law as a dynamic blueprint, a dynamically inviting possibility, a concrete project to be followed out in the personalized concrete situation in which man's *self* presents its demands to an *ego* vitally realizing itself. Monden says that this means on the moral level that the fundamental law in this evolution of the self is "Become what thou art" and this law directs the authentic or inauthentic human development of the person. All the individual acts of the person can be scrutinized in the light of that development. This inner law of growth has in moral tradition been called "natural law." He insists that the classical meaning of natural law which looks upon the dynamic growth of the self has nothing in common with the physical or biological notion of "nature" as it was used in the positive sciences and frequently in ethics in the consideration of sexual problems. It is obvious that actions which are biologically in accordance with nature might in all probability be questionable in the order of morality. Therefore solely because the concept of nature is infrequently used in the positive sciences is no reason to conclude that this is an argument against the use of natural law in the moral sense. The classical meaning of natural law survives despite the inappropriateness of the idea of nature as used in the positive sciences.

Monden is excellent in the clarifications he makes in the concept of natural law. He denies that it is an enumeration of abstract principles or formulations which can be found in many of the older texts in ethics. In some way this cataloguing of moral propositions educed from a natural law shows the influence of the seventeenth and eighteenth cen-

---

[49] Louis Monden, *Sin, Liberty and Law* (New York: Sheed & Ward, 1965), p. 4.

tury theories of natural right. History bears out the view of natural law as an *unwritten law* identified almost with conscience itself which was ever ready to juxtapose the authentic genuine self against the arbitrary written laws of some rulers or states. The principal classical authors have always preserved the notion of the dynamic growth of the real self which was identified with natural law. Aquinas describes natural law as follows: "The rational creature is subject in a more perfect manner than the others to divine providence insofar namely as it shares this providence and becomes providence for itself and for others. Hence it shares the eternal law and possesses a natural inclination towards its authentic act and finality. It is precisely this sharing of the eternal law in the rational creature which is called natural law."[50]

Monden pictures the original meaning of natural law to consist in a *dynamic existing reality,* an ordering and directing of a man "towards his self-perfection and his self-realization through all the concrete situations of his life and in intersubjective dialogue with his fellow man and with God."[51] This view might convey some notion of a static natural law but the picture Mondon offers is consistent with the conviction that natural law is more concerned with man's becoming and that the norm of his action resides more in that becoming than in what he is at present. This dynamic quality of the natural law is incompatible with arbitrary variations that are made in that law because of the individual or the collectivity. The vision is Teilhard's and Monden admits it when he says: "It is precisely the law of evolution, as it appears, for instance, in Teilhard's vision, that an increasing complexity of structures goes along with an increasing interiorization of consciousness, and that this development does not proceed in a steady way but shows, at definite thresholds, sudden total modifications of aspect, situation or disposition."[52] Monden cities J. Onimus[53] who puts the present crisis of conjugal morality in the perspective of an evolutionary morality. Monden's dependence upon Teilhard de Chardin's *The Phenomenon of Man* is evident in the following paragraph:

> Besides wholly new phenomena, running in the line of evolution, *regressions* too and ossifications may occur, which can be judged as such and distinguished from the progressive phenomena only by referring them to the general law of development. It is possible that in evolving humanity some implications of the natural law may rise to full consciousness only gradually, or that moral intuition in its full purity may detach itself only

---

[50] Thomas Aquinas, *Summa Theologiae,* I-II, q. 91, art. 2c.
[51] Monden, *op. cit.,* p. 89.
[52] *Ibid.,* p. 90.
[53] J. Onimus, "Metamorphose du mariage?" *Un Livre pour mes Filles* (Paris, 1964), pp. 179–198.

in a very gradual way from certain representations or projections in which it was caught. It is even possible that, on reaching certain thresholds, the growing moral awareness may show wholly new aspects and forms. Yet not every subjective modification in the moral sentiments of individuals or groups lies in the line of authentic evolution. And it is precisely the awareness of what developing man ought to become, hence the inner and dynamic natural law, which *allows* us to *distinguish* authentic developments from regressions and decay.[54]

In applying this notion of an evolving morality to questions of reverence for life he shows how an increasing reverence for life may bring about a great change in societal attitude toward capital punishment. Again the growing awareness of what constitutes an authentic experience of sexual love may bring about certain changes in the expression of that love. Monden does not see that man could authentically evolve toward a morality of free love, because "that would go against the grain of a humanity which is developing towards an ever more intensive amorization."[55] Therefore for him the actual sentiments of humanity do not constitute the norm, but every law of dynamic evolving growth and self-realization constitutes the *norm of authenticity* of the evolving sentiments of humanity.

Natural law is not only a norm that is located deeply within the human soul but it must also be made *communicable* and become available for education and community organization. As soon as this happens, as soon as it is stated in fixed formulas detailing generally valid rules of conduct, and accepted applications of these laws are made, the vitality and dynamism of the inner natural law seem to disappear. The dangers are great that the law will lose its dynamic quality and that its statements will become abstractions, prescriptions, the language of a determined culture and environment with recognized limitations of a specific mode of thought and committed to an interpretation from a circumscribed philosophical outlook. All these formulations for Monden unavoidably receive a certain *coefficient of relativity*. However, the disclaimer is made at once that this appreciation of change and this inadequacy of every formulation committed to a definite culture and history do not mean that the change is arbitrary. They merely show the plasticity of nature, the malleability of human nature, its openness to endless variation in behavior and conduct that in different places will mean the realization of the inner dynamism of natural law. This inner dynamism of the law is the very norm for every change in its expression. "It is forever in a process of purification from all the images in which a certain time or a certain culture threaten to imprison it, expressing its changeless authenticity in

---

54 Monden, *op. cit.*, p. 90.
55 *Ibid.*, p. 91.

the language and conceptual forms of a new time, a new culture, a new attitude towards life."[56]

Monden's explanation of the real dynamism of natural law shows how inappropriate it is to refer to the *intrinsic and extrinsic immutability* of the natural law which is so closely tied to a static, non-dynamic view of natural law. It also points up the great disservice that is done the vision of natural law as an inner law of becoming and self-realization by characterizing in the past certain acts as *intrinsically evil*. It would be more appropriate to look upon certain values as good and certain disvalues as evil, but it would be wise not to designate any precise definition in terms of specific acts as always vested with intrinsic good or intrinsic evil. The history of the past bears out the embarrassment that falls upon the person who is ready to call something always wrong in the area of sexuality. The slightest acquaintance with the history of the contraception problem in the Church will show that the characterization of contraception as intrinsically evil has become a theological hang-up for many who consider the rigorous meaning of the term and consider that any variation in a position on contraception would be a substantial one in the light of the language used. It seems to us that if the notion of natural law had been one of dynamic growth and of increasing self awareness and self realization, this designation of *intrinsic evil* would not have been used. In other words, if natural law is to be used in morality, the classical meaning of an inner law of growth, a dynamically inviting possibility urging man to become his true self should act as a deterrent from characterizing acts as always wrong or always right.

Monden shows how the basic finality toward self-realization tries to translate itself into the smaller decisions of life but in so doing all sorts of variables are introduced, all varieties of contingent conditions and particular factors. He realizes that this explanation is entirely consistent with Thomas' distinction between primary, secondary, and tertiary principles of natural law. This means that as the person proceeds to more detailed applications of the original moral principle the possibility of error greatly increases. Even the Ten Commandments, which are a practical formulation of certain basic statements of the natural law, have undergone modifications from the original pronouncements in Exodus 20:1–17. The formulas have been removed from various kinds of primitive religious conceptions and antiquated social structures. The process of purification always goes on and while the original formulation may have borne some resemblance to a natural law principle, the final formulation has been made in the light of a specific culture and a particular historical

---

[56] *Ibid.*, p. 92.

situation. Once again this does not mean unbridled arbitrariness in the formulations of the inner law of morality while efforts are made to renounce the static blueprint type of natural law. The dynamic, inner law of growth goes on constantly in the history of each person's individual conscious awareness of his own self-realization. Such a dynamic conception of natural law based on a dynamically inviting possibility, a concrete project to be carried out in the midst of the concrete situation, does not imply a variability in that law in the sense that the variations are arbitrary and under the influence of individual or collective sentiment. The increasing interiorization of consciousness assures that the general law of development will be in accord with the awareness of what developing man ought to become. Man's growing moral awareness of all his authentic human possibilities will bring about in the evolution and development of man a more refined and penetrating respect for life and for the inner reality of genuine human love. This view of human nature as open, evolving, developing as "a dynamically inviting possibility" is extended into the proper area of positive law where the will of the legislator makes the choice between the several possibilities of acting. The positive law seems to be a real restriction upon man's freedom but it is a restriction which ultimately promotes and serves that freedom. Such positive law is by its very nature *changeable* because it is to a great extent determined by the concrete variations in the specific situation. In the application of the positive law in order to make clear the superiority of the unwritten inner natural law, the virtue of equity or *epikeia* was employed. Monden points out how rigidly this term was understood because of the influence of Suarez, who conceived it in such a narrow fashion that it became reductively an objective *principle of interpretation* of the law, some kind of "inner-legal correction of the imperfection or rigidity of the written text of the law." The classical interpretation had been forgotten and Monden shows that *epikeia* in its authentic meaning is a virtue, i.e., a "disposition of the soul, a noble inclination of the heart; it is the decision to make the juridicial serve justice, to keep the law in the service of conscience, and, wherever required, to give unconditional priority to the eternal law of nature written in man's heart over every positive text of the law."[57]

Monden appreciates the contemporary criticisms of natural law and attempts a reformulation of the theory by a more profound conception of an evolving human nature. He is aware of the insights of situational morality and the continued critique of natural law made by the proponents of situationalism. The contemporary insights into man's existen-

---

[57] *Ibid.*, p. 94.

tial concrete nature do not shake his conviction that there is an objective morality grounded in being. He has been criticized for not clarifying the manner whereby "the Teilhardian vision of an increasing interiorization of consciousness" assures the authenticity of man's moral development. However, in his analysis of situation ethics he admits that it contains an appreciation of concrete human nature as realized in specific situations and in different historical periods. This concrete conception of man should be accentuated in any genuine morality because in the past the abstract conception of man frequently minimized the importance of the existing situation. Monden points to the statement from the Holy Office in 1956 which expressed disapproval of certain positions of situation ethics, especially the attitude of over-emphasizing the situation at the expense of universal moral principles. The critical judgment that can be placed upon the more radical forms of situationalism does not extend to some Catholic moralists who have attempted to work into their own thinking all of the best insights of this approach to ethics. Monden describes the philosophical attitude of these Catholic writers as arising from an almost universal, justified discontent with the usual textbook morality. The preoccupation with man's metaphysical being and with the abstract essence of rational human nature leads unavoidably to a consideration of morality which is univocal, universal and essentially immutable in all men. This morality is "negatively protective, fostering infantilism instead of stimulating adult self-reliance; it depersonalizes the human situation of the individual into abstract casuistry; it fragments the organic growth to a Christian fulness of life into a multiplicity of legalistic precepts and prohibitions, worked out into the minutest detail with hair-splitting rabbinism; under the influence of an outmoded form of spirituality, it distorts the unity of body and soul in man into an opposition, and attempts to freeze the evolving picture of man in a static notion of nature; in fact it separates ethics from religion and chokes off the autonomous decision of conscience under a divine authority nominalistically conceived in a merely heteronomous way."[50]

E.   Toward a Morality of Personalism

Traditional morality has always admitted and at times overstated the case for the validity of a metaphysical conception of rational human nature. The contributions of Fuchs, Rahner, Böckle, Fay, Ryan and Monden are in the direction that would now give more importance to concrete, existential, historical human nature. To this end they are open to all the research that has been and will be done in psychology, sociology,

---

58 *Ibid.*, p. 84.

bio-chemistry, and in the empirical and social sciences. If this emphasis on concrete man has come from situational morality, there is little reason why its source should not be recognized while rejecting its excesses. Jan H. Walgrave shows how the value that is assigned to the historicity of morality does not bring with it a relativism but that it will produce a genuine *personalist* morality that will be aware of the incommunicable, unique and ineffable value of the individual human person. Walgrave summarizes his conception of such a morality of personalism:

> The source of authentic morality is the conscience, i.e., our conscious and free acceptance of a call to generosity, and unselfishness. The object of this unselfish existence is the person; the immediate source of this call is also the person. This call is rooted in the autonomous value of the person as such, a value of which we are aware as soon as we express this call in our life, in every genuine encounter, in every genuine dialogue. This call, which makes itself heard unmistakably in encounter and inter-subjectivity, is a basic phenomenon of the human experience. It constitutes the moral experience. All moral demands are nothing but expressions and interpretations of this basic demand, though adjusted to the various situations of human life.[59]

Walgrave describes these situations as complex patterns of life which show aspects that are universally human and apply to all ages because they make up the human condition as such. In addition they display other features common to the historic phase in which men live. Third, they manifest strictly "personal features that are peculiar to my life, my circumstances, my vocation, my potentialities, my responsibilities, my most intimate history. But these three aspects cannot be separated. I do not live in three situations: a general human condition, a social situation of this age and a personal situation. These three one one."[60] In this philosophy the situation therefore becomes highly personalized and concretized; it embraces the contemporary situation at its most concrete just as this contemporary situation is the concrete and historical expression of the human condition in the largest sense. The personal existential situation in which I happen to be is inescapably my own situation and, for Walgrave, just as there is one situation, so there is but one morality:

> I do not subscribe to three moralities but to one only, and this morality is the norm for my personal life, however much it incorporates general norms derived from the general human or the contemporary situation. As Newman says, following the Nicomachean Ethics, every man must make his own moral norms and follow them. This is not laxity or lack of clarity or relativism in moral matters. It does not unsettle morality; it does not open an escape hatch to get rid of, let us say, the great prohibitions of

---

[59] J. Walgrave, "Is Morality Static or Dymamic?" *Moral Problems and Christian Personalism*, Vol. 5 of *Concilium* (New York: Paulist Press, 1965), p. 35–36.
[60] *Ibid.*, p. 36.

the ten commandments; but it breaks through the fixation of morality. Morality becomes personal and dynamic, and so loses its oppressive negative quality. It becomes a positive and inspiring *élan* upward, toward a greater humanity. It does not stand over me with a constant "You may not do this, you may not do that," but it wells up within me with power and zest and says, "I must, I will, I shall." The face of morality has changed. The sorrowful frowning negative handshake is replaced by a glad and positive acceptance, which expresses our growth toward generosity and love.[61]

God calls to account the entire man, the redeemed man, in his absolute uniqueness, in the intimate relationship of nature and grace as he finds himself in the concrete situation. This personal ethics of being is being heard of more and more in Catholic circles, and Franz Böckle points out that the writings of J. B. Lotz emphasize the following features of this personalism. The *ontology of being* under the dominance of material reality must be confronted by an *ontology of existence* under the dominance of person. The Greeks placed the accent upon the ontology of being and this has always influenced the intellectual life of the West. "But today the turning point seems to have been reached when the ontology of existence, under the rule of person, is taking over the leadership for the future of Christianity."[62] An ontology of being is associated with a conception of the being of material reality and a person becomes a being only in the more advanced sense of the being that has been colored by material considerations. However, if we reverse this ontology for an ontology of existence ruled by the concept of person we shall see that even material beings receive new light and deepest penetration. The system of values will be constructed only through the communication of existence to person. In virtue of this system of values the kingdom of being is an ordered hierarchy of good things. The individual person now is looked upon not simply as one out of a class of beings, but is regarded as having a unique personal worth and dignity which have their origins not from any communication from a specific group but which has its foundation in his being called by God. "This singular proper being of the individual and his individual worth stands, as does all being, under the binding will of God. That which is positively individual, insofar as it is more than the 'case' of the general, certainly belongs fundamentally to the content of the concrete demand. Accordingly, the concrete obligation is not only a case and application of a general law, also not *merely* an especially typical case, but it is much more like an individual call, and, likewise, demands an individual answer."[63]

---

[61] *Ibid.*, p. 36–37.
[62] J. B. Lotz, *Scholastik* 38 (1963), 336.
[63] Böckle, *op. cit.*, p. 108.

Robert Johann has accentuated this personalistic view of creative responsibility and has developed the conceptions of responsibility arising from the encounter and interaction of persons. The ethical situation is the response to this encounter with others.[64] The foundation of man's ethical performance is the dynamic relationship of his own person to the Absolute Being and Person of God. Discovery, creativity, intelligent response characterize this ethic of Personalism. In the formation of our moral choices the values and disvalues arising from these interpersonal relations will operate as guides for further ethical actions. These moral codes that are developed are never causally determinative of our ultimate choices. In the interpersonal relation of response we must consider all the possible consequences that might follow in all orders. This feature of the morality of Personalism shows its kinship with the *ethic of responsibility* and the insights of H. Richard Niebuhr, who proposed that the point of departure for a moral philosophy should be a phenomenology of moral experience, of Christian moral experience. In analyzing the phenomenon of responsibility, Niebuhr shows that a human response is never just a spontaneous reflex but an interpreted response or an intelligent response to a question posed by experience. The response also contains the quality of accountability and these features seem to be borne out in the phenomenology of the guilt experience as we tried to show in Chapter Three. The present response is not made only in the light of the past with the appreciation of all the operations of history and situations but it is intelligently aware of all the possible consequences that might follow. Niebuhr considers that within the phenomenology of responsibility there is the final characteristic of our social solidarity.

All the authors whom we have studied are alert to the contributions of evolution, history, existentialism, personalism, and situational morality in the dynamic view of man's nature. Most of them may find some difficulty with the dichotomy of objective and subjective morality, but all of them would admit the validity and inadequacy of a conception of mere metaphysical rational human nature. There is little doubt but that the contemporary thrust of morality is in the direction of an ethic of responsibility in which the dynamic, historical, concrete, empirical, personal elements are more and more coming to the fore. In Chapter One we attempted to show that the *ethic of conviction*, grounded upon *universal* and *absolute* principles, is being challenged in ethics and in the concrete resolution of moral actions, whereas the *ethic of responsibility* is assuming more and more the important place in ethical choices. We consider that the authentic ethic is the resolution of the dynamic tension

---

[64] Robert Johann, "Love and Justice," in *Ethics and Society* (1966), 25–47.

between these two ethics of conviction and responsibility. The latter is getting a larger and more sympathetic audience than the former. We cannot say that it will always be so because man is a being that becomes fully conscious of himself through his relation to nature and to others. Joseph Arntz shows how this implies that we cannot neglect our immediately surrounding reality lest we fall victim to one or another illusion unconnected with the world. "Man's relation to himself, nature and the others is apparently no longer a constant element. This introduces a historical dimension into our 'self' as object. It is, therefore, not only true that the teaching on natural law has a history. *Natural law itself becomes history*."[65] When Arntz raises the question whether on this view of natural law and its history we might finally discover the abolition of natural law his response is in agreement with his conception of man as a rational creature who creates his own possibilities and realizes himself through these possibilities. Man for Arntz is "the being of endless tasks." He achieves himself in each of these tasks. Thus he is not only master of nature at large, but also master of *his* nature. Therefore, to the question whether this view would not mean the abolition of natural law, he replies:

> Perhaps it does, but in a very special sense. We have already seen that natural law is not a goal, and that, in fact a totally new concept of man is beginning to take shape. An abolition of natural law in Hegel's sense (overcoming, fulfillment) is something very different from writing off natural law as out-of-date. It means that natural law has met its truth insofar as we realize that natural law is nothing but the truth of "living together." Natural law is itself the primary evidence that makes itself explicit constantly, and constantly demands to be translated into concrete human relationships. It is the motive force that drives us to give their full human value to all the relationships as they appear within the scope of man's concept of himself at any particular moment. This humanizing process is not arbitrary, but guided and borne by this primary evidence.
>
> If natural law itself is called to achieve its own truth, and at the same time to make itself more explicit and to incarnate itself, it is a historical process. Insofar as this primary evidence imposes itself, natural law is also the motive force in this process, a motive force which "moves as an object of desire moves as goodness and truth move."[66]

History and evolution are two concepts that are receiving a prominence by contemporary scholars in making natural law contemporaneous. The problem is, as van Melsen sees it, that when morality is conditioned by so many uncertainties there is a great temptation to crush this uncertainty by an appeal to revelation and to decide what is natural law

---

[65] Joseph Arntz, "Natural Law and History," *Moral Problems and Christian Personalism*, Vol. 5 of *Concilium* (New York: Paulist Press, 1965), p. 50–51.
[66] *Ibid.*, p. 56–57.

and what is not. This raises the question of the relation of the authority of the Church to matters of natural law. However we should understand that the interpretation within the faith allows also for a history and an evolution. When these factors are neglected natural law becomes more suspect and becomes discredited. This takes place not so much by assigning to natural law things that did not belong there but by a lack of understanding of the way natural law functions as a comprehensive summary of moral first principles.[67] The precise rapport between natural law and the teaching magisterium of the Church requires extended study. We shall summarize the speculation that has gone on in the most recent writings in philosophical and theological journals. There are several areas of division and we shall touch each.

V. NATURAL LAW AND THE TEACHING AUTHORITY OF THE CHURCH

The relevance of the doctrine of natural law in the contemporary world is evidenced by the recent writings that have occurred in both scholarly and popular journals. Vatican II in the *Constitution on the Church in the Modern World* indicates the meaningfulness of natural law in moral questions ". . . the Council wishes to recall first of all the permanent binding force of universal natural law and its all embracing principles."[68] Paul E. McKeever adverts to this interest on the part of Vatican II in order to dissipate any idea that the theory of natural law is out of step with the fundamental spirit of the Council.[69] E. Hamel insists that the latest scriptural writings and the most recent philosophical studies will not displace the validity and the influence of natural law.[70] McKeever investigates the interrelationship of natural law and theology, defining the first as "the complexus of ideas first synthesized under that name in the Middle Ages, and given best expression by Thomas Aquinas. . . . Theology is understood to mean the discipline which identifies, gives an understanding of, and induces reflection upon the divine *revelata*."[71] In order that we can understand the controversy on the role of the teaching authority with regard to natural law, it might be well to oppose the statements of two of the leaders in that controversy.

---

[67] *Ibid.*, p. 59.

[68] *The Documents of Vatican II*, edited by Walter M. Abbott (New York: Guild Press, 1966), p. 292.

[69] Paul E. McKeever, *Proceedings* of the Twenty-First Convention of the Catholic Theological Society, Vol. 21 (1966), pp. 223–241.

[70] E. Hamel, "L'Usage de l'Ecriture Saint en théologie morale," *Gregorianum* XLVII (1966), 71.

[71] McKeever, *art. cit.*, p. 224.

Gregory Baum considers the teaching role of the Church in many of his writings in the light of the recent question on contraception. He denies that the Church's position is infallible for three reasons: (1) the Church cannot define infallibly truths of natural law; (2) a real free consensus has never existed; and (3) it was even questioned at Vatican II. His arguments deserve serious attention because he is one of the most articulate spokesman for this point of view. We shall look to some of his works:

> The Church receives the assistance of the Holy Spirit, to teach infallibly the saving revelation of God, i.e., the faith and morals which Jesus announced to us. The Church also teaches with infallibility in matters which are essential to the defense of the Gospel in the world. But her teachings regarding natural wisdom, and *the meaning and content of the natural law, however true they may be, and however authoritative her voice in proclaiming them, are not and never can be infallible.*[72]

In an elaboration of these same ideas but in a statement in which he takes exception to the contrary position Baum draws the opposing lines in the controversy very clearly:

> I realize that not a few authors, in recent years, have claimed that the Church in interpreting the natural law is indeed infallible. This is wrong. The area of the Church's teaching is revelation. Vatican II, in the *Constitution on the Church*, again repeats the principle that the Church's infallibility is as wide as divine revelation, proposing it and at times defending or explaining it. The human wisdom which the Church acquires and teaches does not belong to the area in which she exercises an infallible magisterium.[73]

Let us look to his arguments. Baum maintains that the Church has the assistance of the Holy Spirit when she teaches infallibly those truths concerning the saving revelation of God. It seems that for him this would include those moral truths and articles of faith which Christ Himself revealed to us. He likewise admits that the Church can teach infallibly those questions which are essential for the defense of the Gospel in the world at large. We might hazard a surmise that Baum would consider that the Church could speak infallibly on the subject of discrimination or genocide because these matters are essentially connected with doctrinal positions on the equality of men and the dignity and reverence for human life. However, when the Church teaches on questions "regarding natural wisdom and the meaning and content of the natural law, however true they may be," such teachings "are not and

---

[72] Gregory Baum, "Birth Control and the Church," *Commonweal* 81 (1966), 286.
[73] Baum, "The Christian Adventure, Risk and Renewal," *The Critic* 33 (1965), 44.

can never be infallible." The Church does teach with authority in these areas but not infallibly. The Jesuits Ford and Kelly disagree completely with this position of Baum and contend that "whatever be the explanation, there can be no reasonable doubt that the Church can infallibly interpret the entire natural law."[74]

The second reason that Baum gives for denying infallibility to the present teaching is the absence of any free consensus. For him the present teaching of the Church on this subject is only part of the ordinary teaching of the Holy See. We would like to consider his words precisely:

> Since the 19th century, this teaching authority, though by no means claiming infallibility, has obliged Catholics, the bishops and the faithful, to be obedient to it; that is to cease reflecting on, studying, discussing the matters thus proposed. They are to be regarded as settled. The reason why the present position on family morality was taught universally in the Church was not because in each part of the Church bishops with the help of their people had reflected on the issue and come to a common conviction, but rather because one position, namely that of the Holy See, was made obligatory . . . the Holy See has decreed, for good historical reasons, that its non-infallible teaching be regarded as the last word, thus preventing the bishops from listening to the Spirit, wrestling with the truth themselves, questioning the echo of the Gospel in their faithful people, and thus leading the entire Church, progressively, to a common conviction produced by the Spirit. If Pope Pius XI had been aware of the doctrine of collegiality and reflected on the pursuit of truth of the whole of God's people, he, the supreme teacher in the Church, would not have written his encyclical *Casti Connubii* as he did.[75]

Baum's statements are strong and the reaction to them was just as vigorous. In an exchange of views on the subject of birth control, Crooker remarked that "this explanation raises difficulties greater than those it attempts to solve." Then Crooker asks the question that is the fundamental crucial question in so much of this controversy on the teaching role of the Church: "How can anyone accept as divinely-constituted a teaching authority that for more than a century has compelled the episcopate to turn a deaf ear to the promptings of the Holy Spirit in a matter of urgent pastoral importance?"[76] Crooker adverts to the words of Baum concerning wrestling done by a great number of bishops "with this thorny problem in direct response to the cries and questions from their people" and then comments: "To suggest that the traditional teaching has been hawked as a sort of party line by a body of uninspired

---

[74] John Ford, S.J., and Gerald Kelly, S.J., *Contemporary Moral Theology* (Westminster, Md.: The Newman Press, 1963), II, pp. 274–275.

[75] Baum, "Birth Control and the Church," *Commonweal*—81 (1966).

[76] Crooker, "Birth Control and the Council: An Exchange of Views," *Commonweal* (January 15, 1965).

ecclesiastical bureaucrats is a calumny and a caricature that cannot stand up under historical examination."[77]

There is still a third reason that is offered by Baum why he questions and even denies the irrevocable character of the Church's teaching on contraception. He points to the fact that the teaching was publicly questioned by Cardinals and Bishops at Vatican II. His final query is that anyone may well ask how can such teaching be an irreformable and immutable doctrine, if "at a solemn moment of an ecumenical council, cardinal after cardinal, and bishop after bishop gets up to propose that the entire position be re-examined?"[78] The substance of this argument for questioning the infallibility of the Holy See on this matter is that there is not adequate evidence to show that the Holy Spirit has provided the Church with an infallible pronouncement: "For this reason it would be irresponsible, at the present time, to say that the whole matter needs no new investigations since the Church has already spoken."[79] Charles E. Curran also raised the same question as the one in the title cited from Baum: "Can the present teaching of the Church on birth control ever change? . . . The entire question is so complex that it is difficult to state, let alone prove."[80] Dupré surveys the doubts and the disagreements and finally says with some resignation: "To me the very fact that there is so much doubt and disagreement on this most fundamental point seems to settle the issue."[81]

In the citations that have been taken from the writings of Baum the discussion on the role of the Holy See with regard to the teaching on natural law has been pinpointed on the controversy concerning contraception. We would now like to bring the discussion to the more general consideration of natural law and the magisterium of the Church by opposing this attitude represented by Baum to the position of Fr. Bouquillon as we find it expressed in his work on fundamental moral theology:

> It cannot be doubted that the *principal truths of the natural moral order* are contained in revelation either explicitly, or at least implicitly. This affirmation is contained in the general principles: the natural order is not rejected by supernatural religion but rather admitted into it; the natural law is not abrogated by the supernatural law, but is received into it. Moreover the affirmation is supposed in the demonstration of the moral

---

[77] *Ibid.*

[78] Baum, "Birth Control and the Church."

[79] Baum, "Is the Church's Position on Birth Control Infallible?" *The Ecumenist* 2 (July-August, 1964).

[80] Charles Curran, "Christian Marriage and Family Planning," *Jubilee* (August, 1964).

[81] Louis Dupré, *Contraception and Catholics* (Baltimore: Helicon, 1964), p. 30.

necessity of revelation with respect to truths pertaining to God and to the natural law; furthermore the same affirmation is handed on by theologians, and is taken as a principle of reasoning by serious authors.[82]

It will be noticed that Bouquillon is speaking of the *principal truths of the natural moral order*, but he also acknowledges that some other authors insist that *all* the truths of the natural moral order are revealed at least implicitly. McKeever shows that there is dispute in this area because Cajetan and de Soto do not go this far in their affirmations.

The lines can be drawn between Baum and Bouquillon. Baum contends that there is a sharp dichotomy between revealed truths and truths of the natural order; Bouquillon, on the other hand, states that the *principal* truths of the natural moral order and perhaps *all* the truths of the natural moral order are revealed. McKeever introduces a further reference to Baum which will allow us to sharpen the differences between Baum and Bouquillon. In the article cited from *The Critic*, Baum makes this statement: "The Church speaks with great authority in the area of human values, but when she is not dealing with the ethics revealed in the Gospel, she is not exercising an infallible teaching office."[83] Baum seems to be distinguishing the *ethics of the Gospel* from the ethics of natural law. The precise differences between Baum and Bouquillon can now be placed as McKeever does: "It is important to notice that in Bouquillon's thought the principal truths of the natural moral order are obviously definable, precisely because they belong to the *revelata*. Baum seems to deny not only that they can be defined as *revelata*, but even that they can be defined as the so-called secondary objects of infallibility. Bouquillon offers the possibility that all the truths of the natural moral order, although not explicitly taught in revelation, could be there implicitly, and therefore could be definable."[84]

In so much of this treatment of the interrelation of the teaching authority and the natural law it has been pointed out very interestingly that only recently has the Church spoken out so frequently on natural law. This was not done with the same frequency in the past.[85] It was only in the mid-nineteenth century that references to the natural law occur with any frequency. The Synod of Arles (473 A.D.) speaks of natural law, but in a generic way when discussing grace and predestination In the fifteenth and seventeenth centuries there are several references

---

[82] Bouquillon, *Theologia Moralis Fundamentalis* (Rome: ed. 3, 1903), p. 23.
[83] Baum, "The Christian Adventure, Risk and Renewal," *The Critic* 33 (1965), p. 44.
[84] McKeever, *art. cit.*, p. 226.
[85] Reed, "Natural Law, Theology and the Church," *Theological Studies* 26 (1965), 40–64; also Regan, *art. cit.*, p. 31–41.

to natural law when the occasion arose for the condemnation of certain specific practices such as fornication, masturbation, and extra-marital coital relations. When the term is used in these documents it is not clarified but merely introduced into the discussion. It seems that Aquinas was the first one to give any extended systematic interpretation to the natural law. From close to 1850 onwards natural law appears more and more frequently in pronouncements of the magisterium. Pius IX gave prominence to natural law in regards to communism, contraception, the immunity of the clergy from military service, the origins of the obliging force of civil laws, the indissolubility of marriage and the question of the possibility of salvation for the unbeliever who is in good faith. Once again, no systematic treatment is given of the meaning and nature of natural law; references are made to it as an argument more often to explain already existing teaching rather than as a theory to propose specific or particular norms of behavior. Regan points out how from the pontificate of Pope Leo XIII onward, the popes, with the exception of Pope St. Pius X and Pope Benedict XV, have continued this dependence on natural law begun by Pope Pius IX.[86] There have been repeated papal statements on the Church's competence to teach authoritatively the natural law not only in principles but also in concrete practical applications. This has been so evident that during the last several years a journal on Papal documents has appeared where confirmation can easily be made of the appeals to natural law made in the teachings of the Popes. The pronouncements in which appeals to natural law have been made concern moral aspects of political structures, the social and economic orders, race relations, the proper conduct of war, marital morality, extra-marital sexuality, problems in medical ethics, and the education of youth. Pius XII can be shown to have used natural law evidence or argumentation more than any other Pope. This repeated use of natural law fascinated one man so very much that he made it the subject of a doctoral dissertation.[87] In addition to the frequency of the use of natural law there is also revealed among all these citations an implicit systematic theory of natural law.

In two important encyclicals, *Mater et Magistra* and *Pacem in Terris,* Pope John XXIII also made references to natural law. We have shown before how in contemporary scholarly articles, in the attempt to update the philosophy of natural law, emphasis is placed on the temporality and the historicity of man. These characteristics of man are brought out also in the documents of Vatican II, especially those two which

---

[86] Regan, *art. cit.*, p. 31–32.

[87] Favara, *De Jure Naturali in Doctrina Pii Papae* XII (Rome: Gregorian University, 1966).

treat of the relationship between the Church and secular society, the *Declaration on Religious Freedom* and the *Pastoral Constitution on the Church in the Modern World*. These references show that the most recent documents of the Church have relied upon the doctrine of natural law to establish the reasonableness of certain positions or to strengthen conclusions the Church has always maintained. It is interesting to speculate on the reasons for the attraction of natural law in these same statements of the magisterium. Joseph Fuchs gives several reasons for this phenomenon: the contemporary Church is more involved in modern social, medical and economic problems than the early Church; the appeal that the Church can exercise in present-day secular society is not by citing Scripture or Tradition but by the approach of reason through the natural law; and lastly, the counter-claims of positivism in theory and practice require answers that are not drawn from the faith but from a means at the service of all men.[88]

Nowhere is the Church compelled to appeal to reason more and more than in the economic and social order where the complex problems of society converge—private property, wages, union membership, taxation, just returns, the responsibility of men toward one another arising from their common dignity and equal rights. It would seem that in all these citations from the documents of the Church at least one ecclesiastical document could be referred to in which a systematic treatment of natural law was offered. Regan points out that there is no such document although recent Popes do speak of various theoretical aspects of natural law.[89] Mention can be made of Pope Pius XII whose use of natural law was more frequent than any other Pope. In various documents which he released he treated of the relationship between the divine order in the world and natural law, the philosophical and theological meaning of human nature and the properties of objectivity, immutability, and the universality of natural law. The closest, therefore, to a systematic presentation of this theory should be studied in the writings of Pius XII. Nevertheless the teaching magisterium even of this controversial Pope does not give to scholars the fullness of explanation for the nature of this theory and leaves to philosophers and theologians the task of arguing to the precise understanding the Popes have had through the years of this doctrine. Regan again alludes to the official silence on the part of these magisterial statements about the principal difficulties that can be raised against the natural law. Most Catholics regard the Church as the protector and custodian of the natural law theory, yet nowhere is there a

---

[88] Fuchs, *op. cit.*, p. 3, note 10.
[89] Regan, *art.* cit., p. 33.

developed treatment by the Church's teaching office of "the Humean problem of the passage from *Is* to *Ought* in moral theory or of the relevancy of cultural and historical determinants."[90] It is because of this omission of a developed theory that the interrelation of the Church and natural law has been studied by philosophers and theologians and different judgments such as Baum's and Bouquillon's appear so far apart. On the specific problem of contraception and the anovulants philosophers and theologians have made references to the documents of the Church and have been challenged by others who do the same. In other questions of medical ethics and social affairs this same procedure is followed by proponent and opponent. Efforts have been made to distill fundamental elements from the Church's teachings about the natural law, and Regan has summarized these features in the light of contemporary discussions:

(1) Together with the revelation communicated in Christ's person, words, and deeds, natural law constitutes one of the two major sources of the moral teaching of the Church. A frequent distinction between natural law and divine positive law contrasts natural law with that found in divine revelation. In a broader sense, both natural law and the teaching of revelation are sometimes called divine law.

(2) The Church's documents view natural law as deriving from God as Creator and divine positive laws contained in revelation as deriving from Him as Redeemer. The Creator-natural law dimension is at times differentiated from the Redeemer-revelation dimension, in much the same way as nature is differentiated from the supernatural.

(3) As the guardian of the Christian moral order to which all men are called in Christ, the Church is likewise the guardian of the natural moral order. This latter forms an integrating element of the uniquely existing supernatural order and does not exist apart from it. Consequently, in accordance with its divinely appointed mission, the Church clarifies the prescriptions of natural law and defends its exigencies.

(4) The nature of man, as God's own work, is the ontological basis of natural law, which forms the rational standard for moral activity and expresses the moral order willed by God. Natural law thus refers to an objective order of morality based on man's nature. Various social institutions, such as the family and the state, find their foundation in natural law.

(5) The ontological basis of natural law establishes its absolute value. This precludes relativism in morals, for the absoluteness applies to more than a few general norms of natural law. Natural law serves as the criterion of all human laws, for no just law can contradict man's being. In addition, the ontological foundation of natural law implies that it remains substantially intact and unchangeable throughout all times and in all places.

(6) The Church never understands natural law as a naturalistic or

---

[90] *Ibid.*, p. 33.

merely rationalistic creation of an autonomous man. The being on which reason reflects and the reasoning power itself flow from God's creative work in man. Both participate in the divine being and in the divine Intelligence.

(7) Many pronouncements use the Pauline theme found in Romans 2. The popes say that natural law is found within man, "written in his heart." Man has the power to discover this law of his being, at least if he is not blinded by sin or passion. In this sense, reason itself is sometimes termed natural law, for reason discovers the concrete good and evil in proposed human activity. In short, the objective basis of the moral order, which is man's being, has its subjective complement in man's rational ability to discover the objective order in the ontological structure of his being.[91]

The above series of propositions present a summary view of the doctrine of natural law, but it does not approach in systematic form the treatment of Aquinas. Neither the methodology in arriving at these principles nor the content itself in any specific way are indicated. For Regan "these propositions state little more than the continuing, valid existence within the Christian moral order of a divinely ordained, universal, substantially immutable, and objective moral order, based on man's nature and discernible by man's reason."[92] Most moralists would agree that if the relativism and subjectivism of contemporary ethical theory are set in opposition to these propositions they themselves will reveal a substantial idea of what the natural law means for the Church. However, if these propositions are scrutinized very carefully we shall see the lines dividing on just how much doctrinal value should be assigned to them. In other words, we shall have the opposing positions of Baum and Bouquillon and more or less moralists and theologians will be ranged in such a way that they find themselves moving in the direction of one or the other. The skeleton framework of a natural law doctrine will be considered by some to be a "matter of faith" while other refinements of the natural law will not be brought within this category. In other words, for some theologians this minimal spelling out of a natural law theory by the Church belongs to the content of the faith. On other areas of the theory there is a possible discussible question about its relation to the faith. Baum would certainly see in much of this what has been called a "creeping infallibility," an inclination toward maximizing papal infallibility by assigning this feature to more pronouncements than appears valid if the conditions for papal infallibility are to be met. Regan shows that there is a qualitative difference in many of the statements of the Popes if careful scrutiny is made of them. Pope Pius XII made hundreds

---

[91] *Ibid.*, pp. 34–35.
[92] *Ibid.*

of statements on moral questions and presented them in different forms—encyclicals, radio messages, allocutions, audiences of scientists, ordinary citizens and parishioners. The conditions and circumstances of delivery, the mode of presentation and the audience to which the papal statements are made should act as a brake against exaggerating the authoritative nature of these pronouncements.

We should clarify here one point. It would seem that the criticism that Baum makes of assigning infallibility to the Church on the truths of natural law would also extend to any statements that are made on the nature and properties of the natural law. In other words, if Baum denies the infallibility in the first case, he in all likelihood would deny the Church's infallibility in proposing a certain theory of natural law philosophy. At least, it seems to us, Baum would not only say that the Church is not speaking infallibly when she says that contraception is against the natural law but she is also not speaking infallibly when she says that these minimal propositions constitute the nature of a natural law theory. If we are correct here the presuppositions of any natural law theory would be outside the pale of infallibility for Baum. In support of the Baum position it might be well to consider how circumscribed and narrow is the extent of this infallible authority as revealed in the *Dogmatic Constitution of the Church*:

> The Roman Pontiff, as the head of the college of bishops, enjoys (infallibility) in virtue of his office, when, as the supreme shepherd and teacher of all the faithful . . . he proclaims by a definitive act some doctrine of faith and morals.
>   The infallibility promised to the Church resides also in the body of bishops when that body exercises supreme teaching authority with the successor of Peter. . . . This is so even when they are dispersed around the world, provided that while maintaining the bond of unity among themselves and with Peter's successor, and while teaching authentically on a matter of faith and morals, they concur in a single viewpoint as the one which must be held conclusively. This authority is even more clearly verified when, gathered together in an ecumenical council, they are teachers and judges of faith and morals for the universal Church.[93]

Regan appears to agree with the position taken above that Baum would simply deny the possibility of the Church's defining any material drawn from natural law alone. Baum would ask the question whether the conditions above have ever been met by any body of bishops or by a Pope speaking on the subject of natural law. Even if they so did speak on the natural law it would not be a proper subject for infallibility because only the *revelata* and what is essentially and absolutely necessary

---

[93] *Dogmatic Constitution on the Church*, par. 25, in *Documents of Vatican II*, Abbott edition.

to explain or defend the *revelata* fall under the Church's mantle of infallibility. Regan observes that it is not necessary to adopt the rigorous position of Baum, i.e. that the *existence, essence, properties* and *applications* of natural law are not within the scope of the *revelata*. Even if we consented to agree that the existence, essence, properties and applications of natural law were within the proper object of the *revelata*, all the other circumscribing conditions for infallibility have never been met. Regan finally states that an "examination of the teachings of the Church presents no certain example of a statement on the existence, essence, or application of natural law which of itself constitutes an infallible definition. As will be seen, this initial conclusion does not exclude the possibility that the constant reliance of the Church's teaching office on natural law perspectives implies that its existence and basic value are articles of faith."[94]

Baum would agree with the first portion of this observation and deny the second emphatically. Some are inclined to agree with him that not only is there no certain example of a statement on the *existence, essence* or *application* of natural law which of itself constitutes an infallible definition but that such a case would be an impossibility because the truths of natural law do not fall under the prerogative of infallibility. The second assertion is certainly stronger than the first, but it does appear to be defensible especially if we consider the remote implications in natural law theory and applications. Surely here the tendency for creeping infallibility should be discouraged. It would seem that the division that has taken place on the question of the infallibility of the statement on contraception (because of the ordinary magisterium of the Church) has made clear that some reputable theologians will not at present accept the irreformability of the doctrine on contraception. The writings of Lynch, Zimmerman, Connell, Gorman, McReavy, Denis O'Callahan, Griscz, Ford, Kelly, and Lambrushini, maintain the widely held position that the Church's teaching on contraception is infallible and hence not subject to change because of the ordinary teaching of the magisterium. On the other side, equally reputable theologians are found who argue that the doctrine can change: Häring, Bishop Reuss, Dupré, Pixten, and Baum. It was argued by some at the time of the release of *Casti Connubii* that the document was an infallible utterance from the very nature of the language that was employed to condemn the practice of contraception. However, as has been suggested before, any assignment of this quality of infallibility should take into consideration the circumstances under which the pronouncement was made.

---

[94] Regan, *art. cit.*, p. 36.

When it is realized that the statement on contraception was occasioned by the decision of the Lambeth Conference which had approved of contraception as morally licit in certain cases, the significance of the strong language can be appreciated. Mega-language has a way of coming back to haunt its user. Terms like *intrinsically evil*, as we indicated before, can become albatrosses around the necks of those responsible. Much has been gained in the contraception question, not the least being the unwisdom in employing the language of over-kill. There is a rhetoric to use and a rhetoric to eschew in papal pronouncements. Clarity is the first quality of any such papal statement but it can be made without the adoption of a rhetoric of demolition. In the encyclical *Casti Connubii* the presumption is made of the existence and essence of the natural law but this material is not explicitly treated in the document which condemned contraception as a practice. Since reference was already made of the strong language that was used in this condemnation it might be well to quote the relevant passage:

> Since, therefore, openly departing from the uninterrupted Christian tradition some recently have judged it possible solemnly to declare another doctrine regarding this question, the Catholic Church, to whom God has entrusted the defence of the integrity and purity of morals, standing erect in the midst of the moral ruin which surrounds her, in order that she may preserve the chastity of the nuptial union from being defiled by this foul stain, raises her voice in token of her divine ambassadorship and through our mouth proclaims anew: any use whatsoever of matrimony exercised in such a way that the act is deliberately frustrated in its natural power to generate life is an offence against the law of God and of nature, and those who indulge in such are branded with the guilt of grave sin.[95]

It was in Vatican I that the solemn definition of papal infallibility was proclaimed. The inclination since 1870 has been to extend papal infallibility beyond the restricted conditions of Vatican I's definition to include, as Regan has pointed out, the canonization of saints, the approval of religious orders, and the doctrinal substance of canon law. The passage from the encyclical above has been considered by some to belong to the *ordinary teaching of the Church* to which, along with other encyclicals, allocutions and decrees the pregotive of infallibility has been applied. It seems reasonable to say that the assignment of infallibility to these documents is going beyond the clear conditions of the definition of Vatican I. In opposition to this tendency to apply the term *infallible* to documents other than the strict definitions, there is the criticism that is made by Baum and others of *creeping infallibility* accompanied by a

---

[95] Pius XI, *Casti Connubii*, NCWC translation. Cf. Leslie Dewart, "Casti Connubii and the Development of Dogma," *Contraception and Holiness* (New York: Herder & Herder, 1964), pp. 202–310.

desire to restrict the range of infallible statements to apply only to those where the explicit terms of infallibility have been met. It is interesting to hear Regan say that "since this position seems perfectly orthodox, a Catholic may hold freely either the restricted concept of papal infallibility as defined expressly by Vatican I or the extended concept as proposed by some theologians."[96] It is understandable that a person's adoption of the restricted concept of papal infallibility with regard to the statements on natural law would mean that he would conclude that the Catholic has no duty to believe as matters of faith any of the propositions on natural law. This has certainly been done by some theologians who have used the criterion of infallibility in the strict explicit terms of Vatican I and have therefore concluded that it is not an infallible teaching of the Church that contraception is immoral. These same theologians would grant the authoritative nature of the pronouncement from the Holy Father but they would not include the condemnation under the prerogative of infallibility. For them the question of change of doctrinal position in the light of history and evolution of the conception of human sexuality would cause no insoluble problems. We cannot help but observe that the freedom of the Catholic to accept either the strict or the extended meaning of the term *infallibility* will mean that the Catholic is free to consider that the statement of Vatican I as far as the object of infallibility is concerned was left fundamentally unclear. Was the definition to be taken *sensu aiente* or *sensu negante*, i.c., was the definition intended to mean that the Holy Father is infallible under these circumstances and the Vatican I statement said nothing more about the object of infallibility; or, on the other hand, was the definition intended to restrict the object of infallibility only to the specific, proper conditions indicated by the pronouncement? It appears to us that to leave the object of infallibility an open question is to invite more and more creeping infallibility, and more and more of the kind of controversy that we have had with regard to contraception.

To accept the extended concept of the object of infallibility leads to consequences that Regan judges to be "important": "Some authors assert that the popes have spoken so frequently and clearly about the existence, essence, and application of natural law that the doctrine has been taught as a matter of faith."[97] Confirmation of this conclusion following from the extended meaning of infallibility can be made by citing Jean-Marie Aubert: "The recent popes . . . have treated of natural law (or of natural right) with such abundance and precision that one cannot doubt that

---

[96] Regan, *art. cit.*, p. 38.
[97] *Ibid.*, p. 38.

this is a truth of faith."[98] Regan maintains that Fuchs seems to draw the same inference about the natural law from an extended concept of the object of infallibility: "These testimonies to natural law and valid natural rights which are given by the teaching authorities of the Church put it beyond all doubt that this is a question of a truth of faith."[99] Fuchs modifies this position in *Natural Law: A Theological Investigation*[100] whereas in another work, *Theologia Moralis Generalis*, he observes that *at least the substance* of the doctrine of natural law belongs to the faith and infallibility can be applied to this more properly: "One can easily concede that, because of its proposal by the Church, the doctrine of natural law, at least in its substance, pertains to the faith; especially if we consider at the same time the tradition of theologians developing under the vigilance of the magisterium and the teaching of sacred scripture."[101] This is a more reasonable position to accept and Regan tends to look favorably upon it. Therefore he would agree with the modified position of Fuchs as expressed in his *Theologia Moralis Generalis* that the existence and substantial value of natural law are articles of faith. The evidence for this is the frequency of the papal references to natural law and the consistent and constant tradition of this doctrine within the Christian community. Most scripture scholars hold this position with regard to Sacred Scripture—that it does teach the existence and basic value of natural law, but McKenzie takes exception to this fact.[102] If the criticism of McKenzie's opinion by McCormick[103] is considered to be a convincing reply, then it might be well to examine the sources for asserting that "the existence and basic value of natural law as a perduring reality within the Christian order is a position maintained by the majority of Catholic scriptural exegetes."[104]

When a position on natural law is taken by the magisterium of the Church, it is only the *core content* of that teaching that is judged to be a matter of faith. What therefore for Regan would be the *core content* of natural law? It would "include the existence of an objective moral order ordained by God and man's capacity to discern the substantial

---

[98] Jean-Marie Aubert, *Loi de Dieu, Lois des Hommes*, p. 18, note 10.

[99] Regan, *art. cit.*, p. 38.

[100] Fuchs, *op. cit.*, p. 6, note 10.

[101] Fuchs, *Theologia Moralis Generalis* (1963), note 9 on p. 70.

[102] John McKenzie, "Natural Law in the New Testament," *Biblical Research* 9 (1964), 1–11.

[103] Richard McCormick, "Theology of the Natural Law," *Theological Studies* 26 (1965) 608–610.

[104] Cf. Regan, *art. cit.*, p. 39 where he refers to the views of Rudolf Schnackenburg, *The Moral Teaching of the New Testament* (New York: Herder & Herder, 1965), pp. 290–293, Böckle's *Law and Conscience*, pp. 49–81, note 3, and Hamel's *Loi naturelle et Loi du Christ*, pp. 18–20.

elements of this moral order."[105] The *core content* of the doctrine on contraception is given by Noonan: "At the core of the existing commitment might be found other values than the absolute, sacral value of coitus. Through a variety of formulas, five propositions have been asserted by the Church. Procreation is good. Procreation of offspring reaches its completion only in their education. Innocent life is sacred. The personal dignity of a spouse is to be respected. Marital love is holy."[106] This limits the *core content* of the infallibly proposed doctrine according to Noonan (and Regan seems to disagree) to these basic values which must be respected within marriage. Others would interpret the basic doctrine to mean that there is an incompatibility between the nature of marriage and the radical determination to exclude positively all children from marriage. If we understand the position of Regan it would be here where his own sympathies would lie. In all of these opinions within the general classification of those who accept the extended concept of papal infallibility we can thus discover a tendency to restrict the statement to a *core content*. Baum would insist that if the lines have to be drawn they should be drawn at the outset by restricting infallibility to *revelata* and interpreting infallibility in the strict conditions of the definition of Vatican I.

There is another category of identification with regard to the papal statements and it is called the *authentic teaching* of the Pope. It is usually applied to those statements that concern the natural law or some other issue and which do not belong to the *core content* for which under the circumstances infallibility might be claimed. Vatican II describes the attitude of the Catholic who is to show "a religious submission of mind and will . . . to the authentic teaching authority of the Roman Pontiff," and a "religious assent of the soul" to the teachings of bishops concerning faith and morals. Regan considers that most teachings of the Church on natural law belong to this classification of authentic teachings, and he examines the meaning of "religious submission of mind and will" as it is critically investigated by John J. Reed. There are two consequences that follow from the nature of this *authentic teaching* which requires the religious submission of mind and will: One external and absolute, the other internal and conditional. The first places an obligation upon the person not to contradict the doctrine in public speech or writing. This does not preclude theoretical and speculative discussion by theologians in scholarly journals and in professional meetings in order to clarify the

---

[105] Regan, *art. cit.*, p. 39.
[106] John Noonan, *Contraception: A History of Its Treatment by the Catholic Theologians and Canonists* (Cambridge, Mass.: Harvard University Press, 1965; paperback reprint Mentor Omega), pp. 532–533.

doctrine and examine all the difficulties involved. In the internal order, this implies the duty of intellectual assent to the teaching and acceptance of the same. If there is some question here that the authentic teaching is not certainly true then a theologian in this situation would be bound according to Reed in the external order but he would not be obliged to yield internal assent. This interpretation of "religious submission of mind and will" is the traditional one that has been given, but more and more it has been questioned. Recently a series of competent articles by a qualified theologian appeared in a non-scholarly journal that was highly critical of the interpretations given natural law in support of the traditional position on marital morality. In other words, this theologian was taking issue with the limitations placed upon members of his profession to express their disagreements and criticisms only within professional circles and specialized journals. This attitude is more in accord with the spirit of Vatican II that seems to endorse the Catholic's freedom of thought and inquiry both in the internal and external orders. This more liberal interpretation of theological freedom appears to receive confirmation from the *Pastoral Constitution on the Church in the Modern World*: "Let it be recognized that all the faithful, clerical and lay, possess a lawful freedom of inquiry and thought, and the freedom to express their mind humbly and courageously about those matters in which they enjoy competence."[107] This wider interpretation has been taken for granted in the flood of writings on the subject of contraception and this in itself had occasioned theologians to consider the application of the doctrine of *Probabilism* because of doubt (theoretical and practical) in this area. We can well agree with Regan that when this more liberal interpretation has been accorded the treatment of the Church's statements on natural law, there will result "an almost unlimited freedom of thought, enquiry, and explicit expression of disagreement."[108] For most scholars this would be a most healthy condition and should have taken place long ago. Especially is this demanded in the field of natural law and its applications where the Church insists upon calling these applications the results of natural morality. If this be so, then these applications should be re-examined by all men and on subjects such as therapeutic abortion and direct killing, all sides of the controversies should be listened to. It is in this way that the efforts of philosophers, theologians and biblical scholars can be combined with scientists of all kinds so that the judgment that will eventually be made will be a cooperative finding of all men who are ethically and morally sensitive to the issues of life and death.

---

[107] *Pastoral Constitution on the Church in the Modern World*, par. 62.
[108] Regan, *art. cit.*, p. 41.

We have not been left without some criteria for evaluating the serious-ness of assent that should be given to a papal pronouncement. Ford and Kelly propose three practical criteria: the verbal formulas used in the statements; the intention of the speaker; and the historical context of the document.[109] If we apply these criteria we shall conclude that the following possess a strong degree of binding force: "Pope Pius XII's condemnations of therapeutic abortion, euthanasia, and artificial insem-ination, and Vatican II's condemnation of indiscriminate acts of war directed against entire cities or extensive areas together with their civilian populations."[110] With some of these cases it should be made very clear that just as the empirical scientific evidence develops through the years so do the applications of natural law. A natural law indifferent to history and culture is a natural law that will be listened to by few. The more fundamental questions of the objectivity, *substantial* immutability, uni-versality and basic intelligibility of natural law can be accepted without being constantly aware of the empirical data which arise to challenge the applications of natural law. We would agree with Regan that most state-ments about the derivation of specific natural law obligations and about the philosophical explanation of natural law are non-obligatory. This ulti-mately means that they *can be* constantly challenged by the empirical scientific evidence which constantly evolves.

VI. Natural Law and the Encyclical Humanae Vitae

Responsible parenthood is the important consideration in every mar-riage. Over the last few years this has been interpreted to include the limi-tation of families to a size in keeping with the health, economic means, and general circumstances of the parents. The encyclical endorses the idea of limitation; the dispute arises over how the limitation is to be effected. For the encyclical the only so-called "natural" contraception is the use of the safe-period. Every other mthod is unnatural and threfore forbidden.

The large majority of the Papal Commission seemed to agree that the purposes of marriage were safeguarded by the intelligent and conscious use of means other than rhythm. In the face of this testimony of the Commission, the encyclical says that "such questions required from the teaching authority of the Church a newer and deeper reflection upon the principles of the moral teaching on marriage: a teaching founded on the

---

[109] John Ford and Gerald Kelly, *Contemporary Moral Theology* (Westminster, Md.: The Newman Press, 1962), note 26.
[110] Regan, *art. cit.*, p. 91.

natural law, illuminated and enriched by divine Revelation." The *Tablet* of London sums up its own reaction toward this position of the encyclical:

> Two questions must inevitably be asked: where is the newer and deeper reflection? What evidence is adduced to support by divine Revelation the teaching of the Natural Law? It is a matter of observation that the whole notion of the Natural Law is now widely rejected It is rejected more often than not because its upholders all too often seem to suggest that they believe in a certain fixed unchanging pattern of conduct as imposed on man from above, a pattern which he must accept whether he likes it or not, whether he sees the point of it or not. But in fact the Natural Law is not imposed in this way. It is discovered by man's use of his own reason, since it is the law of his own fulfillment. As *Gaudium et Spes* itself puts it: "A true contradiction cannot exist between the divine law pertaining to the transmission of life and those pertaining to the fostering of authentic conjugal love." It is indeed difficult not to sympathize with those who have found, by sad experience, that "authentic conjugal love" has not in fact been fostered by attempts to observe the "divine law" as expounded by the Church. They have come to the conclusion that the divine law is discovered through the honest attempts to live a fully human, mutually responsive, dedicated conjugal life.[111]

The Pope's weighty words undeniably take a dominant place in the discussion that is going on. He makes his appeal to reason and the natural law. It is the prerogative of every man to appeal to the same. To be loyal to the faith and to the whole principle of authority will mean that this authoritative, non-infallible, pronouncement will be submitted to more and more probing examination in scientific theological and philosophical journals and elsewhere. This can be most productive in ecclesiology if there is the constant realization that there is in a true sense within the Church varied magisteria, not only the papal and episcopal, but the equally authentic magisterium of the laity and the magisterium of the theologians. Father Daniel Maguire puts it this way:

> Each of these has a role of creative service to the truth, none can be considered as having a quasi-juridical power to stifle or invalidate the other. Each magisterium must be seen as open to the corrective influence of the other magisteria . . . Episcopal consecration does not convey theological expertise.[112]

---

[111] Vol. 222, No. 6689, August 3, 1968.
[112] Daniel Maguire in "Moral Absolutes and the Magisterium" in *Absolutes in Moral Theology*, edited by Charles Curran (Washington: Corpus Books, 1968), p. 88.

CHAPTER FIVE

INTERPERSONALISM, NATURAL LAW, AND SITUATIONAL MORALITY

I. INTERPERSONALISM VS. NATURAL LAW ETHICS?

Natural law is involved in both the *ethic of responsibility* and the *ethic of conviction*. One should not conclude that an ethic ultimately concerned more with principles than with consequences is the only ethic which is grounded in a natural law theory. For, as analysis will show, in the genesis of those reasons which energize a person whose behavior is directed by an ethic of responsibility one must eventually ask, just as he must in analyzing the bases for an ethic of conviction, What is the source of moral action? Is the ethic, whether of responsibility or conviction, grounded in natural law theory or not?

In the previous chapter we saw how a contemporary natural law theory must distinguish between the abstract and concrete human nature. We saw that it is concerned not only with man's metaphysical being realized in a univocal, universal and essentially immutable way in all men, but that it also must take full cognizance of his concrete, existential human nature, as realized existentially in different historical eras and in specific situations. When natural law theory inspects concrete human nature it introduces all the *dynamic inviting possibilities* for man's self realization. Here we want first to show how this contemporary view of natural law theory (the view recommended, as we saw previously, by Monden, Fuchs, Regan, and Fay) is compatible with the notion of *interpersonalism*. Some have been too hasty to derive this interest in the person from sources other than genuine natural law theory. We hold that the harmony between personalism and natural law is greater than the harmony between personalism and any other source; the opposition frequently erected between the two is most unfortunate, particularly when attempts are made to find the source of personalism in an ethic of situationalism completely independent of natural law theory. True, the emphasis in situational morality is on the person in dynamic encounter with other persons in a situation that at its most moral will become agapaic; yet this should not lead one to conclude to a fundamental incompatibility between personalism and natural law theory.

There are many meanings to *interpersonalism*. If we consider it as a contemporary ethical theory, it maintains that the proper genesis of human right is the deliberate mutual interrelationship of reasonable men in a concrete existential social situation. The traditional natural law theory explains the origin of human rights in a more individualistic fashion and refers to rights as coming from God even before he enters into contact with other persons. Josef Pieper expresses this more traditional attitude when he asserts: "Man has inalienable rights because he is created a person by the act of God, that is, an act beyond all human discussion."[1] The more contemporary attitude is given by Robert Johann: "The existence of rights depends essentially on the reciprocity of persons. My creation by God gives me no rights at all in the face of impersonal nature. It is only because I am in your presence . . . that the reality of my personal life first takes on the character of a claim or right."[2] This difference of attitude on examination will be seen to have repercussions on the theology of marital relations and will without doubt develop a genuine authentic phenomenology of marriage. Marriage rights and obligations do not arise from any abstract contract but from personal reciprocity

---

[1] Josef Pieper, *Leisure: The Basis of Culture* (Chicago: Henry Regnery, 1949; paperback reprint, New York: Mentor Omega, 1965).
[2] Robert Johann, in *America*, June 23, 1966.

which takes full cognizance of the interpersonalism in marriage. In this light the finality of marriage, the role of procreation, the significance of the marital act, and the nature of married love should be judged and described.

This interpersonal dimension which is in harmony with a more contemporary view of natural law in its emphasis upon concrete existential man has often been represented as the contribution of a more situational outlook on human nature. Dichotomies have been introduced between the *ethics of personalism* and *natural law* ethics or between a more *essentialist ethics* and an *existential ethics* as if these two are incompatible. Interpersonalism is a characteristic of a genuine authentic natural law ethics concerned with the dynamics of man involved in the historical temporal situation with other persons. To separate this dimension of personalism from natural law theory is to misrepresent the most significant feature of a contemporary representation of natural law. Natural law has always been involved in its considerations of applied practical ethical cases, in an ethics of persons. Raymond Nogar points out how the Christian adaption of natural law contains three elements: (1) the person in the order of nature, with emphasis on objective, passive rights; (2) the person among persons, with stress on active, subjective rights; and (3) personal orientation to God.[3] The virtue and the act of prudence proceeding from the natural light of reason and the movements of man's tendencies were emphasized repeatedly in past treatments of natural law. The reasons were important at a time when the relativity of conventions and the changeable norms of men were held as sufficient grounding for a law. Natural law, on the other hand, was radicated in the eternal law of God as the participation of the rational human nature in that law. This earlier formulation of natural law with its emphasis on prudence and its grounding in eternal law, has been altered in the perspective given in the documents of Pope Pius XII and Pope John XXIII. In *Pacem in Terris*, John XXIII pictures the order of nature as the created plan of God, but then he describes the order of men in society, the principle of which is that "every human being is a person, that is, his nature is endowed with intelligence and free will. By virtue of this, he has rights and duties of his own, flowing directly and simultaneously from his very nature, which are therefore universal, inviolable and inalienable. If we look upon the dignity of the human person in the light of divinely revealed truth, we cannot help but esteem it far more highly. For men are redeemed by the blood of Christ; they are by grace the children and friends of God and heirs of eternal glory."[4]

---

[3] Raymond Nogar, *Chicago Studies* (Spring 1966), 81–92.
[4] *Ibid.*, 83.

The contemporary accent on person over the traditional accent on rational human nature is immediately evident in this citation. In addition, the genesis of moral right is the personal redemption of Christ rather than merely the order of creation. In these two significant ways we can easily conclude to the compatibility in the thinking of John XXIII between a natural law emphasizing personalism and the traditional natural law presentation in which distinctions were made between *essential abstract human nature* and *existential concrete human nature*. This element of *person* is the feature that is most conspicuous in viewing concrete existential Christological man. It is unfortunate, then, if a division is set up between this new awakening of the person and natural law theory as if they could not live in harmony. It might be well to consider the forces that have led to this unfortunate dichotomy. Nogar points to three of these forces which paradoxically placed the emphasis upon interpersonalism in the very act of attempting to undercut the vitality of natural law theory. In representing natural law as overly juridical, legalistic and moralistic, preoccupied with universal essences and the immutable relations of rational human nature, these forces set about to criticize a natural law which was impersonal, indifferent to the concrete existential situation in which men led their ethical lives.

According to Nogar these three forces were the scientific theory of evolution, historicism, and existentialism. By reason of their therapeutic value, advocates of the natural law were forced to reexamine deeply the meaning of natural law so that it could be made relevant to an ethic in which existential and personal dimensions of ethical life are brought to the fore. But the dichotomy which some have erected, on the basis of the criticisms made against traditional theories of the natural law by the forces noted, between natural law and personal values, is false. We shall now try to show why.

Historicism denies that universal, immutable laws can be discovered by the tools of historical research, that it is impossible to find any moral practice which is universally accepted or universally denied. In answer to this criticism exponents of the natural law in turn criticize historicism for its failure to appreciate the multiple facets of human nature: its malleability in the life of different cultures and histories and its desire to discover certain easily reachable results. For the natural law theorist, "the object of natural law is pure object, the intelligible relations and laws of possibility, disengaged as much as possible from the cultural aspirations of this or that group. That such knowledge is possible or impossible cannot be shown on merely historical grounds. Furthermore, historicism suffers mortally from its incapacity to discover meaning within history to substitute for the norms drawn from the natural law it rejects."[5] Existentialism took issue with the objective order of means and ends discoverable by the human reason and concentrated on the concrete unique situation of man in some particular moment of history. The problems that arose to annoy historicism arise even more treacherously when the existentialist attempts to discover in evolving human experience any final moral meaning. Just as the historicist is compelled to become trans-historical in looking for meaning in history, so the existentialist and situationalist becomes trans-biographical in his survey of ultimate significance and meaning. Paul Ramsey shows how this is evident in the situationalism of Joseph Fletcher where, in opposition to an ethic of principle and law, there is an unavoidable tendency to pure act-agapism where meanings and ultimate patterns of behavior cannot be discerned.[6] At the same time there is a corresponding tendency to construct generalizations from these unique cases in a form of rule-agapism. These terms are employed in the ethical typology of William Frankena,[7] where rule-agapism seeks to determine which rules of action are most love-embodying, and act-agapism, which acts are most loving. Bishop Robinson can be shown to vacillate in much the same way as Fletcher between these extremes.[8] This would seem to indicate the necessity of resolving any ethical situation with principle plunged into the fullest meaning of history. However, situationalism, no more than historicism, with its polarization of situation and uniqueness will not reveal to the observer any ultimate meanings. No ethical norm can emerge from an arbitrary particular situation in human history where act-agapism seems to have priority over rule-agapism.

These three forces that have seemingly worked to undo natural law theory have paradoxically operated upon it and brought it to its senses. The importance assigned now in natural law theory to concrete existential historical and situational man is seen by any one aquainted with contemporary presentations of the theory. Man is no longer viewed in a static Parmenidean fashion but as an evolving creature in the space-time continuum just as the rest of nature itself. These three influences upon the awakening of natural law theory have in addition to their negative thrust, which is the denial of natural law, a positive affirmation which is greater freedom, creative realization and personal development. No longer can the moral act be seen as the application of a universal immutable law of rational human nature. The scientific evolution, the

[5] *Ibid.*, 85.

[6] Paul Ramsey, *Rules and Deeds in Christian Ethics* (New York: Charles Scribner's Sons, 1967), pp. 145–225.

[7] William Frankena, *Ethics* (Englewood Cliffs, N.J.: Prentice-Hall, 1963), pp. 42–44.

[8] Ramsey, *op. cit.*, pp. 15–27.

impact of historicism and existentialism have brought to natural law the appreciation that the individual person operating in ethics is creative and free, an incommunicable entity among other persons. As Ramsey has shown, the interpersonal situation reveals both in Fletcher and Robinson the development of a rule-agapism from a series of situations. These rules and principles are synthetic and operational in a large number of succeeding cases but they do not provide the obliging norms that would be acceptable to a natural law ethic. Contemporary thinking has made the philosophers of natural law recognize that just as these three forces were directed to the demands of personalism, so a genuine natural law as it has developed in history could be shown to have the same direction. That direction is toward a dynamic order of nature unfolding in a society of free men where the full realizations of the creative person are to be experienced. Natural law has always been an emerging, evolving, developmental growth in society and has always re-evaluated ends and means in history and culture. The profound value of the individual personal conscience was always an essential part of natural law and became one of the three elements in the synthesis of that theory by St. Thomas. The immutable order of nature was combined with the free creative order of the human person realizable through his conscience. These two orders were placed in proper perspective and orientation within the eternal plan of God. The natural law theory of Locke, Hobbes and Rousseau, so influential on American democracy, developed even more the notion of the free creative person who was independent of arbitrary decisions by civil society.

It can thus be seen that an interest in the person was always the thrust of an evolving natural law theory that was true to itself and conscious of the concrete existential man in history. As Noonan has made clear, the abiding interest of natural law theory has always been in a hierarchy of values rather than in specific rules of action. Procreation as a value in sexuality was upheld at a time when it was being abused by many and the growing self-awareness of interpersonal relations has raised the question whether *love* as a value in sexuality should not now be more emphasized in natural law theory. It is values and their hierarchy that natural law theory recognizes and it is the most fundamental and exigential values of all that the theory proposes. As Nogar says: "Man takes his bearings from ends (values—a more contemporary term); he makes his decisions from rules of action. Any account of natural law which gives the impression that man has written in his heart a fixed set of universal axioms of moral activity, easily arrived at by a quick, infallible, interior glance, is a caricature."[9]

---

[9] Nogar, *art. cit.*, 87.

Vatican II has responded and adjusted to the justified critical charges made by evolutionism, historicism and existentialism. The Council has said repeatedly that there is a supreme value and dignity in the human person; it has stressed the importance of the role of subjectivity in moral decisions. The accent has not been on the legal or juridical order but on the moral and religious freedom and personal responsibility of each individual.

Nogar makes clear in his illustration of the different perspectives of Josef Pieper and Robert Johann that both of them are still within the structure of natural law theory. Johann stresses subjectivity when he differs with Pieper in explaining the genesis of human rights as issuing not from the act of creation of the human person by God but from the mutuality and reciprocity of persons in society. Pieper radicates human rights in the Creator as the fundamental and ultimate source of all rights whereas Johann's interest is in the proximate, specific and actual source of these rights as they are realizable in the concrete. Pieper stresses the objective grounding for these rights; Johann the subjective, and there is little question of the contemporaneity of this latter explanation. For Johann the potentiality and radical capacity for interpersonal mutuality, upon which moral rights are founded, is radicated "in the creative act and is unable to be abrogated by the arbitrary will of man. But the more proximate source of human right is the existing person in reciprocal communication with his fellow-men, not the mere impersonal nature in the abstract."[10] We have already seen how Karl Rahner envisions the possibilities of a formal existential ethics when he compared this with a more extreme type of situational morality. We shall try to show how many of the insights of a form of situational morality can be introduced into a contemporary Christian moral philosophy without compromising the validity of universal moral norms and how this can be done within the structure of a dynamic and more empirical view of natural law. The works of Fuchs, Häring, Janssens, Dupré, Monden, Fay, Ryan, Noonan, and others who have similar orientations can be of invaluable assistance in the development of such an ethic that appreciates the role of interpersonal relations in the explanation of the claims made upon the participants to those relations. The tensions that exist between the three forces of evolutionism, historicism and existentialism on one hand and the foundation-grounds of the nature of man and the creative act of God on the other—these must be resolved in any renewal of natural law theory. Nogar considers that the formulation of Pope John "best correlates the role of God, of nature and of person. The proximate and specific source of human morality is the dignity of the free and intelli-

---

10 *Ibid.*, 89.

gent human person in his interpersonal environment; simultaneously, this interpersonal source is universal, inviolable and inalienable by reason of its ground in the very nature of man; viewed, again simultaneously, from the light of revelation, this interpersonal, natural source of moral right and duty is grounded upon personal friendship with God as children purchased by the redemption of Christ. In the existential human situation these three elements of Christian morality form a single, living norm of decision through the personal freedom and creativity of each man among his fellows. Hence, natural law theory must be interpersonally orientated; interpersonal ethical principles must be grounded in natural law theory; both must be assumed into the interpersonal love of Christ in his mystical body, the people of God."[11]

These three essential components that enter into the resolution of particular moral problems—natural law, interpersonal mutuality and reciprocity, and orientation in Christ are compared analogously "to those historic space flights without which the missions could not have been accomplished: the launching gantry at Cape Kennedy; the ground and manual control systems; the human spirit of achievement. Without the gantry, the rocket fire could not have established the thrust trajectory of the orbital flight. Without the ground and manual control systems, the command pilot could not have maneuvered the space capsule to a splashdown in the appointed recovery zone. Without the spirit of creative industry which gave meaning to the space program and inspired the men, not a single rocket would have been fired. . . . In the question of marriage morality, the natural law is the gantry setting the thrust trajectory of moral decision, Interpersonal discretion and love are the controls which provide maneuverability through the exigencies of a changing human situation. The Incarnate Son of God assimilated the actions of the people of God into himself and gives ultimate meaning and motive to all morality. In our discussions, if one of these elements is missing our mission is destined to collapse. With all of them present, there is a good chance of success."[12]

The Christian moralist who defends the place of natural law in a contemporary ethical theory must acknowledge the fact that he has been forced to see the weaknesses in his own presentation because of the criticisms coming from evolutionism, historicism and existentialism. We would like to consider now the reexamination that has had to be done of natural law theory because of the criticisms from situational morality. To some extent we have developed this theme in the second chapter where we tried to show that the concept of intrinsically evil acts is becoming

11 *Ibid.*, 90.
12 *Ibid.*, 91–92.

non-viable and non-operational in moral discourse. It should even cause the person who reflects on this non-viability to wonder whether from the fewness of intrinsically evil acts there should be any consideration given to them in moral texts. Such acts have to be weighted with so many circumstances that they only become immoral from the determinants that have been placed upon them. Ultimately, the natural law theorist should conclude that there are basic disvalues that are unethical but the problems mount when someone attempts to define these disvalues and to have a definition which is trans-historical, trans-cultural. It seems to us that these fundamental disvalues which most persons accept are incapable of formal definition and that natural law theory is concerned radically only with disvalues and not with acts. This seems to us to represent one of the real insights of situational morality, and natural law moralists can learn from situationalism a freshness of insight into moral reality from the fact that the concept of intrinsic evil is fundamentally non-viable and should not be used. The task of evaluating situation ethics yields to the Christian moralist not only the recognition of error but also a penetration into the moral situation which may help to see and present the truth more clearly. It seems to us that the too facile presentation in texts of Christian ethics of the concept of "acts intrinsically evil in their objects" overextends the true application of the concept and, in the resulting confusion, jeopardizes a correct understanding and application of the Christian moral system. In the following section we shall consider the determinants of the moral act from the point of view of classical natural law theory and from the perspective of situational morality. We shall examine the insights and the blindspots of both.

II. Situation Morality: Insights and Blindspots

It is a simplification in philosophical discussion to dismiss a theory at once by appealing to the refutation of the parent theory to which it partly owes its origin. All of us do this frequently and consider the technique adequate and useful for the immediate purpose we have at hand. We are inclined to sympathize with the principle that there is in the order of ideas something analogous to the Mendelian genetic theory in the order of physical characteristics. If we are successful in discovering the defective gene in the parent theory and in establishing with satisfaction the fact that it is defective, we feel justified in looking upon the descendants as the unfortunate and inculpable inheritors of this genetic endowment. It is not surprising therefore to learn that situation ethics has been sufficiently laid to rest in philosophical oblivion by resorting to the simple device of arguing that this new moral theory carries within itself the defective genes of Protestant theology and ethical relativism.

Now let the point be made clear that we are not denying the value and cogency of any argument that would properly orientate some new speculative theory in its due relation to other theories in the philosophy of ideas. We do recignize the child in the parent and one certain way of identifying the child is to relate the child to the parent. Nevertheless even after this recognition of the child in the parent, the child still remains there to be explained—enigmatic, mysterious and elusive. So does situation ethics.

A.   Denial of Objective Moral Principles

The principal characteristic of situation ethics in its most rigorous form is its resolution of moral problems independently of objective moral principles that are radicated in law. Pope Pius XII, on April 18, 1952, summed up very pointedly the general *esprit* of this new morality:

> The distinctive mark of this new morality is that it is not based in effect upon universal moral laws, such as, for example, the Ten Commandments, but on the real and concrete conditions or circumstances in which men must act, and according to which the conscience of the individual must judge and choose. Such a state of things is unique and is applicable only once for every human action. That is why the decision of conscience, as the proponents of this ethic assert, cannot be commanded by ideas, principles, and universal law.[13]

The situationalist demands that the unique and total situation be considered in the moral evaluation of human conduct. In this confrontation with God in the conscience of man through the unique concrete situation general norms are merely indicative and declarative of God's will, and there is not required the mediation of law to resolve the human moral situation. Absolute moral norms in concrete situations are not valid for the situationalist ethician and law never mediates between the conscience and God. In fact he insists that ethics and religious living become increasingly more and more juridical and moralistic insofar as the mediation of law becomes more and more conspicuous and assertive.

It is not difficult to recognize the parent in the child and to refer to existential ethics' use of private interpretation in the moral situation just as Protestant theology uses private interpretation in docrinal matters. If your background and training is philosophical, you will insist upon referring to this "ethical actualism" (another very appropriate term used

---

[13] Pope Pius XII, "Ad Delegates Conventui internationali Sodalitatis vulgo nuncupatae 'Federation Mondiale des Jeunesses Feminines Catholiques,'" *Acta Apostolicae Sedis* XXXIV, 8 (June 1952) 414, as translated in "The Moral Law and the 'New Morality,'" in *The Irish Ecclesiastical Record* LXXVIII (August, 1952), 138.

by Pius XII) as Heraclitean morality of relativism in a modern dress. These labels satisfy us for a short interval but they do not remove the difficulties that an important consideration of the facts will reveal upon closer examination. Let us consider some of the difficulties that are at once apparent.

B.   Negation of Intrinsically Evil Acts

The situationalist demands in the light of the unique moral situation a confrontation of the conscience with God without the mediation of absolute immutable law. He would equivalently deny that there are any acts that are intrinsically evil in the rigorous Scholastic meaning of that term. Such acts according to definition are always and in every circumstance (*semper et pro semper*) in difformity with rational human nature, prescinding from circumstances and end of agent. No one acquainted with this terminology will deny the difficulty in finding acts that will satisfy this definition. Most manuals in ethics give blasphemy as the sole example and then offer other meanings for the concept of intrinsic evil which water down the original signification. The other meanings for the term unavoidably introduce some minimal circumstances within the context of the object or *finis operis* before concluding to the act's difformity with rational human nature.

We do not quarrel with this procedure in introducing other meanings for the term but we question the silence of the authors in not admitting the problems confronting them when they use the term according to the strict sense. In fact, we wonder whether there is any necessity in the presentation of the treatise on the concrete determinants of a moral act to establish the existence of intrinsically evil acts only in the rigorous sense of the term when there are so few of them to stand up to the definition. Even the case of incest presents difficulties for the moralist, and he finds it embarrassing to call it intrinsically evil from its object in total isolation of the circumstances and motive. The iconoclast Shaw made this one of his targets in *Back to Methuselah*.

It should be understood that we are not saying that there are no intrinsically evil acts in the abstract, but we are insisting upon the difficulties facing the scholastic moralist who would search for such acts in the strictest meaning of that term and who would be satisfied with them after they have been found. It is a more prudent pedagogical method to propose less strict meanings for intrinsically evil acts and to discover multiple illustrations of these than to insist upon the definition for which the fewest possible examples can be found. The impression is frequently left upon students that it is necessary to establish the existence of acts which are always from their objects in difformity with rational human nature, or the structure of this treatise on the moral act will be jerry-built and circumstances will assume too great a role in the moral act. The proposition that there are intrinsically evil acts is defensible for some whether the term is accepted in the rigorous meaning or not, but pedagogically, it seems unwise to establish the proposition on grounds that it is easy to find examples for the definition in the strict sense.

The situationalist, of course, goes much further than the negation of intrinsically evil acts in the strict meaning of the term. He denies also that there are such acts in the concrete. In fact, his argument would be an a fortiori transit from the negation of such acts in the concrete to the necessary denial of such acts in the abstract. This rationalization by the situationalist may need some elaboration.

In the first place, the consideration of a moral act in the abstract is the evaluation of the act from its object or *finis operis*, prescinding from the other moral determinants, the circumstances and motive or *finis operantis*. If the act so considered from its object alone is always in difformity with rational human nature, it is an intrinsically evil act in the rigorous meaning of the term. We referred before to less strict meanings for the concept of intrinsically evil act. One such meaning refers to an act whose object includes a condition within itself, the fulfillment of which is requisite for the act to be considered intrinsically evil. Ethicians refer to taking someone's property as such an act; it becomes evil only if it is an unjust taking that violates the will of the owner. Many examples for this meaning of the term can be given. Possibly the best example to show the several qualifications or conditions that must be placed upon an act before it can be designated intrinsically evil is that of homicide. Homicide, defined nominally as the killing of a man, becomes intrinsically evil only if all these qualifications are superimposed upon it: Direct homicide on one's own authority outside a case of legitimate self-defense and capital punishment. If all these qualifications are assumed into a malleable object or *finis operis* of homicide, then such homicide may be denominated intrinsically evil and the proposition concerning the existence of such intrinsically evil acts becomes easily defensible. However, it should be realized that the expanding object has now included within its walls what are really constitutive and determining circumstances and that without these the object or *finis operis* would be so indeterminate as to render the act a morally indifferent one.

A third meaning for a morally intrinsically evil act arises from the consideration that under normal circumstances this act produces evil consequences. Because these bad consequences consistently follow upon such an act (polygyny and perfect divorce are sometimes cited in this connection), it is called intrinsically evil. Granted the elimination of these destructive consequences under a special providence of God, such acts might become permissible. Thus do some moralists explain the toleration of divorce and remarriage in the Old Testament. Invoking the terminology of formal and material change of law, moralists would call such a change as this not a formal change of law but a change in the matter of the law with the result that we do not have the precise kind of polygyny or perfect divorce which is forbidden always and in every circumstance *(semper et pro semper)*. We can understand that here we have no real change in law but a change in the context of the moral act by special divine providence. It is not polygyny or perfect divorce that is intrinsically evil in itself from its object or *finis operis* but polygyny or perfect divorce with these evil consequences necessarily associated. In other words, polygyny and perfect divorce are against the *bene esse* of marriage and not against the very *esse* of marriage.

C. Cardinal Position of Circumstances

Certainly, if the proposition concerning the existence of intrinsically evil acts has such acts in view, then the difficulties are reduced in finding examples to fulfill this definition. It would also seem to follow from this triple meaning of the term that circumstances do enter more and more into the confines of the object or the *finis operis* and that these circumstances are determining and constitutive *sine qua non* conditions for such acts to be considered intrinsically evil. When we analyze the moral determinants of an act according to object, motive, and circumstances we should constantly recall that even in the abstract there are very few acts that do not include some minimal circumstances within the object itself which are indispensable to the object before any inference can be drawn that we have here an intrinsically evil act. In other words, circumstances are not only required for an act in the concrete but even for an act in the abstract, that is, for an act considered only from its object because the object is clothed with some minimal circumstances that are determining and constitutive.

This becomes most clear in the examination of the truth contained in situation ethics. The situationalist insists upon the primary role of circumstances and motive in the moral evaluation of any act whether the act is considered in the abstract or in the concrete. He denies that there are any acts at all which from their objects are always in difformity with rational human nature. The latter proposition is questionable and contains the fundamental error of existential ethics. The first proposition on the importance of circumstances in the consideration of an act in the concrete is a proposition that is easily understood by the philosopher who would admit the existence of morally indifferent acts in the abstract and the cardinal position of circumstances when these same acts are considered in the concrete. If the situationalist embarrasses us into recognizing the position of circumstances even in the consideration of most intrinsically evil acts in the abstract, then obviously this truth has been clarified by a theory which has manifold errors. Perhaps it is indiscreet to say that we should be grateful to error for this clarification and for the refinement of what some would call a deeper insight into truth. It is no small insight into truth to see that there are the fewest intrinsically evil acts in the abstract if we accept th trm in th rigorous meanining, and that the several other meanings of the term undeniably assume within the confines of their objects circumstances which are necessary to these objects even in the abstract before we can denominate such acts intrinsically evil.

D.   Three Maxims Against Situation Ethics

The interrelationship of the three founts of morality—the object, motive and circumstances—receives added significance in the light of our examination. The latter two determinants in the direct confrontation of the antecedent conscience with God can never modify essentially and substantially the inner nature of the object or the *finis operis* as the situationalist demands. If the *finis operis* of a certain act in relation to rational human nature reveals it to be a deordination, then no circumstances or motive can ever alter this situation. This is merely to assert that the specific, essential and intrinsic morality of any act is derived from the object of the act. Pope Pius XII insisted upon the importance of these sources of morality by proposing three principles of Christianity.[14] First, it is true that God wants primarily and always a right intention. Nevertheless the work itself must be good and the principle of the end justifying the means must not be employed. It has been pointed out by some moral philosophers how the wheel of opposition to Christian teaching has gone full circle. In combatting the forensic morality of the Scribes and Pharisees, Christ had to emphasize the value of the internal act, the motive and the intention, and the insufficiency of the external deed unless it be inspired by the proper motive. In confronting this new theory of situation ethics the Church has to vindicate the insufficiency of the internal act unless it manifests itself in the appropriate external good work. Situation ethics becomes in application a system that is more legalistic and juridical than the system it would displace. By denying that the internal act receives its essential, specific and intrinsic morality from the object of the act and by elevating the motive and circumstances

---

14 *Ibid.* 140–141.

to the status of primary determinants of the morality of an act, the situationalist can only judge such an act by constructing a calculus of motives and circumstances. Eventually he ends up with a moral mathematicism which he thought that he had been correct in identifying with traditional scholastic morality.

The second principle which the late Holy Father recalls in the resolution of the moral conscience is that it is never permitted to do evil in order that good may result. The new ethics is constructed on the principle that the end justifies the means because in the concrete situation the full morality of the act is derived from a consideration of the motive and circumstances and only inadequately from the object or *finis operis*. The latter is considered changeable until the conscience is confronted by God in the light of the other two sources of morality. The third principle pointed out by Pius XII is that there may be situations in which a man, and especially a Christian, cannot be unaware that he must sacrifice everything, even his life, in order to save his soul. The martyrs of all times give adequate testimony to this truth.

E. Circumstance and Motive in Scholastic Ethics

For the scholastic moralist the problem of the formation of conscience is one that does not neglect the importance of the particular circumstances and the motivation of the specific individual performing the act. The personality of the individual is never overlooked; the role of prudence in the moral situation and how frequently this was brought out in the teaching of St. Thomas are points stressed by Pius XII:

> His (St. Thomas's) treatise evidences a sense of personal activity and of actuality which contains whatever true and positive elements there may be in "ethics according to the situation" while avoiding its confusion and aberrations. Hence it will be sufficient for the modern moralist to continue along the same lines, if he wishes to make a thorough study of the new problem.[15]

It is not by the inversion of the sources of a moral act that the personality of a man is found to be worthy of more esteem. A man does not become a moral man simply because his motives are irreproachable. All the determinants must be considered in the evaluation of a moral act. The concept of conscience according to Christian principles allows for a sense of personal responsibility and independence, but only within just and legitimate limits. Those limits are established by understanding precisely the nature of the intrinsically evil disvalue which can never become morally good simply because of the uniqueness of the circumstances in which a particu-

---

[15] *Ibid.*

lar individual is placed. For the situationalist the individual must make his moral judgment entirely on the basis of the actual circumstances in which he finds himself and his conscience cannot be hampered by ideas, principles and universal laws or by disvalues whose very nature is to be intrinsically evil. In substance, the situationalist takes issue with the moral philosopher on the very existence of intrinsically evil acts and denies the concept of a morally intrinsically evil act regardless of how it may be defined.

Situation ethics becomes for its proponents a theological approbative theory of ethics in that the moral evaluation of an act is not to be found in the unauthoritative approvals of human individuals but rather in the authoritative omniscient approvals of God making himself manifest before the individual conscience. To this extent the theory of the new morality participates in a long history of ethical thought. At the present time the formulation of the theological approbative theory is expressed mostly in the works of Protestant theologians who are deeply impressed by the traditional conceptions of the absolute sovereignty of God and the sinfulness and overwhelming helplessness of man divorced from divine revelation and grace. They rebel against the doctrines of man's necessary evolution towards progress and natural goodness. They contend that God reveals Himself not only in historical revelation but also privately in the individual deliverances of conscience. The influence of the nineteenth-century Danish theologian Kierkegaard cannot be denied in this association because he has made so much of the thought of the nature of man and God of the sixteenth-century Reformers pertinent to this twentieth century.

Conclusion

Possibly in the approach taken here towards situation ethics we have only confounded what to others is obvious. However, by an analysis of the theory from within itself we ought to discover deeper insights into the treatise on the determinants of a moral act. In this way we will more easily expose the real roots of the error and absorb the profound truth that is contained in situation ethics. The extreme form of this moral system denies the cardinal role of the object or *finis operis* as the specific, essential and intrinsic determinant of the moral act. There precisely is the error. The insight of the theory, which to us is profound, is the realization that inadequacies arise from any consideration of the determinants of morality in isolation from one another. The theory forces us to admit that there are few acts which from their objects are always in difformity with an adequate consideration of human nature. When we offer alternative meanings for "intrinsically evil acts" we are implicitly admitting that the circumstances in multiple acts together with the objects are the controlling determinant. In fact it makes this moralist wonder whether we ought not to revamp the treatise on the determinants and present it in a different form.

Situational morality has brought into focus the importance of circumstances and motives in the determination of the concrete specific morality of an act. Traditional morality has placed the priority upon the *object* of an act or the *finis operis* of the moral act. In an ethic that is non-telelogical the resistance to such an analysis can be appreciated. However, the fundamental insight into the structure of an act as composed of these three determinants should not be ignored in any clarification introduced through situational morality. We do through rational discourse attempt to reach some tentative meanings for the acts that men posit. These meanings may vary from culture to culture and this in itself should make us wary of concluding that our definition of the act is the one to be accepted for all cultures. We face the embarrassment of the culture in which Abraham lived where it was the customary practice to engage in infant sacrifice and infanticide as a customary act and as something morally good. The empirical evidence would bear out the acceptance of this practice and would occasion problems for anyone who would consider that all forms of infanticide would be in the same moral category. The disvalue of infanticide is not recognized in a culture such as that of Abraham because the more basic disvalue is not just the killing of the child but the *meaningless killing of the child*. It is such killing which reveals the ultimate and basic disvalue, it is unreasonable killing that is the evil in existence on the hypothesis that life and its promotion are the goods that are recognized in all cultures. Situational morality has occasioned this insight into more profound examination of which values are fundamental, basic and exigential in existence. The spelling out of these disvalues is left to the individual culture and these should never be called intrinsically evil.

CHAPTER SIX

SITUATIONAL MORALITY

In our first chapter we held that an authentic morality is one which exists in a state of dynamic tension between what we called the ethic of conviction and the ethic of responsibility. In our examination of contemporary literature on the natural law we saw that much of the criticism directed against a statically conceived natural law rested on the conviction that an authentic natural law must respect the existential, concrete condition of man and that it must allow room for the dynamism of the human person who must act responsibly within the situation in which he is placed. Here we want to show that what is called situation ethics or situational morality belongs to the ethic of responsibility only if it is absolutely serious about all the values and is willing to assume all of the claims and counter-claims that emerge from the situation.

Responsibility is the crucial word in the criticism that is made by the proponents of the "new morality" (also called situationalism or contextualism) and it is this same term which is decisive in any critique of this contemporary ethic. In order to be introduced to the methodology of this situational morality we shall study the work of Joseph Fletcher.[1] It is most important to emphasize that situationalism is a *method* for making ethical judgments rather than an exposition of the *contents* of those judgments. It is concerned with the *how* of approaching moral problems and offers a perspective through the resolution of a moral situation. It specializes in the interrogative form of learning all the relevant facts and elements in the ethical context, and it believes that from the discussion and mutual exchange of several persons more and more of these significant details can be learned. Motivations are sought, the interrelation of one item with another is examined, the apparent circumstances in which the context is viewed are broadened into the real situation in which the person has been performing ethically. This will be shown to be a morality, which, if true to itself, is a most difficult morality but not the *only* morality. It is not the ethic of snap judgment but of reflection and hard extrapolation of consequences. It is characterized by the determination to learn everything one can of the context in which one is operating before one makes his ethical decision. It means that one ought to know himself and know something about psychology in theory and practice before he judges his own moral behavior. It appears as the morality of careful assessment and wise foresight; it knows that it has made mistakes many times and must consider these mistakes before anything else. Situationalism therefore does not provide a solution to the case but an approach and a perspective.

I. THE SITUATIONISM OF JOSEPH FLETCHER

Fletcher's situationalism has no real quarrel with an ethic of principle unless the principles have hardened into laws. Most persons would go along with this attitude because the principles that are considered to be universal are not understood to be universal in a mathematical and analytic way. Fletcher differs from the legalist by making clear that his ethic of conviction is one phrased by "it depends." He is critical of the legalist who enters decision-making situations with a barrel of rules and regulations that are applicable *a priori* and who terminates any further ethicizing by appealing to these universal affirmative or negative precepts.

---

[1] Joseph Fletcher, *Situation Ethics: The New Morality* (Philadelphia: The Westminster Press, 1966). Cf. also his *Moral Responsibility* (Philadelphia: The Westminster Press, 1967).

On the other hand, Fletcher insists that he objects just as strongly to the antinominan who in some gnostic fashion discovers without any principles or general rules just what his ethical behavior ought to be. The judgment for or against Fletcher should be made on the basis of his consistent middle of the road record and of his consistent deeper and deeper analysis of the values and the disvalues of the concrete situation. Ramsey shows that there really can be no Christian morality which is not an thics of conviction or an ethics of rules.[2] Ramsey distinguishes *act-agapism* which appears to be without rules from *rule-agapism*, which consists of synthetic propositions of summary cases of practice. It is Ramsey's position that Fletcher's situationalism issues either into a *pure-act agapism* which elaborates rules which it pretends to avoid or into a *pure-act agapism* which becomes entangled in all sorts of inconsistencies. Ramsey seems to be saying that it is difficult if not impossible to develop an operable *act-agapism*.[3]

Fletcher is not unaware of some of these difficulties. His intention is to aim at "a contextual appropriateness—not the good or the right but the fitting."[4] His situationalism is pragmatic, relative, positivistic and personalistic. The case method that it uses in studying moral situations shows that it is also empirical, fact-finding, data conscious and interrogative and inquiring. The core of this method is outlined by Fletcher as proceeding from: (1) its one and only law, *agape* (love) to the (2) *sophia* (wisdom) of the church and culture, containing many "general rules" of more or less applicability, to (3) the *kairos* (moment of decision, the fullness of time) in which the responsible self in the situation decides whether the *sophia* can serve love there or not.[5] In the structure of this situationalist method it takes something from legalism and something from the antinomians and attempts to stress its own accents of *agape*. If balances can be maintained Fletcher is reaching for the best combination of the Christian tradition and naturalistic morality and for the best operation of the *prudence* of a Josef Pieper. In the development of this theory there are six fundamental propositions:

(1) *Only one "Thing" is intrinsically good; namely, love: Nothing else at all.* Love is the root of all morality. Fletcher agrees with the nominalists who maintain that goodness is only a predicate and never a property. Value is assigned to something only in relation to persons. "Hence it follows that in Christian situation

---

[2] Paul Ramsey, *Deeds and Rules in Christian Ethics* (New York: Scribner's, 1967), p. 145–225.

[3] *Ibid.*, p. 159–176.

[4] Fletcher, *Situation Ethics*, p. 27–28.

[5] *Ibid.*, p. 33.

ethics nothing is worth anything in and of itself. It gains or acquires its value only because it happens to help persons (thus being good) or to hurt persons (thus being bad)."[6] Goodness is not intrinsic or objective but extrinsic.

(2) *The ruling norm of Christian decision is love: nothing else.* The demands of love are the calls that are made to the responsible conscience. An ethics of conviction framed just on law and principle frequently provides an escape from these demands and confers a satisfaction without the real exercise of responsible freedom. There are no ambiguities, paradoxes or agonies for the ethicist of conviction. He follows law and principle wherever it leads unquestioningly; all conflicts with love are only apparent and not real for him. The situationalist realizes that all laws will at some time conflict with love and are therefore only relative, replaceable, compromisable.

(3) *Love and justice are the same, for justice is love distributed, nothing else.* The distinction made between justice and charity or love is not valid according to Fletcher. That distinction has regarded justice as giving a person his due and such giving is of obligation; love is giving something beyond this and such giving is not obligatory. Fletcher looks upon justice as the many faces of love, as the operation of love contextually or situationally. Love absorbs and infuses all the other virtues. Authentic love reaches out for the greatest good for the greatest number of people and it employs calculation, shrewdness, prudence and efficiency. It knows all the angles and convolutions of the situational problem; it studies it from every perspective; it is jesuitical at its best. A short-sighted view of the effects upon one's closest neighbor may bring the judgment of loving action, when if the larger view is invoked the harm and hurt might well be seen by the shrewd observer. Even an act of killing that under normal circumstances might be regarded as immoral may bring ultimate benefits to the general welfare.

(4) *Love wills the neighbor's good whether we like him or not.* Fletcher shows the Christian quality of this ethic in insisting that we must love the neighbor whether we like him or not. Love or *agape* is an attitude, is capable of being commanded by the person, is not just a feeling of benevolence, is impartial because it is primarily other-regarding, concerned with what is most "useful" for the largest number of persons and for those

[6] *Ibid.*, p. 59.

who are most in need. Fletcher reveals his utilitarianism here and his conception of the altereity of real love. He cites Bultmann is saying, "In reality, the love which is based on emotions of sympathy, or affection, is self-love; for it is a love of preference, of choice, and the standard of the preference and choice is the self."[7]

(5) *Only the end justifies the means; nothing else.* All means are morally indifferent or neutral and receive their morality from the end they serve. The new morality declares that everything is right or wrong depending upon the situation. There are no intrinsically evil acts just as there are no universal negative prohibitions. Nothing makes an act good but *agapeic expedience.* Fletcher does not hold that a person should chose an evil means for a good end, because he insists that any means at all to a good end becomes good by the very act that it is related to that good end. He shows his pragmatism even in the selection of his illustrations from the pioneer West when settlers were being tracked down by Indians: "(1) A Scottish woman saw that her suckling baby, ill and crying, was betraying her and her three other children, and the whole company to the Indians. But she clung to her child, and they were caught and killed. (2) A Negro woman, seeing how her crying baby endangered another trail party, killed it with her own hands to keep silence and reach the fort."[8] Fletcher holds that the proper situationist decision was made by the second woman who took one innocent life in order to save many other innocent lives. The only self-legitimating end for the Christian is love and all other means and ends are subordinated to love.

(6) *Love's decisions are made situationally, not prescriptively.* This proposition follows from the distinction between the moral order of love and the juridical order of prescription and law which can never be commensurate. No one can ever tell antecedently to the situation what the demands of love may be in the concrete existential situation, and therefore the rules and laws are never coextensive with the contextual situation to be met. For the situationalist there is no universal affirmative precept, no universal negative prohibition. Some have seen some inconsistency on the part of Fletcher here in this sixth statement of his situationalism. Love's decisions are said to be made situationally and not prescriptively. To prescribe commonly means to order, direct or

7 *Ibid.,* p. 104.
8 *Ibid.,* pp. 124–125.

ordain, to set down as a rule or direction. Now we know that love itself is called "an attitude, a disposition, a leaning, a preference, a purpose." This does seem to imply that it is prescriptive and there is no one who has not experienced in himself or in others the tyranny of love. If love does not prescribe, then it would seem that the situation prescribes value judgments. It is in this whole area of the nature and the role of agape and the situation that Fletcher does not exercise proper clarification in ethics. Nevertheless his insight is a creative one and for Bentham's hedonistic calculus the Christian can substitute "the agapeic calculus, the greatest amount of neighbor welfare for the greatest number of neighbors possible."[9] He defends a teleological theory of ethics although he insists that ultimate ends or supreme values cannot be established.

Fletcher's principal thrust through these six statements is that as soon as we have accepted the Christian ideal of agape we can in the situation formulate rules or norms of conduct. On the subject of premarital sexuality the author denies that there is any moral law which universally forbids all such acts of sexual intercourse as wrong. The very substance of any theory of situational morality is that for the person who adopts it there are no universal moral absolutes. Fletcher makes clear that a young unmarried Christian couple would never maintain that premarital sex is "all right if we *like* each other." The proper attitude is that "loving concern can make it all right, but mere liking cannot."[10] Whether we agree with this judgment or not is immaterial to the fact that Fletcher here offers material for a norm or rule of conduct. He certainly denies that there are immutable natural laws of morality or any system of natural morality. His positivism is as evident as his nominalism, and if the critical reader is jarred by a statement such as "the whole mind-set of modern man, *our* mind-set, is on the nominalists' side," in all probability he will be nettled by another observation that "there are no values at all; there are only things . . . that happen to be valued by persons."[11] Persons certainly are evaluating agents but they exist and move about in a world of values that appear with strong justification to have ontological foundations. It has been pointed out by others that law and prescription are not as death-dealing as Fletcher would make them and that his state-

9 *Ibid.*, p. 95.
10 *Ibid.*, p. 104.
11 *Ibid.*, p. 58.

ment that "people like to wallow or cower in the security of the law" is obviously polemical. The situation can tyrannize just as much as law and prescription. Creative effort has gone into the structuring of law and prescription and creative results have followed from their application. Children do not wallow in the security of family affection; nor do students cower in the presence of a teacher who is able to offer them the fruits of his own scholarship.

II. ASSESSMENTS OF FLETCHER'S SITUATIONISM

Situations are not as discrete and discontinuous as Fletcher seems to think. Each individual situation seems to be unique, unrelated and dissociated from other situations. When this discontinuity of situation is exaggerated there is no question that certain common denominators, explicit or implicit in all situations, are played down. Ethical decisions are always made in the circumstances of the here and now, but some generalizations can be made about values pertaining to human needs and interests. Character penetrates each situation and is developed by the situation as much as it contributes to the elaboration of the situation. Unavoidably the situationalist introduces some set of values into the ethical decision-making. This is evident from a consideration of the medical ethical cases of many situationalists who assert that "no unwanted child should be born." These generalizations would be accepted by the situationalist from whatever source they came, although greater skepticism would accompany the acceptance of any such principles or rules coming from a natural law hypothesis.

The important resolution of the ethical situation is that any one of these generalizations can be put aside in the service of *agape*. Situation ethics admits of only the one absolute of love and the cardinal question in the moral decision is "What does God's love demand of me in the particular situation here and now?" The question is not resolved by the application of a priori rules and principles. This morality has polarized law and principle and has thereby failed in the eyes of the situationalists, who maintain that the ethics of conviction has mistakingly identified law and principle with the totality of ethics. The accusation is made that if morality has broken down it is not the new morality that has caused the breakdown. It has broken down because the contemporary generation no longer puts reliance upon the old prohibitions of natural law or the negative commandments of the Old and the New Testaments and seriously questions most of the presuppositions of the older ethic of conviction. An ethic which appeals to respect and love for one another is understood by a generation that prides itself upon its interest in the empirical, the pragmatic and the verifiable. Mere adherence to the rules and principles of the past has not produced persons of any profound ethical sensitivity.

Just as this criticism of the stringency of the former ethic of conviction can be exaggerated so the judgment made on situationalism can be misjudged, that it is altogether too lenient and relativistic. Nevertheless the truth about situationalism might well be that it is "at once more lenient and more stringent than law morality. It can command hard decisions as well as easy ones—acceptance of martyrdom, for example, when law morality would permit surrender or compromise. It can also say that certain acts are immoral which law ethics would consider technically valid."[12] The situationalist can find the exigencies of *agape* far more self-sacrificing than the ethicist of law. This should be appreciated even when we read some of Fletcher's illustrations which seem to be the lenient resolutions of the ethics of *agape*. For example, he says "even a transient sex liaison, if it has the elements of caring, of tenderness and selfless concern, is better than a mechanical, egocentric exercise of 'conjugal rights' between two uncaring or antagonistic marriage partners."[13] The precipitous critic of this situation should read it over and discover how Fletcher has really exposed the weaknesses of the ethics of law and principle where people respect one another's bodies for not appearing in the wrong bedrooms but never question whether there are internal corruptions of mind and will during the preservation of this pseudo–morality.

It would seem that Fletcher is correct if fidelity to this ethic of love can be realized in the general run of moral situations. This ethic of responsibility is a far more difficult ethic than the ethic of mere law. It is only when one feature of situationalism is taken out of focus (and Dr. Fletcher himself is responsible at times for this misunderstanding) that it gets roundly criticized from many different quarters. President David Hubbard of California's Fuller Theological Seminary complains that "we can talk ourselves into a lot of things in the name of love unless we have some ground rules to play the game."[14] The situationalist's retort would be that there are ground rules and regulations but they never operate as moral absolutes and that in those cases in which the generalization does not apply the reason is simply because *agape* demands otherwise. He would insist that law and *agape* are not necessarily com-

---

12 *Time* (January 21, 1966).
13 Fletcher, "Love Is The Only Measure," *Commonweal*, Jan. 14, 1966, p. 431.
14 David Hubbard, cited in *Situation Ethics Debate* (Philadephia: Westminster, 1968), pp. 24–25.

mensurate, and it is difficult to see how anyone could question this response. The only difficulty is to be found in the sophistication of the one trying to discover the demands of *agape*.

Princeton's Paul Ramsey also raises the importance of the ethics of law and principle and contends that traditional moral principles are authoritative and that "how we do what we do is as important as our goals."[15] In *Commonweal* the Dominican theologian Herbert McCabe argued in much the same way that the new morality offers no criteria to discriminate *agape* from what is really self-interest. The crucial question for McCabe is "How do you know that what you are doing is loving?"[16] Furthermore, situational morality according to him seems to be unmindful of the fact that a person is always operating morally in a community that cannot possibly exist without law.

These judgments against situationalism are not unanswerable. Fletcher might well rebut that the community would be a morally more sensitive and perceptive community if it were not directed primarily by its concern for an ethic of law and commitment. In fact, his approach is applicable to questions of social policy within the community and seems to be very much like the ethic of Christ who overthrew the intricacies and complexities of Jewish law and reduced his own ethical teaching to the dual command to love God and neighbor. We even find traces of this ethic of *agape* over law in the thought of such creative Christian thinkers as Augustine ("Love with care and then what you will, do") and Luther who stated: "When the law impels one against love, it should no longer be a law." These qualities of loving concern and empirical consequences reflect the same qualities that persons have judged to be the substance of real ethical behavior. Situationism itself for Fletcher is a reflection characteristic of an age of experimentation, inquiry and question-asking. This fundamentally explains its contemporary appeal and attraction for twentieth-century man.

If the ethics of law and principle finds its principal hang-up on absolute law, the ethics of *agape* finds its hang-up on the meaning of love. This has been pointed out by many others who press the question upon Fletcher. "What determines whether an action is loving or how love is served?" (asks Milhaven).[17] This difficulty is put in another form by John Coleman Bennett: "Is it correct to say that love as such provides any illumination concerning what is good for the neighbors? To use love as the great simplifier of ethics is to place too much emphasis on the

---

15 Ramsey, "Two Concepts of General Rules in Christian Ethics," *Ethics*, April, 1966, pp. 192 f.
16 Herbert McCabe, "The Validity of Absolutes," *Commonweal*, Jan. 14, 1966, pp. 435–436.
17 John G. Milhaven, *Theological Studies*, September 1966, pp. 483–485.

motive of the one who acts and not enough on the sources of illumination concerning what is good for those who are affected by the action."[18] It would seem that the ethicist of a conviction founded on law and principle and the ethicist of a responsibility founded on love and *agape* have their separate tasks worked out for them if they intend to assist each other in the moral dialogue. The first has to spell out in sharp detail the situation and the importance that he assigns to the situation. The second has to show that the guidelines of the generalizations taken into the ethical contest are great illuminators of concern for neighbor and are put aside only after they prove themselves to be destructive of genuine loving concern. Situational morality insists that we must be frank, grow honest with ourselves and with others, and even dispense with laws, codes and rules of behavior, substituting for them the judgment of love in every situation. It should be equally honest that there are values implicit in the rules, regulations or mere generalizations that accompany the person into the ethical arena and that the weight of these values frequently offsets the spontaneous mistaken judgment that might be made in the name of *agape*.

On the other hand the ethicist of a conviction grounded on law and principle should be candid about the externalism and hypocrisy that frequently accompany an ethic such as this and that it is this external morality that is often misjudged by its adherents as the only morality. The admission should be made that while this ethic of conviction can be at its best completely open to situational modification and correction, it has not in the past been represented often enough in this light. The accent of situationalism should in the dialogue-encounter with the ethicist of conviction assist the latter in the recognition of the inadequacies of the theory in the past in minimizing situational factors and in concentrating upon the command or the prohibition. The accent of the ethics of conviction grounded upon rules and regulations should bring home to the situationalist that he takes along with him a lot of baggage that has molded his character and made him the person he is and that he would put it aside only after assurances in his own conscience that love is not served. It will happen not infrequently that he will curtsy to the very helpful moral generalizations which have made him the person he is at this very moment of moral decision-making.

III. SITUATION ETHICS AND SELF-DISCIPLINE

Situational morality is a mature and sophisticated morality. It presumes knowledge of one's self and of others. It appears evident that it

---

[18] John C. Bennett, *Religious Education*, Nov.–Dec. 1966 (Book Review).

requires, a word not used by Fletcher, a certain degree of asceticism and self-discipline. If the context is to be resolved in favor of loving concern then self-less concern or agapeic love is the desired criterion. We would be wise to take with us into the ethical computer room all of the character-helps and all of the existential knowledge we have of ourselves and of others. The presumption is that only mature persons make mature ethical decisions. How do we prepare persons in maturity and in ethical sophistication? Fletcher would be the first to admit that all the helps a man can bring with him should be brought into the choice of conscience, but he must be willing to put aside whatever would not concretely serve loving concern. The general principles seem to serve the purpose of expressing and reinforcing certain moral attitudes, but the difficulty with even this understanding of the meaning of "general principles" is that this would be presumably a disposition to act in similar ways in similar cases. Nevertheless, for Fletcher there are no similar cases. Copleston comments on this point in Fletcher's ethical thinking:

> In point of fact, there obviously are such things as similar situations which call for similar ways of acting. It does not follow, of course, that we can properly represent the moral agent, when faced with a particular situation, as always, or even generally, sitting down and trying to apply general principles or rules to the particular case. This would be a fantastic misrepresentation of the empirical facts, of the moral life as we know it. But our ways of acting manifest our scale of values and our norms of conduct, even if we do not advert to them. And it pertains to the mature man and moral agent to unify his conduct in terms of values, ends and general principles. A man may alter his scale of values. He may come to think, for example, that there are higher values than those which he previously considered supreme. But the picture of a man jumping from one entirely unique situation to another entirely unique situation without any criteria of judgment which are applicable in more than one situation is certainly not an accurate picture of the moral life. If all situations are unique, one can only add that some are more unique than others.[19]

Copleston goes on to add that he does not want to misrepresent Fletcher because the latter has no intention of atomizing the moral life in this way. The decisions of the ethical agent are not for Fletcher entirely arbitrary and disconnected nor does he show any enthusiasm for a purely intuitionist theory of ethics or for the idea that we can look to the Holy Spirit to inspire us with the right solution to each concrete moral problem as it comes along. Fletcher's teleological theory of ethics with its view of the indifference of all actions until the relation is made to some end

---

[19] Frederick Copleston, *Heythrop Studies* 8 (April 1967), p. 198 (Book Review).

or group of ends rules out the notion of his being arbitrary. In fact, others have criticized him for the cold-blooded ethical analysis in which he engages. However, if it is true that decisions are not arbitrary or disconnected from any individual's ethical past history, the question arises whether the departures from a man's history are going to be as frequent as Fletcher might be implying. If the ethical metanoias are infrequent would it not appear that situational morality is dealing with crises situations and not the ordinary situations in which persons find themselves?

Fletcher makes one appreciate why his ethical choice may finally be the one in favor of the principles which he has brought with him. The scrutinizing of each circumstance and motive in the concrete existential context points out the freedom of the individual in relating seriously each of these factors in their contribution to the service of *agape*. However, if after this scrutiny, the individual discovers that he will make his ethical choice consistent with his past ethical conviction, assured that this conviction has been related to loving concern, then this does not *ipso facto* make him an uncritical legalist. If the legalist would only test his principles in the crucible of *agape*, it would seem that he would still do what he would otherwise have done but the choice would be more Christian and invulnerable to the strictures of situational morality. It might be true that to be Kantian and do what the principle commands out of sheer obedience to the law is less than moral. Fletcher considers such behavior "immoral" but the question might be raised about the imperative of *agape* itself. Is it not conceivable that love itself may demand principles, especially for the very young. If the young person is one who leans more to deontology and principle and less to axiology and love, what would the normal person suggest? Does it not seem that there is the possibility that Fletcher has just the axiologist in mind and the person who can take the strong medicine? We alluded before to the matter of ethical education. Just how is a person trained to be situational in morality—by first being trained in the school of rigid application of principle and rule or by being plunged into situationalism and learning how to swim? We would even be inclined to judge that the best situationalists are persons who have come to situationalism as a reaction against legalism, moralism, pietism or antinomianism. We would think that Fletcher is the capable and competent situationalist that he is because he has learned the hard way that circumstances *do* matter, that acts are not intrinsically evil, that there are no universal negative prohibitions. This reaction is not in violence against one's past biography but because principle and rule do something to the character and only in this way can one with character appraise and judge the existential moral act, do all the prismatic analysis in conscience and exercise himself in selfless loving concern of others.

Situationalism appears to demand a good degree of mellowness and Fletcher has this to a consummate degree.[20]

IV. LIVING ACCORDING TO A CODE VS.
LIVING ACCORDING TO LOVE

Everyone is a situationalist whether he is in the computer room of loving concern or in the Thomistic room of *prudence*. In fact, a comparison with this practical virtue in operation with the situational method of Fletcher would produce some remarkable similarities. To be consistently prudent is difficult and to be consistently situational is difficult too, but both methods have much in common and the Thomist can learn from the situationalist and situationalist likewise from the Thomist. Possibly this explains why some who have been trained more in one than the other search out each other for mutual assistance. Just as the situationalist may under the influence of loving concern put aside principle and rule, so the man of prudence may have to do the same. Examine Josef Pieper's work on prudence and you will find many indications of a fine sense, a delicate appreciation of circumstance and motive. When Fletcher offers a summary statement of his position we might ask certain questions which would bring its provocative intent into proper focus. Fletcher says that "Christian ethics or moral theology is not a scheme of *living according to a code* but a continuous effort to relate love to a world of relativities through a casuistry obedient to love; its constant task is to work out the strategy and tactics of love, for Christ's sake."[21]

What are the problems that we would raise in connection with this statement? It would seem that Fletcher would not quarrel with the individual who lives according to a code so long as he does not live *uncritically* in accordance with that code. Nevertheless from the brief statement above the implicit meaning is that he is opposed to both. We know from his admissions that on most occasions the ethic of conviction grounded on principle and rule will be vindicated. It is only in crises situations where the tension between principle and love will be most poignantly experienced and this experience is not only confined to the situationalist. The man who exercises the proper prudence calculates as much as the situationalist and possibly even more so, and both do the same prismatic analyzing of all of the elements in the concrete existential act before coming to a final moral choice.

It would seem that the target of Fletcher's criticism is not the in-

---

[20] Fletcher, *Situation Ethics*, pp. 95–102.
[21] *Ibid.*, pp. 30–31.

dividual of code-morality but the individual of Kantian code-morality and this is an exaggeration of the man of principle and rule. Most ethically responsible persons follow principle and rule; possibly they should subject their adherence to more criticism in the name of *agape* but it does not represent reality to say that for the situationalist "there are no rules at all,"[22] without realizing that this sounds like the attitude of the antinomian. A re-reading of Fletcher's *Medical Ethics* will assure the doubter that he is not antinomian; in fact, some of his ethical directives are as firm and resolute as ethical directives in some religious hospitals. It is hard to dispose of legalism and the mere assertion that there are no rules for the situationalist does not make it so. Study the situationalist and you will discover other principles and other rules which he puts aside with no great frequency.

Paul Lehmann is critical of the apparent legalism in Fletcher when he identifies in a sort of convertible proposition "situation ethics" and "Christian ethics." "Does he (i.e. Fletcher) really wish us to think that this starkly unique Christ functions in Christian ethics by dissolving complexity both in the analysis and in the actions that go into the making of a decision? If so, then the proposition: 'situation ethics is Christian ethics' and the proposition: 'Christian ethics is situation ethics' are interchangeable propositions. If so, the stark uniqueness of Christ functions in decision-making by a simplistic love reductionism both as regards its 'nothing-else-ness' and as regards its neo-casuistical occasions. Such a reductionism seems strangely akin to the pietism, moralism, legalism, antinomianism which Fletcher rightly abhors and strangely impervious to the pragmatism, relativism, positivism, and personalism which he affirms."[23] Therefore it would seem that the recommendation by Fletcher to abandon any effort to set up a *system* of values on the grounds that all values are extrinsic is not consistently applied by himself. A system of values must not be relied upon but only the method which calls for a person to do that which is *loving* in a given set of circumstances. Love is not a quality or "property" within ourselves or even within our actions. Only God *is* love but what we ourselves do is expected to *serve* love. Law can only be brought into the ethical enterprise when it serves the ends of love. But Norman F. Langford has reservations on Fletcher's calculus of love:

> In his Foreword he asserts that his method is "an old posture with a new and contemporary look. It does indeed have a new look. What this turns out to be is a singularly objective, even blood-chilling application of love by a process of cool reasoning. Fletcher does not hesitate to dismiss the

22 *Ibid.*, p. 55.
23 Paul L. Lehmann, *Bulletin of the Episcopal Theological School*, September 1966.

conflict between love and justice, and to say that justice is simply "love distributed." He is not disconcerted by such a question as what to do if you must choose between rescuing your father or a medical genius from a burning building. The "calculus" of "agape" dictates clearly that the genius must be saved. This is "love using its head." Referring to a decision of the British intelligence service in World War II, "when they let a number of women agents return to Germany to certain arrest and death in order to keep secret the fact that they had broken the German code," he continues blandly that "situational casuistry could easily approve their decision."

But a question remains. Does this "calculus" of love, not, in effect, dehumanize love? Is love, even when it is that unique New Testament love called "agape," so remote from human feeling that it can be exercised with such detachment?[24]

It would seem that most of the questions that have been asked Fletcher have in some way concerned either the erosion of moral absolutes or the proper understanding that he gives the concept of love. Missing from any situation seems to be the idea of grace, and this has been mentioned by some Protestant critics. The problem may not be too serious for the Roman Catholic who considers love or *agape* as entitatively supernatural and, therefore, as virtue and act, accompanied by grace. Missing also is the notion of remorse and guilt. The ethical decisions that result from situational and contextual morality may, according to Fletcher, lead to regret but never to the agony of remorse. The real tension between law and love has gone out of the ethical wrestling, and forgiveness appears to be absent in the glossary of situationalism. The psychologico-moral reactions which result from putting aside the normal restraints against fornication, adultery, abortion, suicide, euthanasia, theft, lying, breaking the law, conspiracy to overthrow a lawfully constituted government, etc. strike anyone to be different in degree from the reaction of regret. In fact, where the conscience has not become so cauterized to these practices, the psychologico-moral experience seems to have many interesting elements that are cognitive, affective, and appetitive and are not so mild and so bland as to be dismissed under the mere name of *regret*. In addition, these genuine reactions have operated as further inhibitions to future practice in the moral behavior of persons in society.

To illustrate this fact we may allude to a question raised by the author in an interview with a famous obstetrician on the subject of abortion. We asked why the American Medical Association has always resisted until the present the liberalization of its professional position on abortion, especially when most doctors regard that it is necessary to per-

---

[24] Norman F. Langford, *Presbyterian Life* (April 15, 1966), 10–11.

form it for reasons other than saving the mother's life. The response was immediate—"No doctor wants to perform an abortion if he can avoid it at all." Now this reaction strikes anyone who understands that the doctor has situationally resolved the moral context in the name of loving concern and yet his reaction is surely stronger than mild regret. Possibly in naming the psychological reaction which results from situationally doing what is not normally done, we might seek out a more meaningful term than *regret*. We are inclined to think that the reaction can be shown to be qualitatively different from regret and we have attempted to offer some phenomenological evidence for this from the study of the psychologico-moral experience of guilt. We may regret having made a mistake in an examination we have taken; but making a mistake in an examination and making the error in situational and prismatic analysis, in a moral situation, involving a possible abortion, adultery, or dropping the bomb, is quite a different matter.

In short, to equate the reaction to a mistake in mathematics with the reaction to an ethical choice to commit an act of adultery is to trivialize the psychology of man. The psychologico-moral experience of having to put aside a law, principle, or rule which, under normal circumstances, would have been adhered to, is not mere regret. At least the qualities of this experience should be examined phenomenologically before the bland substantive "regret" is applied indiscriminately to all such actions which are consistently renounced. A. E. Taylor in looking deeply into the guilt experience has shown how therapeutic this experience has been in the moral life of persons.[25] We have suggested that, despite the situational justification in the name of loving concern, there are still the qualities of the self-condemnatory, the indelible, the inalienable in the experience. To remove them would mean to liberate the person from the principles and the rules that he consistently and normally would obey. To identify these qualities from the experience of a person who in loving concern aborts, or robs, with the obvious reactions of dissatisfaction from having made a mistake is to reduce a psychologico-moral experience to one purely psychological. We wish it were so but phenomenology consistently tells us otherwise. The testimony of the *consequent conscience* is more revealing of the kind of moral resolution of the situation that has taken place in one's psyche than the testimony of the *antecedent conscience* in Kantian morality.

In the resolution of any ethical situation adequate place must be given to the unavoidable tensions that take place. For ourselves this tension is ultimately between an *ethic of conviction* and an *ethic of responsibility*,

25 A. E. Taylor, *The Faith of a Moralist* (London: Macmillan, 1951), Vol. I, pp. 163–210.

but for Fletcher the relation between *love* and the *"cautious generalizations"* which he accepts does not appear to be one of tension or agony. Decisions are made in cold logic or with an aplomb that seems to issue from a computerized intelligence. The cool detachment of the situationalist amazes one if he reflects that it has resulted from an ethical situation in which love often provides little or no illumination concerning what is good for the neighbor and in which the *cautious generalization* may have been put aside too readily. To be told that justice and love are the same and that justice is love distributed and nothing else does not help. It is too simple a reductionism where the claims of justice are wider and more exacting than those of love. This same lack of tension is evident in Fletcher when he says that "once the relative course is chosen, the obligation to pursue it is absolute."[26] John C. Bennett considers that Fletcher has no patience "with those who stress the evil in an action that on balance may be necessary to some calculus, but this is to destroy sources of restraint and almost certainly it will lead us to heedless destruction of some neighbors for the sake of others."[27] Bennett prudently recommends that the relative course should be under constant criticism and that it should be changed and not remain one to which one must be absolutely bound. The intrinsic evil that Fletcher will not accept is an indisputable fact for Bennet, at least in some moral acts:

> To say that no acts have any evil in themselves—not even the bombing of populations nor the torture of an individual to get necessary information to protect other individuals—is to destroy essential sources of restraint. There is another trend in the book that appears in a few places, as in his approval and slight modification of Alexander Miller's statement that "if killing and lying are to be used it must be under the most urgent pressure of social necessity, and with a *profound sense of guilt* that no better way can be presently found" (p. 124). Fletcher prefers "sorrow" to "guilt" but even in this he gives away his case for the view that there is no intrinsic evil in some forms of action.[28]

This same evil that Bennett finds in some more reprehensible acts is the same evil that we ourselves insist manifests itself in the testimony of the *consequent conscience*. If the psychologico-moral experience of guilt is present anywhere it is certainly found in the actions selected by Bennett as containing in themselves evil that everyone admits. The reaction to the performance of acts of killing and lying is quite different from the regret that follows upon some stupid mistake. The qualities of the *self-condemnatory*, the *indelible*, the *incommunicable* and the conviction

---

26 Fletcher, *Situation Ethics*, p. 143.
27 Bennett, *Religious Education*, Nov.–Dec. 1966 (Book Review).
28 Bennett, *ibid*.

that we have *stained ourselves*—all these are revealed in the phenomenology of this unique experience. To be aware of the distinction between guilt and regret is, according to Bennett, to grow in moral wisdom:

> To judge that a particular action is in some situations not the greatest evil does not rob it of all intrinsic evil. To keep alive awareness of this evil is essential for moral wisdom about the total situation. I understand that Fletcher intends to keep in mind all of the consequences, direct and indirect, those that would usually be regarded as evil as well as those that are more readily seen to be good or natural. But his method tends to rivet attention on what is immediate and most relevant at the moment of decision. This may not be as serious in the case of an abortion as it is in the case of the bombing of a city. Also one should give more weight than Fletcher does to the effect of precedent, when in a situation a moral inhibition is broken down which in all but the most exceptional cases is a desirable source of restraint. I am conservative enough to think that this is true of adultery but I know that it is true of torture.[29]

Situational morality impresses us as a tough morality that requires the sophistication of responsibility in all possible relations with other persons. To simplify this form of the ethics of responsibility and to minimize the tensions and the agonies that go on during all this prismatic analysis is to do an injustice to the exigencies of the real situation. We would like to develop some ideas on the demands made by this ethic and the problems that arise for anyone who would judge too easily that the *New Morality* of situationalism is an easy morality. The inference we shall draw from our considerations is that it is undoubtedly true that this morality is difficult but it is also true that it is the morality to which more and more attention is being given. If situationalism is not trivialized in its presentation and application it will offer a more profound insight into the intricacies of moral experience and will be adopted only by those who are willing to accept the demands which go with it.

We might put our question this way: Is situational morality, the new morality too difficult? Is this form of the *Ethic of Responsibility* more difficult to apply than many of its advocates would seem to realize? Do these advocates tend to minimize the situation and to trivialize the full implications of this ethics?

V.   IS THE NEW MORALITY TOO DIFFICULT?

It all looks so easy to say that you are a situationalist and that it is only love that counts. But is this decision-making method of morality so easy and so applicable? Upon reflection it seems true that everyone spells

---

[29] *Ibid.*

out the situation in his ethical decision-making whether he eliminates the categories of objective and subjective morality and questions the existence of universal negative prohibitions, or, on the other hand, allows the distinction to survive and plunges all of the context and situation into the subjectively moral arena with only God as the final spectator. Let me try to clarify what I am driving at.

There is an extraordinary motion picture, *Sundays and Cybele*, with an excellent scene that might help as an illustration. A young man who has been the unseen witness of a departure incident at a private school between a young child and her father overhears the father saying that he never intends to visit his daughter again. The young man thereafter presents himself each Sunday as the child's father and the child willingly cooperates in the deception. On one occasion he brings the child to a body of water and sits with her in conversation on the bank. He takes a stone and tosses it into the water. A swirling circle appears on the surface, grows larger and larger, and as the child studies the expanding circle, he explains to her that this circle will never disappear and no one knows how far it will go.

For purposes of illustration there is no better one than that from this motion picture to understand the meaning and the difficulties involved in situational morality. Mature responsibility is commensurate with the deliberate knowledge and free acceptance of the consequences that follow from this circle, initiated by our moral act in this existential moment of ethical history. Where does that circle go, whom does it touch, with what results for good or evil, how does it develop or undermine our own selves in mature responsibility? The decision-making method of situational morality becomes an enormous calculation and extrapolation of the consequences that unavoidably follow from this particular moral act posited here and now. This is serious business and not a morality of the mere presence or absence of agape. This is a morality which demands self-knowledge, mature experience, a disciplined character, an awareness of others as persons with rights and claims upon us in multiple inter-personal relations, a sensitivity to the short and long term consequences from this moral act. Situational morality is most authentic when it refuses to trivialize the situation. After all, is this not the principal criticism of traditional morality, that it is juridical, legalistic, and indifferent to the agonizing existential moment when the hard ethical choice must be made?

This is the first reason why situational morality is so difficult—in refusing to trivialize the situation, it places the onus on the situationalist to evaluate the consequences that follow from the act, to appreciate the expanding concentric circles that develop from the person's placing his moral toe in the Heraclitean flux. No one wants to trivialize the situation, no one wants to be less mature and responsible than someone else, and situationalism seems only to compound problem upon problem for the authentic choice that has to be made.

Another difficulty with this moral theory of decision-making arises from its attitude toward moral principles, precepts or laws. For the situationalist there is no principle, precept or law that always binds; there is no universal negative principle, precept or law which always obliges. This is not to say that there is no very significant number of occasions when the principle, precept or law does have direct application. Some situationalists refer to the principle being valid and applicable in 98/100 cases, 998/1000 cases etc. Now this should cause problems for any situationalist who wants to establish himself in the very small number of cases where the law does not apply or where, because *agape* would suffer, the law must be put aside. This ought to suggest to the responsible and mature situationalists that a possible deceptive reading of the good might result in a too rapid conclusion that the exceptional has been found. Before this inference can be drawn, should not the wisdom of the law and the values implicit in the law be recognized constantly? Is it not possible that while love may place some moral dimension upon the exceptional case, a certain degree of hubris has been manifest in a summary rejection of the values and the wisdom incorporated in the law? Love and law are not so incompatible that their tension cannot be resolved in most situations to the interest of both. At times it seems that some situationalists represent the extraordinary case as one in which persons can only be loved more if law is loved less. Does this represent the authentic situation? Can it really be established that in a critical case of conflict between love and law, a man necessarily loves a person more inasmuch as he loves law less?

These questions are raised to promote dialogue among the proponents of situational morality, Protestant as well as Catholics. All morality, properly understood, is situational, is aware of the increasing importance placed upon circumstances, motives, historical evolution, the subjectivity of the moral agent. Existential phenomenology provides a proper descriptive appreciation of the complexities of the human moral situation. The point made here is that we should be grateful to some situationalists that they have made us aware of the complexities and that we should equally be on our guard against others who would trivialize the human situation. On the other hand, if situational morality is mature and responsible to the extent that it does not trivialize the human situation, is it a morality that is so easy to adopt and apply with discernment and prudence? Situational morality is a difficult morality but it is the only morality for the mature, responsible, conscientious person. This is the paradox.

Let us look to some other reasons for saying that situationalism is a difficult morality.

Dr. Fletcher has his own problems trying to clarify for others what precisely he means by love or *agape*. Certainly, for this proponent of situational morality, love or loving concern is central in his "new morality." The presence of love is pivotal in the moral life and in ethical analysis everything hinges upon loving concern. Dr. Lachs, professor of philosophy at the College of William and Mary, contends that nowhere are we told in detail what love *is*. In an article in *The Christian Century* he has pointed to the diverse roles love plays in the ethics of situationalism, some of which are incompatible with others. Dr. Lachs identifies the pages in *Situation Ethics* of Dr. Fletcher where these many roles are catalogued.

> Love is first said to be something we do: it is thus (1) an action or a way of behaving (p. 61). This definition is quickly revised: love becomes (2) a characteristic of certain human actions and relationships (p. 63). Again it is (3) the purpose behind the action (p. 61). Toward the end of the book it becomes (4) the motive behind the decision to act (p. 155). Elsewhere, love is (5) an attitude of persons, (6) a disposition to act in certain ways, (7) a preference for certain values, and (8) good will or a conative predisposition to take certain attitudes (pp. 79, 61, 104, 105). And it is also said to be (9) a relation, (10) a formal principle and (11) a regulative principle (pp. 105, 60, 61).[30]

Dr. Lachs concludes that love surely cannot be all these things and if it is identified in all these ways, then Dr. Fletcher has no clear idea of the nature of love.

Dr. Lachs argues that if love is (1), it cannot also be (2) because actions cannot be the characteristic of actions. Again if love is (9), it cannot also be (4), (5) and (6) because relations are not motives, attitudes or dispositions. Further, if love is (3), it cannot also be (10) and (11) because purposes are not principles. Dr. Lachs insists that if Dr. Fletcher holds that love, the only ultimate value for him, is (1) a kind of action, he is unavoidably drawn to the position that right actions are right *intrinsically*; on the other hand, if Dr. Fletcher maintains that love is (3) a motive, (4) a purpose or (5) and (8) a conative attitude, he is ineluctably drawn to the position that right actions are right *extrinsically* from the intentions or personal attitudes of the agent who performs them. Finally, if love is (9) a relation between persons, this should make

---

[30] John Lachs, "Dogmatist in Disguise" *The Christian Century*, Vol. 83, Nov. 16, 1966, pp. 1402–1405.

Dr. Fletcher adopt the position that the moral quality of an act must be evaluated by its tendency to establish such valuable relations.

These are harsh forms of the reductionist type of argumentation and, personally, it leaves many situationalists cold. It is interesting to note that much of this form of approach toward situational morality is not being done by Catholic moralists but by Protestant moralists who frequently can "out-Jesuit Pascal's Jesuit." It seems that a different criticism can be directed at situational morality on the grounds that the love or loving concern of situationalism is most difficult to realize in existential moral situations. Let us develop this point.

What is the love or *agape* that makes an act morally good? It is neither love that is erotic or philiac but a peculiar kind of love that is intrinsically good. Erotic love is selfish love, philiac love is a mutual giving which ceases when mutality ceases. Agapaic love is selfless, completely other-directed, almost sacrificial, perfectly verified in Christ's love of mankind by His death on the Cross. Now, does this distinction made among the 3 kinds of love provide problems for the situationalist who constantly speaks of love and constantly identifies it with *agape*? Is *agape*, selfless love, so easily realizable in human experience? Is it not true that we recognize many acts to be moral and ethical which are not accompanied by selfless-concern? Does it not seem that *agape* is an embarrassing word to use among persons whose highest reaches of affection are philiac? Is agapaic love even a possibility outside of the sacrificial love of a mother, or the heroic act of kenotic love for another creature? In other words, is it sensible to discriminate agapaic love from erotic and philiac and then speak of *agape* as the loving, selfless concern, which gives the moral quality to the human act? If *agape* is selfless love, how many times has anyone attained it? If this selfless love is not required for the morality of an act, might it not be more honest to put aside this word which has so precise and specific a meaning?

By way of summary of the above, it might seem to the nonspecialist in moral science that there are many moral acts that are not accompanied by *agape*, and that there are few moral acts where the love that is present is of a quality, selfless, kenotic, sacrificial, utterly separable from the love that is erotic and philiac. The situationalist may not question this but his persistence in using the term *agape* makes moral acts appear to be almost impossible to realize. *Agape* is an unfortunate word for one who discriminates it from the *erotic* and the *philiac*.

One additional point should be made while on the subject of *agape*. For anyone who recalls the Kantian formula for the moral act, the situationalist formula has almost the same ring. For the Kantian the principle of the moral act was "do *duty* for *duty's* sake"; for the situationalist the principle becomes "do *agape* for the sake of *agape*." Just as any intrusive pleasure in the Kantian moral act might tend to corrode its moral and ethical quality, so any intrusive submission to law and not to love might tend to corrode the moral act for the situationalist. The polar extremes appear to be Kantian deontology and Situational agapaism.

In an article in *Commonweal* called "Law, Love and Politics" (Nov. 25, 1966) Brian Wicker develops the point of the separation between law and love. He refers to Conrad's *Lord Jim* to show examples of completely different attitudes to morality: "firstly, that men are ineradicably social, that it is only in social relationships that men can exist at all and come to any maturity. And the structure of any society must rest upon the acceptance of a code which is not just a rule of thumb, but an unimpeachable fiat which addresses itself imperiously to every man."[31] Terry Eagleton agrees with Wicker and says: "Human beings live by actively interiorizing rules, codes, conventions: we eat, sleep, see, love, think, die according to rules, codes which make sense of our experience and which make that experience humanly possible. A culture is such an active interiorization of rules by a whole people, in a way which makes communication and identity possible."[32]

Brian Wicker continues with Conrad's other attitude toward morality by showing how Conrad insisted that "society is necessarily *criminal*, in that it cannot help exacting from individuals an obedience they cannot possibly give without destroying themselves. To try to give obedience to that extent is, of course, to abandon the very thing that society exists to promote—livable human life. There is thus a contradiction at the heart of human existence that cannot be overcome completely."[33]

In terms of these contrasted moral attitudes that are at the very heart of human existence Wicker finally refers to them in this way: "Legalism asserts a consistent moral universe ruled by 'Law,' situation ethics, a consistent moral universe ruled by 'Love.' "[34] Eagleton admits that he favors the first: "Christians are not virtuous by rejecting rules and codes . . . but by coming to act spontaneously in accordance with them, by appropriating them as the structure of the self; this is what is meant by life in the spirit, life within the creative and restraining definitions of Christ's body."[35] Werner Pelz wants nothing to do with a moral attitude of law and its obsession with moral judgments which he insists have done

---

[31] Brian Wicker, "Law, Love and Politics," *The Commonweal* (Nov. 25, 1966).
[32] Terry Eagleton, "Poetry, Objects and Politics," *The New Left Church* (Baltimore: Helicon, 1966), pp. 31–68.
[33] Wicker, *art. cit.*
[34] *Ibid.*
[35] Eagleton, *art. cit.*

so much harm in Western history. For Eagleton and Pelz there are consistent moral universes but at the heart of the matter there is, according to Wicker, a "paradoxical, inconsistent moral universe; that is, a world in which the irreducible gap between 'law' and 'love' is explicitly recognized as part of the moral landscape. To suggest that, in a pinch, one has to take precedence over the other is just to eliminate the real tension that lies at the heart of morality. For it is at the point of tension between 'law' and 'love' that God's power—the power to reconcile justice and mercy—comes in."[36]

Wicker's analysis is brilliant. It is in the tension between "law" and "love" where consistency breaks down and inconsistency and absurdity appear. But it is precisely here where we become aware of the presence of God in the very tension and agony of our lives. Rosemary Haughton's remarkable book, *Trying to be Human* is a recognition of this tension at the bottom of our lives and she likewise finds much in the article of Brian Wicker that we cited above. In a recent article in *New Blackfriars* she refers to these words of Wicker: "Real moral dilemmas are not cases to be analyzed but agonies to be lived through. The living of these agonies, and the survival of them, *is* the moral history of mankind. And since . . . moral dilemmas have a sociological aspect, because they concern the gap between 'law' and 'love' as it is incarnated at a particular moment and at a particular place, morality has to do with the history of human social structures, that is with our political history."[37]

To polarize "law" and "love" is to deny the moral paradoxes that all of us frequently face in our lives. For example, the paradox is not resolved by the situationalist in the case of a meaningful sexual relationship "outside the Law" by referring to it as *good and right*. It is equally not resolved by the legalist by referring to it as *bad and wrong*. The moral paradox recognizes that agonies are present, that moral consistencies have broken down and that God has introduced us into a situation that can only validly and honestly be called *good but wrong*. Rosemary Haughton's insight into the human situation is penetrating and it is closest to the truth. She has seen what neither polar position has recognized—that in a tension between "law" and "love" tidy moral consistencies break down in agonizing human situations where God is actively present while we work out the moral paradoxes at the very heart of our lives. It is only by faith in the active dynamic presence of God that these moral paradoxes will not find the agonies insoluble for the human conscience. But some agonies will always remain and humility requires that we live with them as best we can.

---

[36] Wicker, *art. cit.*
[37] Rosemary Haughton, *New Blackfriars*, Jan. 1968.

It would seem from the analysis of the hypothetical situation above that it does not help to identify too easily the *right* with the *good* and the *wrong* with the *bad*. It appears that this is done by both the legalist and the agapaist and it might be wise to look towards a clarification of ethical terms before we develop anything else. Let me explain how both the legalist and the situationalist tend to convert the *right* with the *good* and the *wrong* with the *bad*.

For the legalist who contends that there are universal obliging affirmative and negative principles and who accepts the difference between objective and subjective morality, his tendency will be to consider any violation of these principles objectively *wrong* and *bad*. For the situationalist who denies universal obliging affirmative and negative principles and who considers that the distinction between objective and subjective morality is of little assistance in clarification, a meaningful agapaic coital relationship "outside the law" becomes in the concrete existential situation *good* and *right*. This identification does not improve communication between the legalist and agapaist and does not make room for the frequent moral paradoxes where tidy moral coherences break down (as we indicated above). Where these ethical consistencies break down we discover that the verbal identification of the *right* with the *good* and the *wrong* with the *bad* also breaks down. It should make us wonder whether we should not have divorced these terms at the very outset of all discussion of ethical language. Submission of these terms to phenomenological analysis will make clearer what precisely we are driving at. Cases of civil disobedience will be seen to be at times *good* but *wrong* unless the appeal is made to the justice of these cases because of a higher law. Language problems will remain nevertheless even after the concession is made to eliminate the dichotomy between objective and subjective morality. The discovery of the right thing to do under the circumstances of the here and now is never simple. It is the wrestling that must be done by the man of prudence and nothing can be harder for the person who questions the existence of affirmative and negative moral absolutes. What is not in agreement with the principle may in the ultimate consideration of conscience be *good* in the sight of God, and is this not the real meaning of loving concern—to do precisely what the source of Love would want us to do? But how does the ordinary person decide what are the genuine exigencies of love? This decision seems to be known by God but how is it communicated to man? For Fletcher even the Ten Commandments are valid only if the qualifying term "ordinarily" is applied to each one. The ethical decision then seems to rest neither with God nor man but with the situation, but the difficulty with this polarizing of the situation is that the voices may be so multiple and so confusing. Only the command to love is categorically good,[38] but it is not necessarily good to love the law even when the law comes from God who is identified with love by John (1 Jn 4:8).

"Situation ethics is an effort to relate love to a world of relativities through a casuistry obedient to love. It is the strategy of love. This strategy denies that there are, as Sophocles thought, any unwritten immutable laws of heaven, agreeing with Butlmann that *all such notions are idolatrous and a demonic pretension*."[39] Love itself can make the situationalist put aside all the ethical maxims that a person brings with him into the ethical arena. Fletcher develops this notion in pointing out the shifting relativities of each situation: "This situationalist enters into every decision-making situation fully armed with the ethical maxims of his community and its heritage and he treats them with respect as illuminators of his problems. Just the same he is prepared in any situation to compromise them and set them aside in the situation if love seems better served by doing so."[40] Each man must decide finally what are the demands of love in each particular situation and what is one man's calculus of love is not another's. In fact, so shifting and relative is the ethical situation that the calculus of love changes for the very same man at different moments of ethical history. This becomes evident from Fletcher's rejection of ontology or the study that concerns itself with the radical nature of being. He agrees with Sartre that "Ontology itself cannot formulate ethical precepts. It is concerned solely with what is, and we cannot possibly derive imperatives from ontology's indicatives."[41] This seems to leave very little structure to the situation with the result that even the cautious generalizations of Fletcher should be regarded with even more skepticism. The rejection of ontology by the situationalist is incompatible with St. John's ontological assertion that God is Love and that the act of loving results in knowing God. This knowledge is not so much what God does but of Who He is. This seems to be the source for the absolute quality of love. When he rejects ontology Fletcher seems also to reject valid grounds for the absolute character of love. God is no longer offended or his nature in some way violated if love is violated. Love becomes a relative, non-egoistic, agapaic exercise, in fact more intellectual than agapaic. It is discoverable within the situation by a moral choice that is made, not between a series of values and disvalues (because all acts are of their nature morally indifferent and become good if love is present), but between these neutral acts that open up

---

[38] Fletcher, *Situation Ethics*, p. 26.
[39] *Ibid.*, p. 31.
[40] *Ibid.*, p. 26.
[41] *Ibid.*, p. 25.

before man in the concrete existential context. Situational morality accents the context but what remains to puzzle the Christian philosopher is the absence of Christian considerations, such as *grace, sin, remorse,* and *forgiveness.* Does not the omission of these concerns raise many questions about the adequacy of this type of an ethic of responsibility that purports to be *Christian* as well as *situational?.* Is not the ethic of responsibility to this extent trivialized?

The truth seems to be that man demands these Christian elements in any ethic that represents itself as *situational* and *Christian.* We commented on the inadequacy of the term regret where remorse seemed to be the testimony of psychologico-moral experience. The love that is "categorically good," that is "the only one norm or principle or law that is binding or unexceptional, always good and right regardless of the circumstances," the love that as a principle "obliges us in conscience" and that is "the only universal," this love cannot be disassociated from Him with whom it is identified by St. John. In the resolution of ethical situations it should not be divorced from Him because it is evident from phenomenology that man does not possess this love that is indispensable for him to achieve whatever goodness God desires for him. Man's whole being is a testimony to the absence of this love without God giving it to him gratuitously. God is present in such agapaic acts and this gift of His own nature substitutes for the radical incapacity of man to love in such selfless ways. God gives Himself and without Him we cannot love adequately. This seems to be borne out through the evidence of such texts as "There is a new creation whenever a man comes to be in Christ" and "If the Spirit of him who raised Jesus from the dead dwells in you, then he who raised Christ from the dead will also make your mortal bodies live by his indwelling Spirit within you."

Situational morality that finds the reason for the source of morality in a love which is more than erotic and philiac would seem to be reductively an ethic that cannot be indifferent to the reality of grace. If only love is categorically good and this love implicitly is not identified with the love that is erotic or philiac, then only agapaic love is categorically good and we cannot overlook the one Person whose entire existence was a life of agapaic love. Just by contrast it might be helpful to examine how few of our moral acts are agapaic and how many of them are undeniably erotic and philiac with some small traces of selflessness.

Situational morality has many of the same epistemological problems as any morality that represents itself as empirical and personal. If man is not consistently related to God as the source of love, then how does he decide for himself what are the exigencies of love? Fletcher admits this decision must be reached by every man for himself: "Every man must decide for himself according to his own estimate of conditions and consequences and no one can decide for him or impugn the decision to which he comes."[42] No one will question that the moral choice must be a personal one but it surely must be directed by something more than a mere personal estimate. Does this not seem to mean that according to Fletcher "the only categorical good," the law "that obliges in conscience," "that is binding and unexceptional" is the personal estimate of this individual man? Every man is his own casuist and this is the conclusion of Fletcher. "We must favor a casuistry in which every man is his own casuist when the decision-making chips are down."[43] If a study could be made of the prismatic analysis that goes on in several hundred persons, it would be fascinating to see whether this casuistry terminated in anything higher than a love that was erotic and agapaic. Agapaic love is to be determined by the judgment of the individual and if this is so, that it is only a matter of opinion, then it would appear that the categorical, absolute and universal nature of his love has been compromised. That the absolute quality of love does seem to be compromised in Fletcher's situationalism appears clear in the comment that he makes regarding a citation from Cicero. Cicero said, "Only a madman could maintain that the distinction between the honorable and the dishonorable, between virtue and vice is a matter of opinion and not of nature." To this Fletcher replies, "This is *precisely and exactly* what situation ethics means."[44] It is difficult to understand how the absolute, categorical and universal features of love are left unimpaired in this multiplicity of ethical situational options.

There is a consistency to much of this situational morality and the problems that arise in the epistemology of ethical choices receive no help from the Holy Spirit or from conscience. Conscience is rejected as "inspiration of an outside decision-maker, in the guidance of the Holy Spirit or a guardian angel or Jiminy Cricket."[45] Huckleberry Finn's consideration of conscience was along the same lines as Fletcher's: "If I had a yaller dog that didn't know more than a person's conscience does, I would poison him. It takes up more room than all the rest of a person's insides, and yet it ain't no good, no how." With such disenchantment with conscience and the Holy Spirit we come to some fascinating decision-making which raise questions about their agapaic-quotient. One example is given of a young unmarried couple who "might decide, if they make their decision Christianly, to have intercourse (e.g. by getting

---

[42] *Ibid.*, p. 37.
[43] *Ibid.*, p. 44, p. 37.
[44] *Ibid.*, p. 77.
[45] *Ibid.*, p. 53.

pregnant to force a selfish parent to relent his overbearing resistance to their marriage)."[46] The possibilities of self-deception as to the agapaic relation here, the question about the use of alternative means, the interrogation of others as to the wisdom of such a procedure, even the suggestion that possibly God might be of some assistance before this coercive measure is employed on the parents, all these finally are put aside by the agapaic calculus of the two persons who, just possibly, are the least reliable to settle the ethical quandary.

Such an ethics is undoubtedly situational even if the depth and the width of the situational analysis can be questioned. What one can seriously wonder about is "Is it Christian?" If we look to the ethical behavior of Christ with regard to adultery, Our Lord reacts in a different way than situationalism appears to react. For the situationalist adultery must always be submitted to the crucial test of loving concern and if this is promoted then adultery can be situationally justified. Does Christ resolve the problem of the woman taken in adultery in exactly the same way? Of course there was the additional problem of the relation of the Pharisees toward this woman. But He never asked the woman whether there was a situational defense for what she had done. He did not ask her what Fletcher would ask if the problem arose concerning adultery. For the situationalist the reaction is to submit a concrete existential case where adultery might be right and another where it might be wrong. But how does Christ behave toward the adulteress? He does not resolve the problem by disposing of the law and stating that it must serve the situation in the name of loving concern. He does not seem to say that adultery is morally indifferent until a concrete case is submitted to him for a provisional and then final answer. He does not absolutize the law as the legalist is represented as doing in the person of the Pharisees. They were anxious to see whether He would put aside the law in the name of love or charity and therefore be in opposition to their understanding of morality. On the other hand they watched to see whether He would dismiss charity in the name of law and thereby recognize their conception of morality. The Pharisees would have subjected Christ to criticism in either event. However, if we read John 8:3–11 carefully we shall find that Our Lord neither discarded the law in the name of charity nor discarded charity in the name of law. He was the wisest of all situationalists in resolving the tension that existed between law and love and therefore his first reaction was to place the law of adultery in proper perspective and to ask the Pharisees who were accusing the

---

[46] *Ibid.* Norman F. Langford (*Situation Ethics Debate*, p. 261) calls this "ethics in cold blood," Fletcher accepts this description.

woman: "Let him that is without sin among you be the first to throw a stone at her." Christ implied that if the law was to be cited by the Pharisees against the woman then they should be consistent in allowing the law to be cited against themselves. This willingness on the part of the Pharisees would indicate a real genuine concern for law and not an idolatry toward the law. That they had an idolatry toward the law was revealed in the aftermath of His remarks. They left and silently admitted their unwillingness to be judged by the very law that they directed against the woman. Christ therefore made clear that judgment was to be made by God and no one else. He would equally show that forgiveness belongs ultimately to God and therefore He forgave the woman, not by saying the law did not apply, or that she had not possibly sinned in the act of adultery, or that her psychological reaction should be one of mild regret because of a possible wrong ethical situational resolution, nor did He give indication that remorse and guilt were not proper to her. He simply said "I do not condemn you." In fact He implied that her wrongdoing was not only a possibility but an actuality because He advised her against future adultery and said: "Go and sin no more." Christ must have known that some of the situations in which this woman entered were experiences that were performed with loving concern. In those, as in the case in *Situation Ethics*, participants were better disposed to accept themselves and others as a result of this relationship. Nevertheless, Christ does not relativize the law; He held on to the law but liberated it from the charge of legalism with love and forgiveness.

The true question that the situationalist should ask himself in the computer room of ethical analysis is not what does love demand but what does the Person Who is Incarnate Love demand. It would not hinder the analysis to look at some of His own resolutions of moral situations as they are given in the Gospels. He never denies the existence of law or the fact of wrongdoing. He never denies that man can transgress the law of God. However, if we examine the total picture of situational morality we shall notice that the conception of the judgment of God is completely missing. An Anglican scholar brought to my attention the absence of any discussion of sin in *Situation Ethics*. He pointed to the significant fact that the word *sin* did not even appear in the index and he suggested that it was plausible to expect the absence of the word *forgiveness* as well. He was right about the omission of any discussion on *forgiveness* and his sharp mind at once asked me how valid and adequate was an ethic that had no room for *grace, remorse, sin, forgiveness*. Law without forgiveness creates a very serious problem but it is an unnecessary problem because forgiveness is the prerogative of God and is one of the greatest gifts of God to man.

The judgments of God in matters relating to life and death are submitted to the same crucible of loving concern and they can put aside just as summarily if they meet the test. Fletcher calls the opinion of Dietrich Bonhoeffer on the subject of abortion to be "shocking and inexplicable."[47] Bonhoeffer suggested that "the question of whether the life of the mother or the child is of greater value can hardly be a matter of human decision."[48] Bonhoeffer may be wrong and Fletcher may be right but both have presuppositions on the nature of life and it requires no elaborate research in the Gospels to discover whose presuppositions are more compatible with Christian value. If we reread the comment of Fletcher on Bonhoeffer we are forced once again to ask whether there is a trivialization of both the situation and of the Christian dimension of the ethical situation.

Situationalism faces the difficulty of trivializing morality in the denial of the dichotomy of objective/subjective morality. By making all morality subjective and situational, by denying that there are any acts, however definable, which are intrinsically evil, the situation should have become the real ethical computer room for situational analysis. The problem is that the room too frequently is much too small to contain all the elements of the ethical situation and the situationalist likewise suffers from contextual claustrophobia. Instead of asking many questions about the situation and how it arose before offering a tentative ethical resolution of the demands of loving concern, he holds that the decision-making is spontaneous and brief. The person who is trivial will inevitably trivialize the situation in which he happens to be. He will ask of himself and others very few questions about the empirical consequences of the act that might follow. The succession of such trivial ethical decision-making only compounds the trivial nature of the situationalist. He needs all the help he can bring into the situation and he should not be told that he can dismiss even the judgments of God in the name of loving concern which is reached by his own casuistry. To allow the ethically naive to decide that in this situation adultery is an act of love and therefore moral for him is to make demands on him which he will tend more to minimize than to magnify. What is the true legitimate situation for him—is it one that his own naiveté has created or is it the one that results from a succession of situations in which God's judgment on certain acts has been very easily dismissed?

[47] *Ibid.*, p. 38, Cf. Dietrich Bonhoeffer, *Ethics* (New York: Macmillan, 1965), pp. 175–176.
[48] Bonhoeffer, pp. 175–176.

How much of the situation is already structured before this situational decision-making takes place? How much of the structure is altered by the rapid spontaneous ethical resolution of the naive?

The three leading situationalists employ the example of the young sailor who is helped by the prostitute to attain for the first time a satisfactory coital relationship. Bishop Robinson appeals to this story in *Never on Sunday* in order to show that only love "makes something right or wrong."[49] H. A. Williams praises the prostitute's act as one of "charity which proclaims the glory of God."[50] Dr. Fletcher expresses more caution in the words: "we could, we might, decide that the whore is right."[51] The comments of the Anglican Usher-Wilson are very much to the heart of the matter: "None of the three raise any question about how the girl came to be a prostitute and what brought the man to her room, but surely if the situation is about to decide a matter of right or wrong these are questions which should be taken into consideration. One situation leads to another in an endless procession. Is man to be content with the meager crumbs of love and humanity that these situations permit or does he need, by a clear cut moral decision, to break out of a vicious circle, make a pact with God to listen to His voice and obey His laws thus creating a whole new set of situations free from pettiness and in line with God's unique plan for humanity?"[52] In other words, one of the crucial questions that should be considered is not whether the situation should be so important as to determine the demands of loving concern, but whether it might not be better to undermine the situation in which one happens to be, create an entire new situation, and begin all over. Most would agree that this should be done but can it be done by the ethically naive who are advised that love is the only absolute? The situationalist has to enter the new situation with a quality of character that has been formed by having made the proper options "according to the strategy and the tactics of love." This is placing responsibility in the right place, but it may be placing it upon persons who are either not prepared for assuming such difficult decisions or who may have been better prepared by the ethic of legalism. Who can tell?

How to incarnate love in the concrete existential situation has been the interest of many recent philosophers and theologians. Fletcher himself, according to George Roelder, supports his own method "by

---

49 Bishop John Robinson, *Christian Morals Today* (Philadelphia: Westminster Press, 1964), p. 18.

50 H. A. Williams, cited in paper of Usher-Wilson, chapter IV, *New Morality*, p. 32.

51 Fletcher, *Situation Ethics*, p. 126.

52 Usher–Wilson (Anglican priest, will publish book on *New Morality*).

thirteen references to Jesus, eleven to Luther, eleven positive but three negative references to Brunner, nine postive and three negative to Bonhoeffer. William Temple and Paul Tillich are called upon nine times each, followed by H. Richard (not Reinhold) Niebuhr with seven. Most contemporary theologians are cited. The Lutheran Joseph Sittler is described as a sympathetic situationalist."[53] To a greater or lesser degree Fletcher calls upon Bernard Häring, Josef Pieper, Jacques Leclercq and others. Most recently the writing of Bishop Simons has produced a Roman Catholic writer whom Fletcher admits has gone beyond any other in the Roman tradition to resolve ethical problems situationally, and to question the existence of all moral absolutes except the one moral absolute of love. On this nerve end of the discussion whether there are no moral absolutes but love alone, Milhaven raises some very gnawing questions:

> To evaluate Fletcher's affirmative answer, one would have to raise certain questions which, in the judgment of this reviewer, Fletcher barely touches on and certainly does not answer with adequate clarity. What do the maxims, the "cautious generalizations," tell the individual? How do they illuminate the problem? And how are they adduced from experience? Only after one answers these questions can one see whether the maxims always permit exceptions or not. Furthermore, what determines whether an action is loving, whether "love is served"? What, specifically, does love strive to bring about in the loved? Is there a hierarchy of goods which the "good will" of love should effectuate in the loved? Perhaps Fletcher's vagueness on this subject of love explains why he is vague on the content and formation of the practical maxims. Fletcher's strange silence on both these points may arise in part from a lack of an intrinsic humanism. As he sees it, man should love himself, not for his own sake, but for the sake of other men. Other men he should love not really for their own sake, but for God's. To love a person is not to respond to his unique value as a person, but to imitate God in caring for this person independently of his deserts or worth. This extrinsicism will surely rebuff most thinkers in the Catholic tradition and indeed most humanists.[54]

Herbert McCabe in his *Commonweal* exchange with Fletcher puts his finger on the same nerve and as does Milhaven in his reference to the *extrinsicism* in this type of ethical thinking.[55] Richard A. McCormick illustrates this extrinsicism in the statement of Fletcher that "sexual intercourse may or may not be an act of love," and contends that "if any activity can count as loving, we begin to sense that the the word has lost its content, because human actions have lost their significance."[56] McCabe interprets the sentence of Fletcher to mean

---

[53] George Roelder, *Book News Letter* (June–July, 1966), Augsburg Publishing House.
[54] Milhaven, in *Theological Studies* (September, 1966), 483.
[55] McCabe, *Commonweal* 83 (1966), 429.
[56] McCormick, *Theological Studies* (December, 1966), 616.

that there is no *intrinsic* value to sexual intercourse. With this Fletcher would agree because all bodily behavior, any somatic action, is neutral and indifferent and receives whatever value it has from the loving concern that accompanies it. Sexual intercourse, like any other somatic act, is per se neutral and indifferent and becomes an act of love only because minds and wills make it so. This extrinsicism of situational morality might provoke some questions on the nature and content of this humanism. Is human sexual intercourse different from non-human sexual intercourse only in the sense that the one *can* become an act of love and the other remains forever neutral and indifferent? Is it only minds and wills that make sexual intercourse an act of love; without this elevation by minds and wills, has it no value *per se*? Now this appears to us to be an implicit and unavoidable dualism on the part of Fletcher. If goodness can only come from the psychical sides of ourselves, our minds and wills, and goodness can never come from our bodies, then this introduces a real dualism into situational morality. It appears to us that human sexual intercourse has *intrinsic value as an act of love*, is *per se* an act of love, and this meaning and significance can be abused by the circumstances and motivation in which it is performed.

McCabe also sees human sexual intercourse as *per se* a loving act; for Dr. Fletcher, it is neutral and indifferent, it has no intrinsic value in itself. All somatic behavior is the same—amorphous, gray, indifferent—until it is elevated and redeemed by loving concern, which comes only from minds and wills. For Fletcher the body is indifferent and awaiting elevation by the loving concern of *agape*. Reductively, this theory involves an inescapable dualism of the physical, somatic and corporeal, on one side, with its indifference and moral neutrality, and the physical, mental and volitional on the other. Which explanation is more compatible with existential experience? Is sexual intercourse of its nature an act of love, open to all varieties of misuse and abuse by minds and wills, or is it an act of the body without any *intrinsic* value until the loving concern of *agape* accompanies it? There is an oversimplification in regarding the human personality and a reductionism of all human acts to a neutral and morally indifferent status because there are no intrinsic values except the intrinsic value of love.

Wilford Cross has developed this critique of Situation Ethics in his objection to the "radical oversimplification of human personality that is present in the method in that it largely disregards values, virtues and conscience, and the human structures by which we usually make our moral decisions."[57] The complex mechanisms of psycho-

---

[57] Wilford O. Cross, in *The Living Church*, May 22, 1966.

logical decision are not adequately considered in a method of solving moral problems that reduce all the complexity to two elements: love and the situation. Cross admits that for Fletcher love is a calculus rather than an emotion and that it includes the classic virtues of justice and prudence. To this extent love is to be governed by common-sense and subject to reason and the position of the situationalist is not an irrationalism committed to the absolute and unqualified emotional aspects of love. The inclusion of the element of prudence finds Fletcher very much in agreement with many of the observations of Josef Pieper in his extraordinary work on this cardinal virtue. Love for Fletcher is volitional and mental and these features are constantly exercised in any decision-making. However, when it comes to real ambiguities and paradoxes involving situation and love, it is sometimes hard to see which should be controlling. Cross asks some of the right questions in this regard:

> At times, in situationist ethic, one is never quite sure what ought to dominate, the sheer determinism of the situation or the cognitive-affective attitude of love. There seems to be an ambivalent shift between the pressures of the situation and the motivations of love. For instance, in the case of a wife who is most unhappy with a husband with whom she cannot make any sort of emotional or personal accord, and who is hungry for companionship and love, does the situation of lovelessness become the determining answer to whether one should respond to her need, or does prudential love, concerned with justice, dictate the answer? Situation ethics, as it is so far developed, does not provide a precise answer. Clearly in this case a love that destroys the relationship between wife and husband or the possibility of relationship, would be destructive and therefore is not the creative, fulfilling love that Fletcher is writing about. Does this understanding of love as creative dominate or does a situation of obvious need and sexual hunger dominate? If you are going to deny the validity of all lawful guides, such as the notion of "adultery" and talk only about love-applied-to-situation it seems to me that contradictions between the physical and psychological demands of the situation and the just, prudential following of love-alone do arise. And Fletcher does not allow us to seek guidance from the crystallized experience of moral and civil law, which would be, in his terms, "prefabricated morality."
>
> Once you have set aside as irrelevant the guiding structures of law on the objective side, and conscience and values on the subjective side, and reduced morality to an issue of love applied to situations, you are navigating in channels which have not been mapped and buoyed.[58]

Despite the evident fact that certain "earthquakes" in our social and intellectual environment have altered the old channels, it is still true that cautious moral generalizations and maxims that summarize human

---

[58] *Ibid.*

experience should not be put aside without strong and demonstrable reasons. The structures of the situations in which most men find themselves have not been so substantially undermined that these generalizations can be put aside lightly without doing something to the character of the man and the structures of future situations. When the ethical problems concern social issues and a multiplicity of persons reacting with different inter-personal claims, situational ethics requires these cautious generalizations even more. Love and situation may be controlling in personal issues involving two persons in a sexual encounter and justice may not be appearing too frequently but in problems of war, strikes, racial issues, justice asserts its demands more and more. Cross admits that situationist morality can deal with the sexual revolution but "can it deal, in social context, with the cybernetic organizational revolution of modern industrial society? This side of the ethic calls for far more attention than Professor Fletcher's book has given to it."[59] Even in the narrow situation of two persons resolving their sexual encounter in the name of loving concern the possibilities in this area of self-deception should be emphasized and the empirical verifiable values of other alternatives should be assessed.

We have often acknowledged that one of the insights of situational morality is the non-viability of the concept of intrinsic evil but we would not want to leave any impression that evil is not a graduated thing and that certain acts are not more reprehensible than others. It would be relatively impossible to redeem some of these more repugnant acts as acceptable because they are the best that one can do or because they are done with loving-concern. Cross raises this point also and mentions rape, murder, adultery, mayhem, sodomy and other "dangerously uncreative actions." "The effort of situationist ethics to declare that no acts are intrinsically wrong seems to contradict common experience."[60] Fletcher would have to be consistent in maintaining that just as there is nothing intrinsically good but love, so there is nothing intrinsically evil but hatred. Cross would insist that these acts mentioned by him are very close to acts of hatred, if we understand the reasoning implicit in his selection of examples. We might also judge that it would be impossible to accept genocide being brought about in loving concern for persons. These evil acts that appear to be the closest to the concept of intrinsically evil acts bring back the same problem that was raised by Fletcher's observation that "sexual intercourse may or may not be an act of love." We maintained

59 *Ibid.*
60 *Ibid.*

that it was more in accordance with existential phenomenological experience to say that sexual intercourse is per se an act of love and that it can be undermined by the person who performs the act in hatred of the person he ought to love. We might continue the reasoning here and say that existential phenomenological experience would bear out the fact that certain gross acts are acts of hatred per se and that it is almost impossible to understand how these same acts could be done with loving concern when they contain so much intrinsic hatred of persons.

The reservations we have made before on the problems of introducing situational analysis into the ethical choices of a majority of persons are also made by Cross:

> In any case, a great majority of people are going to have to be guided by prefabricated morality for the simple reason that they are not sufficiently mature and their values are insufficiently personalized (in the sense of being conventional and not authentically their own). There arises also a problem of the moral education of children and the molding of the conscience. Despite the stifling effects of taboos and legalism, man becomes a socially successful creature under the tutelage of law and value.[61]

In other words, Cross seems to be saying that the best situationalist is the one whose character has been trained and developed by law and intrinsic values, the very elements that Fletcher would hold up to scorn. Nevertheless, situational morality is open to the possibility of becoming a morality of real genuine responsibility. Despite the shortcomings, despite the blindspots of some situationalists, situational morality offers the insights that must be respected in the elaboration of an authentic ethic. We agree with Cross when he praises these insights of situationalism:

> Despite the necessity of pointing out these dimensions where situationism is inadequate in its pioneering stages, it is obvious that Fletcher's book places its emphasis and discovers the spring of morality precisely where a Christian moral system should discover its first principle. This is the primacy of love in Christian ethics. Its second axiom, the flexibility warranted by the situation, is equally essential. Given these guiding principles, and with a lessening of reductionism and simplification, situationism can work out the problems of its inadequacies in time. At any rate, Professor Fletcher has written a book that cannot be disregarded in all subsequent writing and development of Christian morals.[62]

---

[61] Ibid.
[62] Ibid.

CHAPTER SEVEN

An Authentic Contemporary Christian Ethic in Outline

Here we want to recapitulate the essential features characterizing an authentic contemporary Christian ethic. We have made some general observations on such an ethic in the first chapter, and we then attempted to show that there is a basic insight in situational morality and that is the non-viability of the concept of intrinsic evil applied to specific acts. Fletcher would say that there are no universal negative prohibitions, and that the concept of intrinsic evil is of no value for fruitful discussion in moral discourse. Fundamentally this is true, because acts have to be spelled out in such a way that the radical evil circumstance that makes the act immoral is contained within the essential definition. Nonetheless, this does not rule out the awareness and consciousness that every man has of evil and guilt. For this reason we

151

developed the phenomenology of guilt and moral evil and tried to show how the testimony of the *consequent conscience* could be brought to bear in the elaboration of a contemporary ethic. The qualities that we considered to be present in an authentic experience of moral evil and guilt could be of some service in approaching situational morality which minimizes the role of remorse, guilt, evil, and forgiveness. In a subsequent chapter we articulated the place of a contemporary interpretation of natural law in an ethic that proposed itself as relevant and Christian. This meant that theology and philosophy would be considered in the re-evaluation of the place of natural law in the ethic of conviction. Next, in assessing the value of situational ethics we saw that it stressed personal responsibility, recognizing the complexities and ambiguities of concrete moral situations. Our general criticism of Fletcher's situationalism was that it was not responsible enough, not radical enough, and it gave the impression of trivializing responsibility rather than accentuating the difficulty in its application. Situational morality is a difficult morality, and should not be represented simply in terms of love and situation without showing the latitudes and longitudes of both love and the situation. Traditional morality can be shown to be most concerned with situational circumstances and just as difficult to apply. To characterize traditional ethics as application of law to case with little exercise of the prudential reasoning is a caricature of Thomistic morality. To characterize situational ethics as the application of love to situation is to trivialize and caricature this ethic of responsibility. We shall show how situational and contextual both ethics must be in order to be authentic, contemporary and Christian.

I.   SOME BASIC PROPOSITIONS

Let us place in a series of propositions what we have suggested thus far as the structure of such an ethic.

Proposition I: We propose in the first place that the authentic ethic for today is the one resulting from the personal resolution of the dialectical tension that exists between the two ethics, the *ethic of responsibility* and the *ethic of conviction.* The first ethic places its ultimate concern in personal consequences and empirically verifiable evidence of those consequences. The second places its ultimate concern in principles with more or less indifference to consequences. We suggested that situational morality absolutizes and polarizes the first ethic, whereas traditional morality absolutizes and polarizes the second. Our own position is that a person cannot consistently, constantly, and uniformly operate on either ethic but must live on both in dynamic, dialectical tension, which is resolved in the personal decision of conscience.

Proposition II: The few moral absolutes that do remain in the ethic of conviction are in the order of sexuality and direct killing, and we speculated whether these two are any longer moral absolutes validated by a sufficiency of empirical verifable evidence. For example, we asked whether the empirical evidence for contraception outweighed the evidence against it. We suggested, therefore, that it would be difficult if the question were answered in the affirmative for anyone to say that contraception is intrinsically evil and therefore there is a prescriptive principle against it.

Proposition III: Contemporary culture is characterized by a deflation in doctrinal absolutes and also in moral absolutes. We submitted that any value such as life, promise-keeping, fidelity, etc. should be seen in a constellation of values. No value should be so polarized or absolutized that it is no longer viewed in the concrete existential experience where it is surrounded by a multitude of values which have to be harmonized and synthesized into a reasonable *gestalt*. It is not only the physical universe that is complicated and intricate; the moral universe is a congeries of values and disvalues, and the moral option requires the agony of decision in bringing them all together into some ethically tranquil pattern.

We attempted to show that the criticism that is often made of another person arises from the judgment of the critic who considers that the person criticized was bound by one of the two ethics above but not by the other. We illustrated this with the example of Hochhüth who holds up the Holy Father to scorn because he did not speak out more articulately in condemnation of the killing of the Jews. Hochhüth judged that the Pope was obligated primarily if not solely by the *ethic of conviction*, that is, the Pope as Pope should have spoken out even though the personal verifiable consequences might have been deleterious to Christians and to their Churches. On the other hand, *Commonweal* criticizes the present Pope with regard to his silence on the possible change in the contraception position, arguing that the Holy Father is obligated primarily, if not solely, by the *ethic of responsibility*. In this ethic the personal empirically verifiable consequences are seen to favor a change in the present legislation on contraception, according to *Commonweal*. The profound commitment in faith and love is promoted better in a marriage where contraception is accepted than in one where the only available means for responsible parenthood is the exercise of the practice of rhythm which in so many cases just does not work successfully. Now just as in the first case Hochhüth advises the Holy Father not to calculate or mathematicize the possible destructive consequences to the Church on the grounds that he is bound to speak out according to the directives of the ethic of conviction, so in the second case the Holy Father is advised to calculate and to mathematicize on the grounds that the evidence is in favor of a change. There seems to be no admission that the *ethic of responsibility* is present in the first case and the *ethic of conviction* in the second. This certainly trivializes the moral situation in both cases and removes the agony, the paradoxes, the ambiguities of the moral choice that the Holy Father made in the first case and the choice that faced him in the second. Should Pius XII not calculate and mathematicize the consequences that follow upon his own people? Should not Paul VI be governed by what he is convinced is possibly a principle that cannot very easily be altered? The critics of both can be simplistic, but not the one who has to make the paralyzing moral choice which resolves the dialectical and practical tension between the two ethics of *conviction* and *responsibility*. This choice is made by the one who is ultimately responsible, and it is no easy judgment to dance between the two ethics in what might be for the person the dance of death.

If we realize that the authentic choice of any person is the resolution of the tension between these two ethics, then only with trepidation will someone judge the moral choice of another. He will with only the greatest reluctance advise the person after the choice that he was immoral in not being directed more by one ethic than the other. We are considering not only the two cases above but the judgment made on Paul VI by Charles Davis on the subject of contraception. One enters another's moral conscience with the possibility of playing the role of God before whom the original choice was made and to whom the moral agent will be responsible.

Proposition IV: The concept of an intrinsically evil act is no longer viable and operable in moral discourse. To spell out within the basic moral object or *finis operis* all the adjuncts that construct the act physically and morally is to add a sufficiency of adjuncts so that the term becomes almost an analytic proposition. We construct this definition of murder in *direct killing of another man on one's own authority outside a case of legitimate self-defense and capital punishment*. How viable is this in discourse with persons who would add or subtract from this definition? The non-viability of the concept of intrinsically evil acts is one of the insights of situational morality.

Proposition V: It seems that some Christian values such as physical life are not so patent, so luminous, so empirically verifiable that the ethic of convicition can be supported by the empirical data. We shall develop this point in a subsequent chapter, but we have already given the example of rhythm and contraception and raised the crucial question: In responsible families committed to faith and love does the commitment to faith and love receive more assistance from contraception or rhythm? An editorial in *America*[1] suggested that authorities might be well advised to take seriously the medical evidence favoring the deepening of this commitment to faith and love resulting from the practice of contraception and to question the reasonableness of the defense of rhythm when the empirical evidence in the phenomenology of marriage is against it.

Proposition VI: With college students a more sophisticated ethic should be suggested. They should be encouraged to be faithful to their principles within the structure of their ethic of conviction but they should be encouraged to develop much more the ethic of responsibility where the ultimate concern is the personal consequences that follow from personal choices. We should admit that the propositions, *moral values are personally beneficial* and *moral dis-values are always personally non-beneficial,* are not convertible unless we are considering the person essentially and not existentially and phenomenologically. In other words, an exaggerated polarization and absolutization of physical life can lead to a minimization of the quality of existence. This seems to be true in assuming an absolute position on the subject of abortion. We shall elaborate upon this later.

Proposition VII: We should clarify for students the great difference in responsibility between *descriptive knowledge or cognition* and *evaluative cognition.* In the first the response is solely cognitive; in the second the response is complete and personal—it is cognitive, affective and appetitive. There is no responsibility even on the cognitive side if the cognitive reaction to an imperative is evaluationally negative. In other words, if the response cognitively, affectively, appetitively (i.e. the reaction of the total person) is negative to an imperative then there is no evil in acting against such an imperative.

Proposition VIII: We should make very clear what the new Dutch catechism says so well and with such truth: *The last word lies with*

---

[1] *America,* "Contraception and the Synod of Bishops," September 30, 1967, p. 339.

conscience, not with a doctor or the confessor. There is nothing more necessary, more primordial, more radical, more fundamental than conscience in which takes place the personal resolution of the dialectical tension between the two ethics of conviction and responsibility. Here, after all the evidence is in from all sources, the person stands before God and makes the paralyzing moral option.

Proposition IX: Conscience might be better defined than as "the last practical judgment of the practical prudential intellect commanding an act to be done or forbidding it to be done." This definition would look upon conscience as a response with evaluative cognition and freedom of one person to the Person and not just of a person to law. A person is the communicating existent who stands at the convergence of a series of relationships arising from his encounter with another person. A person meets structured experience and other persons in these experiences with values and disvalues similar or dissimilar from his own.

Proposition X: It seems to us that the situationalism involved in the ethic of responsibility is compatible with a Christian conscience in the explanation that we suggested for a genuine ethic, which results from the moral resolution of the dynamic tension between this ethic and the ethic of conviction. To polarize the ethic of responsibility is to polarize a certain kind of *utilitarianism;* to polarize the ethic of conviction is to polarize a certain kind of *juridicism and legalism* that conceivably could destroy. Recall the valid logic applied to the air-raid shelter case in a journal, where, according to the author of the article, the person who owned a shelter could legitimately deny the entrance of anyone whose presence would tax its resources.[2] If the one seeking entrance into the shelter should persist in his efforts to do so, the owner could legitimately look upon him as an unjust aggressor and he could, if necessary, shoot him. This is an ethic of conviction, valid dialectic, refined logic—and no love. Recall the arguments, all tidily logical for rhythm and against contraception which if applied would terminate in a lessening of the commitment of the two parties, in faith and love rather than in a deepening of this commitment. Once again the logic involved in the ethic of conviction was evident; the appeal to personal values was absent. We are getting back to our original point. Is the ethic of conviction always borne out in the empirically verifiable results that are beneficial to persons? The ethic of conviction

---

[2] *America,* Sept. 30, 1961.

ought to be open to modification when empirically verifiable personal results do not bear out the values implicit in this ethic. In addition, even if the empirically verifiable results are borne out in a particular case in opposition to the principle or the ethic of conviction, is the ideal always a moral imperative?

Proposition XI: It seems to us in the light of scholarly articles appearing in several journals that the following are examples of the erosion of moral absolutes: (1) It cannot be shown apodictically that masturbation is always wrong. (2) It cannot be shown categorically that pre-marital sexual relations are always wrong. Reductively we are saying that exploitative or irresponsible sex morality is an absolute; non-exploitative sex morality cannot be shown to be always wrong and bad. To say that all non-exploitative sex is wrong and bad is to bend the empirically verifiable evidence to the defense of legalism and to demand as a matter of obligation what may be the ideal in human sexual relations. Once again it cannot be shown apodictically that all non-exploitative sexual behavior is wrong and bad.

Proposition XII: It seems to us (and we shall develop this at length in another chapter) that if mediate animation can be shown to be a respectable position, scientifically, philosophically and theologically, then the situational context involving other values would warrant justifiable abortions as a moral good in the first three months of pregnancy. This requires further analysis. We are just offering it here in order to give an example of the genuine ethic which is the moral resolution of the dialectical tension between the *ethic of conviction* and the *ethic of responsibility.*

II. A "Symphony of Values"

In all these propositions we have been implying or saying explicitly that no one can live consistently on one ethic without invoking the other at all times. In the history of ethics the one assumed an importance over the other but both were always used in the resolution of ethical problems. To polarize and absolutize the *ethic of conviction* is to produce in ethical behavior a legalism and a juridicism which are the principal targets of situational morality. However, to polarize and absolutize the *ethic of responsibility* is to introduce into ethics such a concern for empirically verifiable consequences upon persons that the values and wisdom implicit in principle and law are neglected or scorned. We find this overreaction in some situational ethicians who have become almost as antinomian as they have become obsessed with the overriding priority of *agape*. Both ethics are needed and it is not to deny the importance of the *ethic of conviction* to state that the *ethic of responsibility* is finding more of a hearing.

The moral absolutes that have been proposed in the past have been questioned over and over again and empirical evidence for the values represented by these absolutes have been demanded. In a culture where so many ethical decisions are reached by an appeal to the two criteria of "everyone is doing the same thing" and "my behavior is hurting no one" the authority for any value implicit in the moral absolute cannot be any longer just the voice of Church or parents. If there are values, then they have to make themselves present in the phenomenology of the lives of the persons who are challenging them. We think that this has been attempted with good success by Peter Bertocci in *Sex, Love and the Person,* where he addresses himself to the question of the college student who sees nothing wrong in premarital sex for an engaged couple. Science for this student has eliminated the fear of pregnancy and his background and education has removed the fear of God. Bertocci answers the question with empirical evidence of the awesome view of sex as a gift. Starting with a consideration of marriage he introduces delicate and tender examples from the lives of persons he knows and reinforces his point through their experiences. It is the sense of values in a home which makes the difference between a house and a home, passion and love. These values must be applied to a person in a concrete existential situation. The relation of these values to the growth of personality is shown and a vigorous case is made for the place of sex and love only in marriage if sex and love are to have their total meaning. He raises questions whether the fear of restrictive codes and of self-righteous, insensitive moralism leads thinkers like Fletcher and Robinson to conclusions that would not cultivate the very creativity they want:

> In their attempt to avoid idolatry, to relate morality to personal growth at the expense of principles, do they really escape a relativity in morals that knows no direction? On what grounds can they defend love as the absolute, especially when they do not provide light to its meaning (and cannot do so, I suggest, apart from some pattern of values)? In other words, it is not enough to say that freedom, or the love of persons, is the absolute value—especially if one does not provide also a criterion of value that will keep freedom from becoming emasculated power, and love from becoming self-absorption or sentimentality. What is at issue is not only the meaning of Christian love but the justification for any particular view of what it involves . . . unless there is a supporting theory of values to guide us as we try to love our enemy and our friend as persons, it will be easy to do almost anything in the name of love.

At the same time, it is not enough to propose as I do that there is an ideal pattern of values for all persons and that there are guiding principles and policies by which we do and can criticize our rules and codes. For the basic principle is that persons ought to respect and encourage the growth of values in themselves as persons in every situation. This is the minimum meaning of love, but it needs explication in terms of some such pattern of values as "the symphony of values" to be proposed.[3]

There is something to be learned from Bertocci that is of value for both the *ethic of conviction* and the *ethic of responsibility*. Admittedly, the first is on the defensive now to show that the values it has been proposing to persons do have empirically verifiable advantages and benefits for the persons concerned. These have to be made clear by the ethician of conviction when he is challenged to produce the evidence. On the other hand, the values that are implicit in the moral principles ought to be admitted by the ethician of responsibility and that admission should be made concerning the largest number of cases. Where the empirically verifiable evidence does not support the value involved and where this fact is adduced by the person of responsibility it seems to us to be unwise to claim that in the face of the absence of this evidence the moral principle still stands with the same or equally obliging force. The empirically verifiable evidence has become the criterion for the presence of value, and if the value is admitted as something worthwhile it appears to us that where the evidence is not present we ought to see the possible presence of another value manifesting itself with a different empirical face. In the ethic of responsibility we find frequently the presumption so much in favor of the resolution of the ethical situation in the name of loving concern that there is little presumption given to the presence of the values incarnate in the principles. We have referred to this as the over-reaction of the ethic of responsibility toward *agape* and the overreaction of the ethic of conviction toward the values implicit in the principles. The first ought to be more aware of the high probability of the presence of these values except in extraordinary cases, and the second ought to be more aware of the possible absence of *agape* in being too ready to respond to principle and law. This is especially true for the Church which, as the documents of Vatican II emphasize, is "in the world of today" and in this world of today there is a concern for persons, for empirically verifiable human values which are not always present in the observation of law for its own sake. The message of Christ must be meaningful to a world that looks upon responsibility as measured by the concern a person has for other persons.

---

[3] Peter Bertocci, *Sex, Love and the Person* (New York: Sheed & Ward, 1967), xii.

The norm of what is good or bad as Bertocci seems to develop it is the traditional one—whether or not an action is in keeping with human dignity. This last proposition is not convertible with adherence to a moral absolute as such. The action must correspond to a love which strives to help men to the fullest possible development of their personality in responsible freedom. In the application of this general norm the actual, consistent behavior of men can and should be a reason for asking ourselves the two questions posed by Father W. Molinski S.J., Professor of the Free University of Berlin: "One is whether the moral values which we uphold are precisely and justly estimated. The other is whether, if so, they are being propounded in a way which can really be convincing to our contemporaries."[4] The meaning here is clear and demands empirically verifiable evidence when the subject of the prohibition against pre-marital intercourse is considered. It is refreshing to hear this said by Father Molinski:

> There can be cases in fact where popular reactions and general behavior can be closer to the mark than theoretical morals. By this I mean that in the actual situation which confronts us today, we must recognize that the usual reasons given against pre-marital intercourse need to be re-examined. And many of our attitudes need revision if proper help is to be given to young people so that they can integrate their sexual development into their personality.[5]

We would reiterate that if contemporary culture is characterized by a deflation of doctrinal absolutes and moral absolutes then this is so in face of the growing demand for showing that in the moral absolutes the values to persons are always in evidence. The demand is frequently followed by the suspicion and then the denial of the presence of these values to the person. Cases are shown where the moral absolute does not produce the values to the person and while it may be plausible to say that in principle and in the largest number of cases these values are realized, this cannot lay the grounds for a categorical obligation to observe the absolute where the values are not present.

We suggested before that there has been an erosion in moral absolutes in the face of these demands for empirically verifiable defense of the absolutes and that the last two areas of erosion are *direct killing* and *sexuality*. For this reason we are indicating here how the ethic of conviction representing that there is at least in principle a dis-value in pre-marital sex has to alter its case from the type of defense offered by a St. Thomas. Father Fuchs has made a very close study of the ethics of sexuality according to St. Thomas. Molinski refers to this study and points out how the evidence has shifted through the reason-

---

[4] W. Molinski, *Herder Correspondence* (December 1966), p. 370.
[5] *Ibid.*

ing of Thomas and how it has been altered up to the present. Where the evidence in some cases has become so fragile and so weak, is it reasonable to contend that there is a universal negative prohibition against pre-marital sexual intercourse? Thomas based the condemnation of such a practice on the argument that it was against the good of human nature because the education of children inevitably suffered. Consider the reception this reasoning would get from an ethic of responsibility in which children do not have to result necessarily from such a relationship. Even in his own day when the objection was made that such intercourse need not mean any injustice with regard to the woman Thomas replied that it was an offence against the neighbor because it is detrimental, once again to the children. He never shows the possible wrongness of pre-marital sex by arguments derived directly from the dignity of the Christian. Molinski concludes from the non-cogent evidence of Thomas and from his non-appeal to personal dignity:

> But it is clear to us today that we must consider human sexuality as a gift through which human love can be expressed in a unique way, and hence, that it has a specific human significance which cannot be found on the infra-human levels of life. *The arguments of St. Thomas, who bases his conception of sex on the equivalence of this biological urge in man and beasts, can no longer be convincing.*
>
> The Christian position is definitely this: it is only in the stable security of indissoluble marriage that the self-surrender of the sexual act can fully correspond to the dignity of the human person.
>
> But this is an attitude which is based on the Christian understanding of man. Arguments of a purely rational nature can never attain the force of this act of faith. Reason can put forward a number of very impressive arguments to show that marriage is indissoluble. But, personally, like many other theologians, I should not dare to rely on my own rational arguments and the limitations of human wisdom to insist upon the indissolubility of marriage, even in tragic cases, as strongly as we do when we are guided by the convictions of our faith.[6]

In applying this same norm to pre-marital sex Molinski admits that it cannot be shown that the universal negative prohibition against such a practice is supported by empirically verifiable evidence. Reason and human wisdom cannot show that there are no cases at all where the evidence would favor pre-marital intercourse. In fact, it is legalism and juridicism at its worst if someone were to insist upon the retention of the universal negative prohibition in a case where interpersonal values are present and the only dis-value in evidence is the absence of the juridical words of marriage. As Molinski states: "Our attitude to sexual matters is ultimately determined by a conception of man which

[6] *Ibid.*, p. 371.

derives from revelation. This should make us wary of hastily condemning and despising those who have convictions of their own which do not coincide with what we have learned."[7] To repeat what we stated in proposition XI above—it cannot be shown categorically that pre-marital sexual relations are always wrong. This is true, we would insist, not only with respect to the subjective morality of the persons concerned, but even with regard to the objective morality of the situation observed by the best criteria we have for so judging. This conclusion is reasonable in a culture that is enlarging its view on the meaning of personality and that is convinced that "human sexuality is a gift through which human love can be expressed in a unique way which has a specific human significance that cannot be found on the infra-human levels of life."[8]

The cautious generalizations in the situationalist which are part of the equipment to be used in decision making should be seen to contain the values of past experiences which it would be foolhardy to thrust aside. They are illuminators, according to Fletcher, although at times one fears that they are given too little opportunity to show their light and relevance. They would seem to apply in almost all cases but the extraordinary ones. Presuppositions and priorities show their hand when we are advised early that the situationist "keeps principles sternly in their place, in the role of advisers without veto power."[9] Is it the part of wisdom to consider that the cautious generalizations of years should be treated lightly by the ethically naive whose experiences have been few? Once again it would seem that only those who have existentially lived and been trained in such a way that character is one of steel and conviction can become the best situationalists. How is one best prepared to assume the situationalist role? By situationalism itself which keeps principles in their place or by an ethic of conviction grounded in unquestioning obedience even though the latter is an unsophisticated morality? Paradoxically the best situationalist in the ethic of responsibility is the man who has been trained for it in the school of the ethic of conviction. Reductively this means in the education of the young that we must admit some time in their ethical development that they are being trained in one ethic in order that later in their existence they can apply the genuine ethic. For ourselves the problem is even more difficult in pedagogy because for us the genuine ethic is neither situational responsibility nor the ethic of conviction taken by itself but the resolution of the tension that exists between the two. The problems in pedagogy are enormous and one

---

[7] *Ibid.*, p. 371.
[8] *Ibid.*
[9] Joseph Fletcher, *Situation Ethics* (Philadelphia: Westminster Press, 1966), p. 55.

of the great tragedies of many religious persons is that they have never been introduced into the profundity and sophistication of ethical choices. However this is an objection that can be thrown at any one who trivializes the serious and almost terrifying decision of conscience, and our grievance against traditional morality can be directed with equal validity to the situationalist who minimizes the quality of the cautious generalizations which he carries with him into the ethical context. In fact, the criticism that can be directed at both moralities is that they are not radical enough and are not sufficiently aware of the insights and the blindspots of each other. Let us develop this in order to construct what we have been offering as the genuine ethic for contemporary man.

Fletcher is not completely convinced of the situationalism involved in traditional morality. We have seen that most moral acts are indifferent in their morality if they are considered from the point of view of their fundamental moral objects. In order for these acts to acquire even the generic quality of the moral good or the moral evil they have to be constructed with certain minimal adjuncts or situational circumstances which not only account for the physical totality of these acts but also provide them with their moral determinant. Take, for example, the universal negative prohibitions of the classical ethic of conviction and you will find them to be highly situational. Trying to locate the situational components in the definition of lying is a case in point. There seem to be at least four reputable definitions of a lie, depending upon which circumstance the proponent of a particular definition considers to be the real situational factor that explains the malice of the lie. Thomas considered every difformity between speech and judgment to be a lie; Augustine added the concept of "intention to deceive" which for Thomas was required for the full meaning of a lie but not for its essential quality as a lie. Grotius distinguished between formal speech contrary to the mind to one who has no right to the truth, which he called a *falsehood*, and formal speech contrary to the mind to a person who has the right to the truth, which he called a *lie*. Dorzynski refined Grotius' definition to localize the evil of the lie in the violation of the right of a person not to have his intelligence undermined by deceptive speech. No one can fail to recognize that there is no disagreement among Thomas, Augustine, Grotius, Dorzynski about the necessity of introducing situational factors into the discussion of the constitution of a lie. The real problem for each of these philosophers is which situational factor is the explanation for the fundamental, radical, ultimate evil of the lie. This is the case not only in the definition of a lie but is true of every universal negative prohibition. All are defined situationally. The problem of the older morality was not in the admission of circumstances and context into the act; it was the problem of localizing the real essential circumstance or situational factor that constituted the real evil of the act. Once this factor or these factors were discovered, classical morality declared that the acts so constituted were always wrong. We granted to the situationalists that the difficulties in the construction of definitions for even the simplest universal negative prohibitions proved that the concept of intrinsically evil acts was non-viable and not very helpful in moral discourse. If one does not object to the inflation of the fundamental moral object by a series of situational factors that make up the physical integrity and the moral quality of an act, then the concept may still be used. However, just the consideration of the difficulties involved in the construction of such a basic act as murder will make clear to anyone the trouble we have in spelling out the words "unjust killing of another man."

Putting aside these problems of definitional construction, classical morality maintains that if adultery is conceived as the symbolic sexual act of total unconditioned commitment with a person other than the person to whom one is committed, then this act of adultery is regarded as always wrong despite the situational variables that may be introduced. Likewise if the killing of another person is of an innocent person and is done on one's own authority intending this death of an innocent person as an end in itself or as a means to a further end, then this act of killing is regarded as always wrong. There is no disagreement on the necessity of situational factors for both classical morality and situational morality. Where the crucial division takes place is in the denial by the one and the affirmation by the other that the radical, fundamental, essential evil in the act can be overridden by other situational factors in the service of loving concern or *agape*. This is the real point of departure between the ethic of conviction grounded on universal affirmative and negative imperatives, and the ethic of responsibility represented by situationalism, whose ultimate concern is the empirically verifiable set of personal consequences which can outweigh the essential malice that is present in the otherwise evil acts (these consequences are always submitted to the criterion of loving concern).

If situational morality has not been overly conscious of the situationalism in classical morality, classical morality has minimized the importance of love in the totality of the act. In doing so, however, there has been a more profuond regard for the ethical machinery involved in the human act, which has always in the classical tradition found three ethical factors to be the specific determinants for the morality of the act. In addition to the essential, intrinsic, generic nature of the act, these three factors are: (1) the qualifying circumstances; (2) the foreseen effects of the act; (3) the motive of the act. In criticism of the older morality it might be said that the question of the status of love was resolved by assigning it to the third determinant, the motive for the act. While it may be true that love was minimized in assuming the role of motive, classical morality concluded that an act could be morally evil if any of the three ethical factors in addition to the intrinsic act itself were evil. The principle of "*Bonum ex integra causa; malum ex quocumque defectu*" demonstrates that classical morality looked upon goodness as indivisible and demanded goodness from each of the determinants. Situationalism takes issue with this and maintains that goodness is divisible and that the totality of the act must be decided by a calculus of pluses and minuses. It seems to us that the mystery of the moral act is not appreciated if any of these determinants is trivialized. In the assignment of love to the status of motive, classical morality may have trivialized love; but situationalism strikes us as leaving love in the status of motive and circumstance and elevating it into an over-riding importance at the expense of trivializing the act itself, and frequently the other determinants as well. James Burtchaell considers that despite its name, situation ethics does not revolve on situation at all:

> Fletcher moves about—messily at times, it seems—from motive to consequences to situation. *But the crucial factor in the method is motive.* The system really should be called intention ethics. What is novel about it is the claim that any action, in any situation, with any consequences, is good if it is an action of love, and evil if an action of non-love. Love, urges Fletcher, is the only norm, the only measure. All ethical judgment must therefore revolve around purpose. It is essentially indifferent what forms a man's behavior takes, provided this behavior be the outward expression of inward caring. No one can ever be blamed if his intentions were good. In other words, the moral value of a man's deeds is wholly contained in the purpose he brings to them. It is precisely this axiom which I feel to be both the pivot and the weakness of the entire system. The New Moralists are saying that the moral value of an act is what you put into it. They neglect, it seems to me, that it also involves what you get out of the act.[10]

This criticism strikes us as pointed and valid. If the role of love in the classical tradition was minimized in being given the ontological role of motive or intention, it was only because the act itself was assigned the essential generic intrinsic position in the moral scale. Situationalism, on the other hand, appears to preserve the role of love as belonging to motive or intention and then proposes to elevate it in importance over all other determinants, even the act itself, defined in the most careful way. There is little surprise then to find moralists asking questions of the situationalists concerning the justification in the name of loving concern or *agape* of

---

[10] James Tunstead Burtchaell, "The Conservatism of Situation Ethics," *New Blackfriars* (October, 1966), p. 11.

such acts as rape, sodomy, genocide, cheating, adultery, etc. Even the moral act itself must be submitted to the judgment of loving concern and whether that act be one of rape, sodomy, genocide, cheating, or adultery, the crucial question to determine the morality of the situation is whether they are done in the service of loving concern. A strong case can be made out for classical morality that implicitly more love was intended and ultimately reached in respecting the roles of all the determinants, than in the New Morality which is willing to sacrifice all determinants in the name of an explicit intention of loving concern.

We have frequently called upon phenomenological experience through the chapters of this book and we would like to consider its testimony from the point of view of the consciously known free acts that we place. If we examine seriously the activities of a normal day it is amazing how few are free and not circumscribed in some way by habit and routine. If this is so, then it would seem to follow that there are few acts in which the person stops short and reasons situationally in a very adequate way. No doubt we do reason situationally, but phenomenologically the testimony seems to be that the normal resolution of the situation is by the ready application of the cautious generalization to the particular matter in hand. Occasionally the person enters the situation as a full and true person who reflects seriously on all the circumstances flowing from his moral act, and tests whether the cautious generalization should be put aside against the claims of loving concern. Single actions do not make the same demands on us and do not draw from us the full resources of character and personality. These actions are not considered to be decisive in our lives and to many of them we give short shrift. Nevertheless it is the catalogue of these insignificant acts which forms the character and disciplines it for the real serious situational encounters in which reflection and calculation will be indispensable. As Fr. Burtchaell develops this relation between the deeds we perform and the intentions that we have he sees this relationship not as a separable duality but as "as dialectic between this fundamental option (let us say, our fundamental selfishness or selflessness) and the complex of individual actions."[11] There are so many of these insignificant actions of our lives which do not involve the whole personality or character and are not memorable at all. But over a period of time certain individual or characteristic traits and trends begin to appear, personality indices are in evidence and there is a discernible topology in our lives. If we acknowledge that this is so in the phenomenology of our own experience and the admitted experiences of others, then it is a legitimate criticism to say that Fletcher points out very convincingly that purpose

---

[11] *Ibid.*

and intention shape deeds, but he appears to neglect the converse of this fact, that deeds shape purposes and intentions. From a series of unreflective heterosexual encounters in which intention and purpose were not seriously considered, we wonder how situationally successful a person will become in the one relationship where purpose and intention are so paramount. The interaction of deed and intention is developed by Burtchaell:

> What I do and what I am are constantly interacting upon one another. My character discloses itself in what I do, yet can be shaped and modified by changes in what I do. My life works from the inside out and *also* from the outside in. In Christian terms, the state of grace and the state of sin refer to this deep level of fundamental option which is forming and stabilizing itself over the course of a lifetime. It would be difficult to localize conversion or serious sin within any singular act, and unobservant to assert that there could be much short-term oscillation between one fundamental option and its opposite. Yet these states are slowly entered and reinforced by the swarm of minor daily deeds. Fletcher, it appears, acknowledges only a one-way traffic: he points out—quite well—how purpose shapes deeds, but neglects that conversely deeds shape purpose.[12]

This is an excellent insight in criticism of situational morality. Situationalism, in developing its basic truth that the intention and purpose of loving concern are of fundamental importance, has not given equal significance to the truth that this intention and purpose are most probably authentic and genuine only because they have themselves resulted from a series of actions that have produced character and discipline in choices. The purpose and intention of loving concern can and should be determinative in some way of the morality of the act. But in situationalism very little importance is apparently assigned to the question—just how the situation is constituted and just how it terminates in this purpose and intention. Deeds shape purposes and intentions, and this fact should be accentuated as much as Fletcher's favorite converse of this proposition—that purposes and intentions shape deeds. The difficulty here, it seems to us, arises from the problem of judging the situation resulting from deeds when the dichotomy between objective and subjective morality has been cast aside. This requires some clarification. Fletcher cites the story of the Puerto Rican woman in Bruce Kendrick's account of the East Harlem Protestant Parish.[13] "How are we to 'judge' the Puerto Rican woman. . . . She was proud of her son and told the minister how she had 'made friends' with a married man, praying God she'd have a son, and eventually she bore one. The minister, dear silly man that he is, told her it was okay if she was repentant, and she replied, 'Repent? I ain't repentin'. I asked

---

[12] *Ibid.*
[13] Bruce Kendrick, *Commonweal* (January 14, 1966).

the Lord for my boy. He's a gift from God.' She is *right* (and this, by the way, does *not* mean that a situationist approves in the abstract of the absence of any husband in so many disadvantaged Negro and Puerto Rican families)."[14]

Herbert McCabe comments on this attitude and answer of Fletcher: "No, not in the abstract, just in the concrete."[15] "She is right" is a betrayal of the revolution that is required in East Harlem. Of course such a woman caught up and lost in the jungle of the acquisitive society may be blameless, may be a saint, and of course the first thing that matters is to understand and sympathize with her immediate position; but she is *wrong.* To say she is right is to accept, as she does, the social situation in which she lives. A genuine moral judgment cuts deeper than that; it questions such a "situation" in terms of something greater. When we say "You can't apply the same high moral standards to slaves as you do to us" we accept slavery as an institution. Of course to punish or condemn the slave for lying or stealing is to hit the wrong target; it is the masters who bear the blame but the blame is for the slave's wrong action.

It is here that we see how all three positions, that of the minister, Fletcher and McCabe, are captured by the morality of *praise-and-blame.* The minister, in characterizing the conduct of the woman in terms of *objective* and *subjective* morality, qualifies the morality by saying that she acted wrongly (adultery is *objectively* wrong) and that she is guilty (she is *subjectively* guilty of committing adultery). McCabe considers the whole situation and concludes that she has acted wrongly but is not *subjectively* guilty because the guilt really belongs to those who are responsible for Harlem. Fletcher breaks through the *subjective-objective* dichotomy and concludes from her good motives and from the total situation that she has acted rightly and is not guilty. Burtchaell points out the short-sightedness of this praise-and-blame ethics in all three cases and contends that situational morality is not radical enough as an ethic of responsibility. Fletcher does not sufficiently emphasize that the Christian often has the duty of re-structuring the situation as much as he possibly can and not merely yield to it, convinced that if he performs an act in such a wounded situation with loving concern he will be doing the right thing. But if Fletcher's ethic is not revolutionary enough neither is McCabe's, because there is some resignation in the face of the evil of Harlem when he remarks that it is likely that "such a woman, caught up and lost in the jungle of the acquisitive society, may be blameless, may be a saint." Harlem is the cesspool of evil because the persons who have produced Harlem

---

14 *Ibid.*
15 Herbert McCabe, "The Validity of Absolutes," *Commonweal,* Jan. 14, 1966, pp. 435–436.

have destroyed the body and the soul of the residents who are imprisoned there. The tragedy of Harlem is really faced when in the praise-blame ethic as applied by McCabe the woman has been made to assimilate the evils of Harlem and to become less of a person. We fail to see this tragedy in its deepest dimensions if we acknowledge that the evil of Harlem has made the woman act wrongly although she is subjectively guiltless. To be compelled to accept the evil so that there is little freedom left is the heart of the tragedy—it does not help her in this ultimate evil to characterize her conduct as objectively wrong but subjectively she is without guilt. Burtchaell develops this weakness in the praise-and-blame ethic:

The myopia in a praise-and-blame ethics is that it ignores the dialectic between singular acts and overall orientation, deed and intention. A morality that is concerned with guilt or innocence thinks of acts only as responsible expressions of the self, and neglects that they are also shapers of the self. Now the fact that repetitive evil actions incur guilt is extrinsic; the intrinsic, and to my mind more important, fact is that they make the doer less loving. A young boy who grows up in Harlem may, through no fault of his own, take his recreation by slashing automobile tires, robbing drunks, petty thieving, and taking heroin. It is absurd to suggest that, since there is no malevolence involved and he is the creature of his situation, he is doing right. It is irrelevant to say that he is doing wrong, but that the guilt falls upon others. The tragedy is that morally he has been destroyed by a course of actions which he may have entered with no particular evil intent. A young girl who knows no better may take to bed with her new boy-friend every week, simply because this is the accepted way of showing affection and holding a partner in her milieu. It is simply not meaningful to call her guilty or guiltless. What can be said is that she has corroded through unwitting misuse her own capacity to love. A north-country mine-owner in the last century may have taken it for granted that young women and children were effective workers if put to crawling through tunnels, dragging loads of coal. He probably did not choose overtly to exploit them, yet gradually and imperceptibly the situation was likely to make him exploitative, and to kill his sensitivity and respect for persons. A child brought up in an unstable home has harm done to his loving-power that is not of his own choosing. Sin, it seems to me, has too often been imagined as a responsible decision to do evil. What I see of it seems rather to be a suffocation of responsibility through repetitive actions which generally avoid any open decision. We have made "good" into a legal metaphor corresponding to "responsibility" and "guilt"; in a world where there is all too little responsibility but much evil, it seems not the most helpful metaphor to employ in theology, Old or New. Remember that in Christ's parable on judgment the condemned are sent away for offenses that were unwitting; by doing unloving things they had become unloving, to their surprise.

Consequently my distress for the East Harlem woman is that with the best intentions, with the worst situation, she has done something that has hurt her. *And my distress with the New Morality is that it is shallow and legalistic. It ignores that there are false, selfish, and evil actions which, regardless of our motives for performing them, can corrupt our ability to love, and that moral value is somehow objective as well as subjective.* Situational variables may anaesthetize us to moral pain or mitigate the damage, but damage there is. We cannot long go through the notions of lovelessness without one day waking up to discover we have killed our love. Like Pontius Pilate.

One of the great weaknesses of the Old Morality is its refusal to allow for extraordinary exceptions in its absolute laws. Indeed, the weakness is in using the notion of law at all. *The New Morality's criticism of this weakness is disappointing because it is so half-hearted and conservative.* It shares the Old idea that morality has to do with guilt or innocence, with responsibility. It thus ignores that much of the evil we do is not due to our evil intentions and purposes, but to the evil values that our cultural milieu foists upon us. A situation ethic should recognize more clearly that our situation is to a large degree evil, and that our worry should be to defend ourselves against the false values accepted in our society. Ethics cannot afford to be individualistic, when so much of the lovelessness in individuals is inherited from a bad society. The Christian's duty is so often to fight free of his situation, though he may be destroyed in the process. Like Christist.[16]

This provides an interesting and fascinating twist to situation ethics. The true situational morality should therefore recognize the evil in which we happen to enter and resolve to be concerned not only with the predicates of our own ethical actions, not only with the intention of loving concern in which these actions are performed, but to do something about the evil in which we happen to be. This situational morality would become more radical, less conservative, suffering not from the same illness as the old morality structured on a praise-and-blame ethic but fundamentally committed to the alteration of evil structures in the situations that are so evil. Ultimately, this means less concern with ourselves and the praise-and-blame predicates that will be applied to our own actions and more and more dedication to the heart of the matter—the ethical revolution in society that will reduce the quantity of evil in which we are all engulfed. We will reduce the evil in its causes rather than finding the presence of evil as an adequate explanation for an action of ours objectively wrong but subjectively without guilt.

We will test the real worth of the cautious generalizations in order to assure ourselves that they are not perpetuating false values or values that are no longer operational and wise. We shall not discard them too easily as if they were derived from too little experience and from too little testing. Instead of a readiness to discard the cautious generalizations in the service of loving concern this re-examination of the generalizations may lead to the ethical choice of breaking the situational structure in which

---

[16] Burtchaell, *art. cit.*, p. 13.

one happens to be and which is so corroded with evil. Moral reality will expand in its dimensions and ethics will be seen to include not only persons but non-personal nature as well. Here again we shall see that situationalism is not radical enough in its approach to ethical choices. These arise from relations of one man to another person, but also from his relations to nature and to God. The second of these has not been touched upon with much seriousness by Fletcher, and criticism of situationalism from this vantage point has been made with great validity by Richard L. Means.[17] Means refers to Albert Schweitzer's saying that "the great fault of all ethics hitherto has been that they believed themselves to have to deal only with the relation of man to man."[18] Fletcher is represented by Means as dealing piecemeal with man's relations to his fellows "without even suggesting that man's relation to nature—to the physical and biological world—raises questions of moral behavior." The oversight is seen as due to the general psychological and subjective tone of much current social criticism. It also represents the "revolt against formalism," the scorning of abstract and sweeping interpretations of man and nature that was once the passion of American social scientests. Likewise Harvey Cox's *The Secular City* is "set in an urban world in rather extreme isolation from the surrounding problems of resources, food, disease, etc. The city is taken for granted and the moral dimensions of Cox's analysis are limited to man's relations to man within this urban world, and not with the animals, the plants, the trees, the air—that is, the natural habitat." Morality, radical morality touches not only the relations of persons with persons but the relations of persons to nature. Means sees this neglect of ethics in man's relation to nature a moral crisis for man. It involves the actual social consequences of myriad and unconnected acts. "The crisis comes from the combined results of a mistreatment of our environment. It involves the negligence of a small businessman on the Kalamazoo River, the irresponsibility of a large corporation on Lake Erie, the impatient use of insecticides by a farmer in California, the stripping of land by Kentucky mine operators. Unfortunately, there is a long history of unnecessary and tragic destruction of animal and natural resources on the face of this continent."

An issue becomes most moral when it touches persons, and especially when it is existential and appeals to our own experience. This neglect of the ethical dimension in our experience arising from our relation to nature has produced the moral crisis to which Means refers. He documents this neglect and shows how serious this crisis really is: "It is a historical one

---

[17] Richard L. Means, "Why Worry About Nature?" *Saturday Review* (December 2, 1967).
[18] Means, *art. cit.*

involving man's history and culture, expressed at its root by our religious and ethical views of nature—which have been relatively unquestioned in this context." The historian of medieval culture, Lynn White, Jr., brilliantly traces the origin and consequences of this expression in an insightful article "The Historical Roots of Our Ecological Crisis."[19] The author contends that the Christian notion of a transcendent God, completely removed from nature and breaking into nature only through revelation, removed spirit from nature and therefore allowed for an easy exploitation of nature. In an ethic only of extrinsic values this neutrality to nature can become even more evident than in any other moral theory. In the classical morality in which ethical relations emerge from man's threefold role of *subordination* to God, *equality* with other persons and *superiority* over the world of nature, this criticism of a personal ethic, concerned primarily with the second relationship, may not be so telling. Whatever the explanation for this neglect of the moral implications of our actions with regard to nature, it is obvious that many social critics seem to avoid the issues. The fear on their part may be an unwillingness to accept the charge that one anthropomorphizes or spiritualizes nature. Means himself suggests, on the other hand, that the refusal to connect the human spirit to nature may reflect the traditional thought pattern of Western society wherein nature is conceived to be a separate substance—a material, mechanical substance—and, in a metaphysical sense, irrlevant to man. He develops his view of nature:

> It seems to me much more fruitful to think of nature as part of a system of human organization—as a variable, a changing condition—which interacts with man and culture. If nature is so perceived, then a love, a sense of awe, and a feeling of empathy with nature need not degenerate into a subjective emotional bid for romantic individualism. On the contrary, such a view should help destroy egoistic, status politics, for it helps unmask the fact that other men's activities are not just private, inconsequential, and limited in themselves; their acts, mediated through changes in nature, affect my life, my children, and the generations to come. In this sense, justification of a technological arrogance toward nature on the basis of dividends and profits is not just bad economics—it is basically an immoral act. And our contemporary moral crisis, then, goes much deeper than questions of political power and law, of urban riots and slums. It may, at least in part, reflect American society's almost utter disregard for the value of nature.[20]

An ethic of responsibility that concerns itself with the empirically verifiable consequences upon persons of the actions that are placed by ethical

---

[19] Lynn White, Jr., "The Historical Roots of Our Ecological Crisis," *Science* (March 1966).
[20] Means, *art. cit.*

man must come to grips with this view of nature and man's responsibility toward it. This deepens and broadens the situation more and testifies to every situation as inclusive not only of persons in individual and social relations but also of nature and man's role in nature. It would seem that neither situational morality as an ethic of responsibility nor the classical morality of the ethic of conviction has been radical enough in the total consideration involving God, other men and non-personal nature. Situation ethics has often simplified and trivialized the amplitude of the situation; love has been superficial and short-sighted and has not been of the selfless kenotic kind that is distinguishable from the erotic and the philiac. The older morality, concerned with law, rule, and principle has consigned love to the role of motive or purpose which confers an accidental extrinsic sort of goodness upon the moral act. Nevertheless, both of these ethics are required in moral behavior and neither of them can be put aside without absolutizing the other. The more contemporary ethic and the more acceptable one in the present ethical climate is the ethic of responsibility—the ethic concerned with persons, empirical evidence of the results of our actions upon persons for good or ill, the ethic of love over law, the ethic of the present existential moment of history as love reveals its demands in the situational context. My own misgivings against the priority that is being assigned to the ethic of responsibility is that it creates a distortion of the real nature of ethical decision-making. For ourselves there will always be the dialectical tension between the two ethics of conviction and responsibility and only the personal conscience at this precise moment of existential personal history will be able to do all the prismatic analyses and the parabolic dancing that have to be done. It strikes us that it is unrealistic to deny this tension in conscience, and neither situation ethics nor classical morality of conviction sophisticates the conscience adequately. There is a simplification and a reductionism about situational morality which often approaches the simplification of the very morality it scorns. After requiring that love be present in every ethical act it has often been trivialized and claustrophobic. Love has not been taken seriously enough and if it had it would not lightly discard the love and wisdom that have gone into the cautious generalizations that are present in the particular situation. An authentic contemporary Christian ethic is an ethic of tension between the two ethics and the agony of resolution of this tension is profoundly personal and ineluctable. This is the ethic we propose—more radical than either, more sophisticated as one's ethical history develops. We intend to propose this ethic and to apply it to some concrete problems.

CHAPTER EIGHT

STERILIZATION: DIRECT AND INDIRECT

I. INTRINSIC EVIL AND STERILIZATION

In chapter II we discussed the non-viability of the concept of intrinsic evil and the problems that befall any moral philosopher who is too ready to characterize a practice in these terms. We find this happening in discussions that take place among moralists on the subject of sterilization, and this is evident to anyone who has followed the arguments on the issues of the anovulants. Let us begin by referring to what has already been said about intrinsic evil and sterilization. Sterilization in itself is morally indifferent; indirect therapeutic sterilization in the presence of a pathological disorder is morally good; direct punitive sterilization would be acceptable to anyone who accepts the DeLugo position on the lawfulness of direct

174

killing of an aggressor in the case of legitimate self-defense. If the DeLugo position warrants direct killing of a criminal in these circumstances, then, a fortiori, direct sterilization of a criminal can be allowed because to intend directly the death of the man himself is something more serious than to intend directly the mutilation of his generative system. The further problem with the moral dimension of sterilization is the formidable question involved in the controversy over the anovulants: if the anovulants result in temporary sterilization, may such a sterilization be *directly* intended in the absence of a pathological condition such as menorrhagia, dysmenorrhea, or an irregular menstrual cycle? In other words, may this kind of sterilization be intended as a means for the further good of marital intimacy and in the presence of serious psychological reasons? To say that direct sterilization is always wrong, to say that indirect sterilization is licit only in the presence of a *physical* pathological condition, is to narrow the area of moral dialogue.

II. Are Arguments Against Direct Sterilization Cogent?

This was what was tentatively said in an earlier chapter. We would want to carry the discussion beyond what was said there and to introduce into the problem of direct sterilization some provisional resolutions of our own. We want to raise certain questions which throw doubt upon the cogency of classical arguments against direct sterilization. We want to show that the term *direct sterilization* has been confined to a narrow interpretation of the person and that even the term *indirect sterilization* has been considered as moral only under circumstances which respect the physical organism but not the psychological, the psycho-somatic or the total person. Our reflections therefore will center on the concepts of both indirect and direct sterilization and we might begin by re-examining indirect sterilization and the reasons for the lawfulness of such sterilizations. We remarked above that an indirect therepeutic sterilization is permissible in the judgment of most moralists if there is a mediating pathological condition. This pathological disorder is always a *physical* pathological disorder related in some way to the organ affected. This in direct sterilization is referred to as therapeutic but it is therapeutic in a very narrow and circumscribed sense of the term. The therapeutic effect is directly intended, e.g. in the case of woman suffering from a cancerous uterus in which the hysterectomy will result in the death of the nonviable fetus. The latter death is only indirectly intended in excising the pathological uterus. This excision is productive of two effects, the restoration of the health of the mother (direct intention) and the death of the fetus (indirect intention). The pathology is physical in origin; the cancer is due to a disease which has an organic physical cause. The effect of this cause is seen in the inability of the organ to do what that organ would normally do.

Another example is the substantial undermining of the uterus of the woman resulting from repeated Caesarean sections. If in the judgment of competent medical men these repeated sections have so undermined the uterus that it is pathological in the sense of being unable to discharge the purpose of the uterus in carrying the fetus, then the sterilization that results from the hysterectomy is referred to as an indirect therapeutic sterilization.

In both the cases offered here, the pathology is due to physical causes which have undermined the organ which will be sacrificed in the operation. Moralists see little difficulty in these cases and they are the ones, especially the first, which are employed to illustrate the indirectly volitional act applied in medical-moral cases. However, there are other cases where the causality of the disordered organ may be due more to psychological, psycho-somatic or even psychiatric causes, and we are asking now whether in justifying indirect therapeutic sterilization we have not narrowed down the root cause of the disorder to the physical and closed off the etiology from other causes. In fact, is this not even implicit in the term that has been selected for the disorder—it is referred to as a *pathological* condition, emphasizing a physically disordered condition produced by a physical organic cause? We wonder whether in narrowing down the causality to the physical we have difficulties in presenting the evidence which is "most clear to the light of human reason."

It has frequently been my conviction (and I have expressed it to competent doctors) that the following propositions are almost convertible: "Good medicine is good morality" and "Good morality is good medicine." Have we not in our restriction of the term *pathological* put obstacles to our claim that the proposition is convertible? Would not ethically responsible doctors have a wider range of meaning for *pathological* and if our own is more narrow, how can we possibly say that we are proposing reasons which are clear by the light of human reason? Whose human reason? Whose human reason would be accepted by a reasonable third party who would listen to both definitions, one more circumscribed, the other wider, more acceptable by scientific men who know, more personal in its applications? My suggestion is that if we want to be taken seriously by professionals who are as sensitive and perceptive as we are in ethics and morality, we ought to listen to their judgment of what pathology means in its etiology and its effects. We can certainly accept a more confined meaning of the term, but let us not say that this narrow interpretation is evident by the natural light of human reason. Let us admit that we accept the meaning on some other ground. This criticism of the ethic of conviction, especially as it is presented in Roman Catholic circles, is valid and legitimate. Clarity of the reasons for certain practices in medico-moral problems has not been recognized by many competent, ethically responsible doctors. It is time to recognize this lack of clear evidence for the positions that are taken in Roman Catholic circles. Much of the criticism of natural law ethics is in this very area of medical procedures.

III. The Problem of Direct Sterilization

So much for the present concerning the term *indirect sterilization*. The problems that we touched upon are more difficult in nature and number when we turn to the issues of *direct sterilization*. In fact it would appear that as soon as this term raises its head all further speculation comes to an end. This was the situation with regard to the publication of Janssens' "Morale conjugale et progestogènes."[1] The article appeared in the same year as the publication of the book of Dr. John Rock, *The Time Has Come, A Catholic Doctor's Proposal To End The Battle Over Birth Control*. In it Dr. Rock maintained that the recent discovery and perfection of the progestogene (the "pill") provided a solution to the birth control question which could be accepted by Protestants and Catholics. In America the immediate reaction was devastating and almost completely negative. The Jesuit Richard McCormick summarized the position of Dr. Rock and the theological and philosophical respectability conferred upon it by Janssens as follows: "Janssens argues that use of progestins contraceptively is morally acceptable because it is morally similar to periodic continence: it (1) is not a direct sterilization even though it is a positive intervention; (2) leaves the natural structure of the act intact; (3) represents less of an intervention than periodic continence insofar as the ova are not destroyed but conserved."[2]

Very few American moralists accepted Janssens' argument that the use of the pill is ethically comparable to the practice of rhythm. What most American moralists immediately seized upon was that the deliberate frustration of ovulation is a *direct sterilization*. This was the crucial point and if the pill suppressed ovulation, this was a sure case of *direct sterilization*. John Lynch, S.J., expressed this attitude when he observed: "Theologians have universally conceded until now . . . that the direct suppression of a generative function as such (that is, direct sterilization) is in-

---

[1] Louis Janssens, 'Morale conjugale et progestogènes," *Ephemerides Theologicae Lovanienses* 14 (1963), 787–826.

[2] Richard McCormick, "Whither the Pill?" *The Catholic World* (July, 1966).

trinsically immoral.[3] Michael O'Leary said much the same thing: "The use of any drug for the precise purpose of inhibiting ovulation in a woman in order to prevent conception is nothing more than *direct contraceptive sterilization* and as such is a grave offense against the moral law."[4] These two citations are examples of the unfortunate use of the term *intrinsic evil*.

Archbishop Roberts was not the first to see the inconsistency in permitting a *direct sterilization* as a punitive device and later calling it intrinsically evil if it were done as a contraceptive measure: "How is it wrong . . . to grant me for the good of my family, what according to many Catholic theologians, the state could impose forcibly on me as a punishment if I committed a crime?"[5] Furthermore, it can be shown that "some of these same moralists who label as *per se* immoral the use of steroid pills as direct sterilization agents, uphold at least one exception: namely for women who face inevitable danger of rape. (This opinion was given, for instance, in the case of certain nuns in the Congo.) This inconsistency of thought is inexplicable."[6] To designate an act *intrinsically evil* is to use a megaton term when a milder one would not have exposed the user to the inconsistencies mentioned in the cases above. Other moralists do not agree even within the same tradition on what is so basic, namely, *the intrinsic evil of direct sterilization*. In *Louvain Studies* Francis W. Swift points out these inconsistencies:

> If we follow the reasoning of Fr. Lynch and Fr. McFadden, these two cases could never be allowed because they both certainly are examples of "a direct suppression of a generative function as such"—which Fr. Lynch says is "intrinsically immoral." And certainly he would also accept the principle that the end does not justify the means. Fr. McFadden could certainly never condone the case in the Congo; for here the nuns would be taking the pill "for the precise purpose of inhibiting ovulation," in order to prevent conception. And this, he says, would be direct contraceptive sterilization and "as such a grave offense against the moral law." For when a moralist teaches that a certain action is intrinsically evil, under no circumstances can it be said to be morally permissible. The argument that these nuns were under no obligation of undergoing pregnancy can equally apply to many married women under certain circumstances. All such considerations, however, are irrelevant when one is talking about an act which is called *per se* intrinsically evil.[7]

---

[3] John Lynch, "Notes on Moral Theology," *Theological Studies* (June 1964), 242.

[4] Michael O'Leary, "Some Thoughts About the Oral Steroid Pill," *Jubilee* (March 1964).

[5] Archbishop Thomas D. Roberts, Introduction to *Contraception and Holiness* (New York: Herder & Herder, 1964), p. 20.

[6] Ralph J. Tapia, "Overpopulation: Possible Solutions," *Homiletic and Pastoral Review* (August, 1965), 937–938.

[7] Francis W. Swift, "An Analysis of the American Theological Reaction to Janssens' article on 'The Pill,'" *Louvain Studies* 1.1 (Fall, 1966), 32.

Francis Connell explains how the case of the nun in the Congo is not a *direct* sterilization: "I believe that *she may lawfully use this means (the pill) to prevent conception.* I cannot see any essential difference between her act and the act of a girl who uses a douche after a sexual attack. Both perform contraceptive actions, but are not guilty of the sin of contraception since sexual intercourse has been forced (or will probably be forced) upon them; their act of sexual union is not voluntary."[8] This response points up the verbal gymnastics that have to be employed after the strongest language has been used in calling every act of *direct sterilization intrinsically evil.* Even after this reply other moralists are not satisfied with the explanation because the admission is made in the first place that the intention to prevent conception is not necessarily immoral, i.e., it can be morally acceptable under certain circumstances. In the second place, Connell recognizes that the *means* (the pill) used to prevent this conception is also not necessarily immoral, but can be justified in certain circumstances. The intention to prevent conception and the means used are admitted to be not immoral *per se* but justified under certain contextual circumstances. Consequently, why is the act moral in the case of one and immoral in the case of the married woman, who has morally valid reasons for preventing another conception and for whom the rhythm method is not possible? This is the reasoning of Janssens and he receives support from Van der Marck, although their precise point of difference is precisely the kind of sterilization brought about by the progestogene steroids. Janssens contends that to postpone ovulation is nothing more than "a kind of *temporary indirect sterilization* which the Church has always considered legitimate for serious reasons."[9] Van der Marck takes a slightly different position when he claims "this direct effect of the progestogene steroids when used for fertility control is the postponement or delay of ovulation rather than any real suppression of ovulatory function . . . consequently there is no question of sterilization in the genuine sense of that word."[10] If direct temporary sterilization were intrinsically immoral, Van der Marck argues, it could not be allowed even for therapeutic reasons. Lynch refuses to accept this reasoning of Van der Marck and takes issue with it: "Merely to call the contraceptive use of the pill 'fertility control' instead of calling it 'direct temporary sterilization' does not furnish any theological support for the position. Such terminology simply amounts to saying either that the end justifies

[8] Francis J. Connell, "Delaying Ovulation," in Answers to Questions, *American Ecclesiastical Review* (December 1964).

[9] Gommar DePauw, "The Pill Controversy," *Homiletic and Pastoral Review* (June 1964), 752.

[10] Cf. Lynch, *art. cit.*, 241–242.

the means or that the means is not immoral. The first is inadmissible. The second begs the question."[11]

Much of this discussion must strike persons of a different philosophical tradition as intolerably anachronistic. Because it takes place among persons of the same tradition and concerns what appears to others as minuscular points in philosophy or metaphysics, interest soon wanes and the exchange is not fruitful at all. It ought to be done in the company of competent medical men to whom the ethical and moral positions are offered for consideration. Terms should have an acceptable meaning for all the participants and they should not be associated with just one tradition and be foreign to others. For example, in a dialogue on radio with Dr. John Rock he had occasion to mention that the term "temporary sterilization" is not very meaningful for the doctor; in addition he observed that the term "anovulants" to his knowledge hardly ever occurs in medical literature. If this be true, then how can philosophers and theologians speak of the convertibility of the proposition that "Good Morality is Good Medicine" and "Good Medicine is Good Morality" when there is not enough dialogue going on among the different disciplines? When terms are ambiguous even among the persons who are in the same discipline and the same tradition and when these terms are almost completely unused by the other disciplines, what can be expected in the absence of real exchange and real clarification?

We are convinced that there would be helpful alterations in ethical and moral procedures in medical practice if more of these extra-mural exchanges were taking place and if the intra-mural discussions would admit specialists from all relevant disciplines. What we have developed within the last several pages has been the differences that exist among theologians and philosophers on an intra-mural problem of *direct sterilization, indirect sterilization,* and whether *every direct sterilization is intrinsically immoral.* Lynch observes that the discussion points up very emphatically that "the enunciation of our principles with respect to contraception and sterilization is in sore need of considerable refinement if we are to resolve satisfactorily certain apparent contradictions in our applications of those principles to newer and more complicated problems."[12] On the question of direct sterilization Lynch clarifies his own position this way: "*it would appear legitimate to suggest that divine natural law need not and does not condemn all direct sterilization, even of the innocent, and that the Church in her teaching never deliberately chose to give that erroneous impression.*"[13] We shall make use of this evidence in developing later

---

[11] *Ibid.*
[12] Lynch, "Notes on Moral Theology," *Theological Studies* (June 1965), 258–259.
[13] *Ibid.*, 261.

what we shall offer as discussible cases for legitimate direct sterilization.

The subject of *direct* and *indirect sterilization* with regard to the pill was the theme of the address to hematologists on September 12, 1958 by Pope Pius XII. It is the statement to which the opponents of Janssens' position always appeal in their conclusion that the use of the pill for contraceptive purposes is an example of a *direct sterilization*. We would like to cite this paragraph because we shall be referring to it in order to show the ambiguity in the term *direct*:

> Is it licit to prevent ovulation by means of pills used as remedies for exaggerated reaction of the uterus and of the organism, although this medication, by preventing ovulation, also makes fecundation impossible? Is this permitted to the married woman who, despite this temporary sterility, desires to have relations with her husband? The answer depends on the person's intention. If the wife takes this medication not with a view of preventing conception, but solely on the advice of a physician, as a necessary remedy by reason of a malady of the uterus or the organ, she is causing an *indirect sterilization* which remains permissible according to the general principle concerning actions having a double effect. *But one causes a direct sterilization, and therefore an illicit one, whenever one stops ovulation in order to preserve the uterus and the organism from the consequences of a pregnancy which they are not able to stand.* Certain moralists pretend that it is permitted to take drugs for this purpose, but this is a mistake. It is necessary likewise to reject the opinion of many physicians and moralists who permit the use of them whenever a medical indication renders a too early conception undesirable, or in other similar cases which it will not be possible to mention here; in these cases the employment of drugs has as its end the prevention of conception by preventing ovulation; there is a question, therefore, of *direct sterilization*.[14]

From this statement we can conclude that a *direct sterilization is one intended as an end or as a means to an end* and that an *indirect sterilization* is one of two effects from an action in which the intention is to achieve some other purpose even though sterilization is foreseen as an unavoidable concomitant. In the case of the pill, these purposes may be the alleviation of dysmenorrhea, menorrhagia, or the regularization of the menstrual cycle. The sterilization becomes direct even in these cases where there are the two effects in the event that the contraceptive effect, the sterilization itself, is intended. It is here where persons from other traditions begin to raise questions about the reasonableness of these definitions in practice and how realistic they are in experience. If the intentionality of a person using the pill should be fixated upon the sterilization effect even in the presence of those conditions that warrant the use of the pill, the sterilization becomes direct according to the meaning as-

---

[14] *Acta Apostolicae Sedis* 50 (1958), 735–736. Cited by Dupré in *Contraception and Catholics* (Baltimore: Helicon, 1964), p. 54.

signed to it in the statement above. The difficulty in attempting to show that these definitions are realistic in practice is not too simple. Is it not true that frequently if not always the reason for the practice of rhythm is the exercise of responsible parenthood, which in more realistic terms is the avoidance of the next child? Is this not the dominant intent in the exercise of periodic continence? Is it the complete answer to say that the means are indifferent or morally good when we examine the intentionality and discover that the intentionality is not *indirect* but *direct*? Is it not true that the intentionality is not indirect in this case? Although it is possible to conceive the case where the contraceptive intention is not present (and hence indirect), the intentionality in the largest number of users focuses precisely and primarily on this end.

It appears to me to be unrealistic to say that the contraceptive intention accompanies an act which is indifferent in itself and that the contraceptive intention only affects the act in a non-essential way. It seems to me that the contraceptive intention is present as much in rhythm as in condomistic intercourse, but the freedom from possible conception is more obvious in the latter than in the former. What I am saying is that the intentionality in most situations involving rhythm is direct intentionality and not indirect and that it is realistic to admit the direct intentionality and not to conclude that it is always wrong. It seems to me that we have minimized the contraceptive intention in rhythm because the act in which it is found, i.e. rhythm, is of itself morally indifferent while we have magnified the intention in condomistic intercourse because we have been restricted by Pius XXII's condemnation of condomistic intercourse.

It is more realistic to admit that a contraceptive intentionality can be as *direct an intention* in rhythm as it can be in the exercise of condomistic intercourse. However, if this admission is made of the presence of such intentionality in rhythm the next step is to admit the ethical and moral goodness of such an intention. I would want to illustrate the same problem here with another example.

IV.   "Direct Intentionality"

Possibly the example of the implications in the meaning of *direct killing* will point out how intentionality is direct even where there are two or more effects as long as the "evil" effect is the one intended. Direct killing is obviously killing *intended as an end or as a means to an end*. Such killing can be accomplished either: (1) by an act which is by itself, *per se*, lethal, productive of death. For example, it would be difficult to see how anyone could say that he is not intending his death directly if he takes a good amount of poison or if he thrusts a knife into his heart. (2) It can take place by an act productive of two or more effects, but the effect of death is the one intended by the act. In this second case the act is one in which death could possibly have been indirectly intended while some other effect which also resulted from the act had been directly intended, but here and now, the intention is focussed on the death of the person. This is precisely what seems to take place by a realistic re-examination of the use of rhythm by many persons. The intention not to have the child by the use of rhythm appears to be just as direct an intention as the intention of death is direct in the illustration. The tendency is to regard the intention as more indirect than direct because the means used in the case of rhythm is morally indifferent. The intention then becomes the *end of agent (finis operantis)* which in some way changes the morality of the act, but not in the manner which we maintain is more realistic—changing it in virtue of the intention being *direct* and not *indirect*.

As soon as we qualify an act as *direct*, ethical issues have to be resolved; whereas if we qualify it as *indirect* all ethical issues are taken care of. The suspicion that this is true arises in the discussion of abortion. Richard McCormick, S. J. puts the question this way: *"Is direct abortion always direct killing?"* Let us examine his words:

> The phrasing of the question contains several implications. It implies, first of all, that there is a legitimate distinction between direct and indirect killing. It further acknowledges a difference between direct and indirect abortion. Direct abortion, for instance, describes a lethal action performed with the intention that death should follow for the fetus. Indirect abortion refers to an action designed and solely intended to achieve some other purpose even though death is foreseen as an unavoidable concomitant. The distinction, it must be noted, does not immediately assert that direct killing is right or wrong. Nor does it claim to be able to classify clearly all lethal interventions. It simply identifies direct intervention as something recognizably distinct from indirect taking of life. It only highlights the meaning of the action.
>
> Secondly, the question implies not only that direct killing is different from indirect killing, but that direct killing is generally morally wrong, and that indirect killing need not be. *I realize that the distinction and the conclusions based on it have been challenged in some theological circles, and that in non-theological circles they often elicit a patient smile.* Nevertheless I am convinced of their general usefulness and validity. If one abandons this distinction, he can no longer recognize the difference between legitimate military targeting, with collateral civilian death, and counter-society bombing. He is forced to be either a pacifist or an obliterationist. I shall accept here the fact that this distinction represents a reasonable and charitable effort to respect the equal sanctity of both or several lives that may be in conflict.
>
> *It has been commonly taught for years that direct abortion is direct*

killing—and therefore immoral, since *it is accepted that direct killing of the innocent is immoral.* This teaching received a classical challenge in the mother vs. child dilemma. Such an instance is, of course, extremely rare in modern obstetrical practice. But it does serve to focus attention on the principles involved.[15]

We would like to draw several implications from Father McCormick. Not every case of an abortion that is intended as an end or as a means to an end is *eo ipso* direct killing. If we examine the two definitions of direct killing we shall see that not every abortion intended as an end or as a means to another end is necessarily associated with intending the death of the fetus. In fact, we should mention here two things: (1) McCormick loads his definition of direct abortion by calling it "a *lethal* action performed with the intention that death should follow for the fetus." (2) He later accepts some plausibility for a distinction of Paul Ramsey which leads him to admit that to intend directly the abortion of the fetus may be associated at the most with his incapacitation rather than with his actual death.

In attempting here to clarify the term *direct* we hope that we have dissipated some of the ethical clouds that hover over the term. What I am trying to say is that we do not legitimate behavior by too quickly resorting to an implausible use of double effect when really what we have at hand is an action with direct intentionality which requires explanation and rationalization. We should not retreat from the more realistic attitude of admitting that many volitional acts of ours are direct volitional acts whether they be direct sterilizations, direct abortions, direct killings. When they are, and necessity demands their being placed, we ought to re-examine the premises and presuppositions which forbade them in the past. We shall touch upon some of these cases of direct sterilization and direct abortion with a view to expanding the area of ethical discussion.

Before we advance to an analysis of broader interpretation and moral warrant for direct sterilization, let us consider some of the consequences from the dual meaning of *direct killing* which we gave above. The first kind of direct killing was by an act which of itself, *per se,* is productive of death, lethal of its nature. The second was such direct killing by an act productive of two or more effects in which the effect of death is the one intended by the person. Now, with these two meanings, one stressing the very nature of the act itself, that it is *per se* lethal, and the other stressing the element of intentionality, difficulties should become evident to the discerning. There are cases where the action is direct by the very

---

[15] Richard McCormick, "Aspects of the Moral Question," *America* (December 9, 1967), 718.

reason of the act but hardly direct in virtue of the intentionality. One should begin to wonder whether the only real case of directly volitional behavior is the act which would include both elements at the same time, *per se* lethality and intentionality for that end of death.

Let us illustrate. Apparently in some cases it is possible to sever one element from the other. Consider the case of a soldier who is willing to undergo such a transfusion of blood for his friend so that his friend will live that the quantity of blood is necessarily connected with his own death. Certainly this act is direct by virtue of the very act placed; it is the donation of such a quantity of blood as will cause his own death. Yet can it be said that in the order of intentionality this effect of death is willed by the donor? Which intention realistically is uppermost in the behavior of the donor—is it not the intention to save his friend at any cost? Is this not a laudable intention? Therefore it would seem that an action is direct in virtue of the very act placed but hardly direct from the point of view of conscious intentionality. Of course, the conclusion to this might well be that direct killing can be most laudable and we would be the first to agree, but we would also judge that comparable cases of direct sterilization can be just as laudable.

Another example of a possible severance between act and intentionality is the case of a mother who suggests to the doctor that he perform some medical action whereby she herself may be incapacitated for further existence but the child in her body may be saved. The suggestion seems to involve an act, direct from its very nature, yet in the conscious intentionality this intention of the woman's own death is hardly adverted to. What is adverted to primarily if not solely is to save the child. Ontologically it may be true that one and the other are associated; this may be true and as we state the case, they are, but are they so in the order of associated intentionality and is not intentionality stressed in the very definition of the word *direct* (to intend as an end or as a means to an end)? The speculation that we have done here on the apparent separability between action and intentionality was occasioned by similar speculation on constructing a valid realistic definition for suicide. The problems were many.

V.   Direct Contraceptive Sterilization

So far this chapter has concerned itself with the difficulties that are faced by someone within traditional moral philosophy and theology with the concepts *indirect or direct volitional behavior*. The distinction between the two is helpful and basically clear. It is in the sophistication of the discussion on the precise implications in both that even the intra-mural debate becomes refined and microscopic. Little wonder that those outside the tradition find problems with terminology and consider the terminology irrelevant and anachronistic, when in the presentation of realistic experiences admission is not made of the inadequacies in these terms as they are tested by these concrete existential situational cases. We would prefer to turn to a particular problem here involving *direct sterilization* where it would seem that there is need for some latitude in the moral judgment that has been made by moralists. Considering what we have said thus far about *direct and indirect* sterilization, we might briefly repeat that most moralists would permit *direct punitive sterilization* but not *direct contraceptive sterilization*. In other words, *direct* sterilization is indifferent in its morality and receives its moral quality from the circumstances in which the direct sterilization is performed. Now we would like to defend the proposition that such a direct sterilization is warranted not only as a punitive device but also in certain circumstances as a contraceptive measure where other values are situationally involved. We ought, I maintain, to re-examine the traditional evidence that is offered against such *direct contraceptive sterilization*. The evidence may appear not to be as demonstrable and clear "by the natural light of human reason" as we have thought. Evidence is historically conditioned, and just as the evidence against contraception in general has eroded in its probative quality, so the evidence has weakened in the case of *direct contraceptive sterilization*. It might be well to consider this evidence as it is seen by many responsible men as ethically perceptive as ourselves for whom the prohibition of *direct contraceptive sterilization* is not as clear or as unambiguous as we might think. There are many factors involved in the discussion, medical, psychological and economic, but we shall consider the traditional arguments against this direct sterilization and speculate whether we ought not to make some alterations in the light of new developments.

Others have raised the question of re-examining the evidence and we shall make references to them. Quentin de la Bedoyere elaborates upon the ethical position of the secularist who would show the morality of the case for *direct contraceptive sterilization*.[16] Certainly there are situations in which there are justifying circumstances for the conscience decision not to have any more children. Pius XI in his encyclical *Casti Connubii* in 1930 admitted this himself and suggested some of these justifying circumstances. Responsible parenthood has been accepted by all moralists as a moral end in marriage; the differences take place on the election of the means.

---

[16] Quentin de la Bedoyere, "Sterilization and Human Reason," *New Blackfriars* (1967), pp. 152–156.

Some situations are so serious that the only way in which the risk could be responsibly avoided would be either by a total and permanent abstention from consummated sexual intercourse or by a *direct contraceptive sterilization*. The first alternative carries with it the inevitable psychological tensions and discord in the marriage with the serious consequences for the tranquillity of the family, including the children. The second alternative involves the willed permanent incapacitation to have another child. Under ordinary circumstances this loss of fertility would be substantial but in the case under consideration this loss is not present because there is the duty in conscience not to have another child. Is it realistic to oblige a married couple to refrain permanently from marriage relations in order to preserve the integrity of a faculty of fertile intercourse which ought not to be exercised in the realization of this effect? In other words, if the only alternative is permanent abstention from sexual intercourse with the concomitant risks to the stability of the marriage, is it realistic to say that this obligation is always present in such situational contexts? Let us examine the response that is usually given to this dilemma. It is suggested that there is greater harm done to the marriage and to society by *direct contraceptive sterilization* than one at first might suspect. In order to confirm this contention the defender of the traditional prohibition is compelled to offer adequate reasons for the *universal negative prohibition*. If the position is correct which we have been presenting through these chapters, then the priority of the *ethic of responsibility* is going to show itself in its demand for *empirically verifiable* evidence which will support the universal prohibition. Does the empirical evidence support the prohibition or the situational permissibility of direct contraceptive sterilization? Let us examine the case for the defense of the negative moral absolute concerning this type of direct contraceptive sterilization.

The argument customarily proceeds from a denial of ownership of a man over his life to the admitted fact of stewardship or legitimate right of use of his body. This legitimate right of use is shown in the application of the *principle of totality* to justify mutilations on the non-reproductive organs of the person; and the application of the *principle of double effect* to justify mutilations on the reproductive organs of the person. In other words, the only justifiable sterilization would be an indirect sterilization and not a direct contraceptive sterilization. The Christian moralist takes seriously the notion of stewardship and the two principles of *totality* and *double effect*. For example, a woman may undergo a hysterectomy if she suffers from a carcinoma of the womb even though sterilization may result and the possible death of a non-viable fetus. The argument is that despite these losses there is an overriding gain to the totality of the body and the concomitant effects of sterilization and fatal death are indirect effects and not direct. However, where the hysterectomy is done solely to sterilize as a contraceptive measure, this is not justified because the body would suffer the loss of an important organ of the total person without compensating or overriding gain. There is stoicism in the contention made in the traditional presentation and Quentin de la Bedoyere notes this: "Fertility is never in itself a source of danger to the body; it only becomes indirectly so as a result of a voluntary act of sexual intercourse. Therefore its neutralization is a diminishing of the totality of the body and thus a betrayal of stewardship."[17]

It is difficult to understand how in any personalistic view of marriage it can be said that the act of sexual intercourse is voluntary without at once emphasizing its nature as part of the commitment of the two persons in faith and love to which they have a right and a duty. The real question is within this context of the nature of marriage as a deep permanent commitment in faith and love testified to symbolically by an act of consummated sexuality, whether men and woman should forego this symbolical expression with the obvious results for the stability of their marriage, the deepening of their relationship and the inevitable consequences for family life. We consider that within this more relevant and meaningful revelation of the profundity of sexual love, we ought to reconsider the evidence which would as in the past suggest the only alternative to be permanent abstention from the very relationship that stabilizes their marriage and deepens the commitment in faith and love. In the light of this awareness of the phenomenology of sexual love we would maintain the the *principle of totality*, which has been invoked in the past for justifiable mutilations, has become too circumscribed and narrow in scope, that it has considered the primary totality to be that of the body and the subordination of a part of the body for the realization of the physical health of the whole body. We consider that the new theology of marriage requires a reassessment of this *principle of totality* to include not only the body but larger and more significant totalities to which the body itself might be seen to be subordinated. We realize why the *principle of totality* has been interpreted narrowly in the past and what risks there are in the application of wider meanings for the principle where man might be regarded not as a person with dignity of personality but an object maneuverable among other objects. To widen the principle of totality might just as easily work to the disadvantage of personality as to its growth and self-realization. The principle of totality concerns physical parts of the body in due subordination and relationship to one

---

17 *Ibid.*, p. 154.

another. This relationship is of the physical order unlike the moral and juridical relationship that exists between men and society or among men themselves. Within society man is not subordinated to the state as the different limbs and organs of man's body are subordinated. To accept such a subordination of man to the state is ultimately to destroy the integrity of his personality and to reduce him to the ontology of an object among other objects. The parts of man's body might be considered to be means toward the body as a whole, but men in society are never means but ends. For these reasons theologians have always been wary of enlarging the concept of the *principle of totality* in fear of reducing man and his role in creation to a mere means for the ends of society.

Recognizing the enormous difference between the physical union of the parts of a man's body in relation to the whole of his body and the moral and juridical union of men in society, is there not a unique kind of union in marriage itself, a specific and proper kind of totality that belongs to marriage and to no other community? There is the moral and juridical union of minds and wills, rights and duties that have been usually treated by moralists under the formality of the matrimonial contract. In addition to this union of minds and wills fixated upon the goods within marriage there would seem to be a union of another order to which the Scripture refers and to which our Lord himself referred. In Matthew 19:5 we read "For this cause shall a man leave his father and mother and shall cleave to his wife and they shall be in one flesh. Therefore they are not two, but one flesh." Likewise the union between Christ and his Church has been compared to the union of man and woman in sexual union. St. Paul develops the notion of mystery that is found in the significance of the marriage union and it would seem from the mystery of marriage that certain inferences can be drawn as to its nature. The individuality of the two persons is not destroyed or lost but is transcended and can only be properly regarded against the background of the totality of marriage. Quentin de la Bedoyere develops this relationship of man and woman forming a true totality, that of two in one:

> The link that binds is of a corporal nature; it occurs at the level of the "flesh." In fact this link is more radical than the moral link; it persists when love is dead, even when the marriage has been repudiated. A closer investigation of this corporal link involves impenetrable difficulties. It is one that is not superficially visible—as if the married couple grew into each other like siamese twins. It persists even if the couple are physically separated from the moment of their marriage vows until death. Without scriptural authority we should have no means of knowing of its existence at this static permanent level. But it also exists at a dynamic level in the actual "living out" of the marriage union. Here an important distinction must be made. The ordinary acts within marriage (which might be de-

fined as any act which is aimed at promoting the purposes of the union) can only be regarded as expressing the underlying union and fostering the love that accompanies it. They may be more, but we have no authority for saying so. On the other hand, the act of sexual intercourse falls into a different category. St. Paul is dramatically explicit about this. He says that an act of sexual intercourse with a prostitute makes one flesh out of the two participants (1 Cor. 6/15 etc.). Since in his example there is no love, no intention to generate and a single occasion is visualized, it must be that the act, of its very nature, effects the mysterious union that is at the root of marriage. Therefore it cannot be a mere optional act which happens to be permissible within marriage; it actually brings about the union, completing and existentializing it at its dynamic level. A marriage within which sexual intercourse does not feature as a recurrent expression is deficient in this important dynamic element; the unity of the two in one flesh suffers thereby.[18]

The nature of human relations and the evidence of sexual psychology seem to bear out the point in the Pauline argument. Sexual intercourse makes the two become "one body" and "body" in this context represents the total being—body, mind and spirit. The whole person is involved in coital relations and not merely the genital organs. The act takes place not on the circumference of experience but at the very centrality of man's existence as a personal duality of body and spirit. It can never be considered just the act of an individual because it always involves another individual in such a manner that the participants can never again be as they were before they engaged in this union. Sherwin Bailey in *Sexual Ethics* explains how once the act is done, it can never be undone because its effect, though imperceptible, is indelible and repetition only serves to deepen the impression made upon the personality, either for good or for ill.[19] This is the radical explanation why St. Paul can say that the personality has been touched in this relationship in a way different from other relationships, why this is true whether the union be with a prostitute or with one's married partner. Man and woman in this relationship always become "one flesh" and whether they realize it or not they are deeply and inextricably involved with one another in a relation which expresses the essence of their attitude toward other persons. Comparing and contrasting the two unions in marriage and in prostitution Bailey says: "If they are husband and wife, their act is an act and a promise of love, a disclosure of what lies too deep for utterance and yet must be told, a distillation and concentration of the meaning of their common life—or so it should be, if they are growing in knowledge of what marriage really is. But in prostitution or casual fornication man and woman equally declare their true nature, and become united in common irresponsibility

18 *Ibid.*, p. 155.
19 Sherwin Bailey, *Sexual Ethics* (New York: Macmillan, 1962), p. 88.

and mutual exploitation. Not only does the use of another person for mercenary or lustful ends leave its marks upon the character, but continual treatment as a means of self-gratification eventually impairs the capacity for true relation of any kind."[20]

It would seem to follow from this view of sexual relations that a marriage in which there is an abstention from such relations suffers as a marriage. This is not to deny that such abstention because of special graces from God and for extraordinary reasons may not produce a unity in the order of spirit which could not otherwise be achieved. There is no intention to reflect upon those unions in which mutual vows of chastity may have been taken or a union such as that of Our Lady and St. Joseph. However, we would agree with de la Bedoyere who maintains that such unions precisely as marriage unions were defective. Marriage is more integral and more perfect as marriage when the union between man and woman is a total union of body and soul. It is not just a union of spirit and its radical nature demands the totality of union "which occurs at the level of the flesh and this can only be brought about in its dynamic aspect by sexual intercourse."[21]

Now let us return to the marriage case outlined at the start of our speculation. The alternatives that the parties confronted in the concrete were either permanent abstention from sexual intercourse or direct sterilization. There were adequate reasons why in conscience they should refrain from having additional children. A case in point might involve the physical health of the mother but her condition is one which does not permit the application of an indirect sterilization. If phenomonology has revealed a clearer understanding of the nature of marriage, if the nature of marriage is such that it introduces a different totality to which the married parties must direct their minds and wills, does not this new realization of the uniqueness of marriage offer some assistance for the resolution of the above dilemma? In other words, is there not present in this view of marriage the recognition of the duty and the right that two persons have to deepen the union "which occurs at the level of the flesh and which can only be brought about in its dynamic aspect by sexual intercourse?" Abstention from such relations then acquires a more profound meaning in that it involves as well the abstention from what those same acts radically mean—the union in one flesh which union is dynamized by sexual intercourse. Something happens to the very status of the marriage as a marriage when abstention takes place. Is the loss here greater or less than the loss sustained by the sterilization?

It can be seen that the moral issue is still resolved by the application

---

[20] *Ibid.*, p. 89.
[21] de la Bedoyere, *art. cit.*, 156.

of the *Principle of Totality* but the principle has now been widened to recognize the special and unique union of marriage as we found it in the scriptures and which is now testified to in the phenomenological experience of many married persons. The totality now is not just a body related to another body but the union of the two in one flesh. Fertility might be considered under normal circumstances to be an important part of this union and the contribution that it makes is a substantial one to this totality. However, there can be circumstances similar to the one we described at the outset, where fertility may not contribute to this totality but may actually damage this totality because it precludes the dynamic element which is actualized in sexual intercourse. Applying the Principle of Totality under these circumstances the gain to the totality in not precluding the exercise of sexual relations counterbalances the loss to the union occasioned by the direct sterilization. The larger totality has been promoted in the sacrifice of one of the parts which is the faculty of fertility.

We characterized contemporary morality as more committed to the ethic of responsibility than to the ethic of conviction. The first is concerned with the personal empirical verifiable consequences that follow upon the act; the latter is rooted in the acceptance of universal affirmative and negative principles. It would seem that the wider horizon that has been given to the meaning of marriage and the empirical evidence in cases similar to the one we have been considering would suggest that the classical arguments for the prohibition of every *direct contraceptive sterilization* are not compelling. The conclusion is not that the prohibition should not stand but that the prohibition is not one that "the light of human reason makes most clear." The universality of the prohibition is in the light of the continuous and evolving theology of marriage difficult to establish and the empirical verifiable evidence is not on the side of universality. While it is clear to us that it cannot always be shown to be wrong that a person in certain concrete circumstances would decide in favor of a *direct contraceptive sterilization* the resolution of the ethical problem for the individual conscience would be the result of the tension that exists between the two ethics of conviction and responsibility. The individual conscience would have to assure itself that the totality of marriage is being damaged by the abstention from sexual relations and the refusal to make the serious ethical choice of a direct contraceptive sterilization. To make this option the person has to call upon the best resources of the ethic of responsibility and the ethic of conviction and to resolve satisfactorily the tension between the two. Difficult, yes: but it is the only authentic contemporary ethical way to exist.

CHAPTER NINE

THE MORAL PROBLEM OF ABORTION

Contemporary culture testifies to a deflation in doctrinal and moral absolutes. The moral absolutes are the mainstays of the ethic of conviction and with the erosion of moral absolutes there is a concomitant erosion in the ethic of conviction. Moral absolutes have to offer empirical evidence to prove their right to exist as absolutes in the ethical enterprise and this is not to infer that the evidence is not there and possibly abundant in some cases. What is being seriously questioned is the quality of the evidence in all cases to bear out the universality of the affirmative and negative principles. Moralists in the ethic of conviction who are anxious to preserve the status of the moral absolutes resort to a re-examination of the very acts that have been either commanded or forbidden. The human act has been exposed to more and more illumination and the precise technical meaning of the elements of the act have been re-appraised. The ethic of conviction is living in difficult times when prag-matic, empiricistic students are demanding that the moral absolute either "speak up or shut up." Either the moral absolute must show empirically that the loss is substantial if a certain disvalue is placed or it must admit that in conflict with other values and disvalues the moral absolute just does not situationally apply. The demands that are being made upon the ethic of conviction are those that the more contemporary ethic have been raising—the concern of this ethic is the empirical verifiable good or bad consequences that follow upon persons acting and re-acting in personal relationships. This ethic grasps at the dimension of truth contained in that criterion of morality which says "everyone is doing it and it is harm-ing no one."

There is no doubt that this expression of the guideline in the ethic of responsibility is open for observation and verification. It is certainly criticizable as an ethic but it has discovered something vulnerable in the ethic of conviction and the nettling that is done is therapeutic. We observed in an earlier chapter that this nettling of the ethic of conviction has been recently concentrating its operations upon the two areas of *sexuality* and *direct killing*. It is here where the moral absolutes have been secure in philosophical and theological writings within the Church. How-ever, more and more these moral absolutes have been undermined *as absolutes* and strong empirical evidence has been offered against them. In the area of direct killing the over-riding issue in the United States and in England has been the abortion problem. There are legal and political dimensions to the problem but we shall consider in this chapter the moral issues involved and then suggest some tentative provisional resolu-tions of these issues. A recent International Conference on abortion brought out many of these ethical issues and served to emphasize the great differences that exist among persons of the same general background.

I.   Reflections on the Crucial Question

It would be interesting to participate in a controversial discussion in which emotive language would not be used. One wonders whether such a discussion is even a possibility. When the social issue is abortion and involves persons with different philosophical and theological presupposi-tions discussing questions of life, the quality of life, the right of the person, the inter-relation between the legal and the moral orders, it seems that emotive language has a tendency to increase and multiply according to some law of rhetoric. The end result is the generation of more intense heat and less clear light.

Vatican II has called for a dialogue with other churches, some of whose representatives favor liberalization of present abortion laws. It has also recommended dialogic exchange with secular humanists, many of whom support the relaxation of these laws. The "sincere and prudent dialogue" between these participants cannot be unmindful of the teaching of Vatican II on the sacredness of life. In the *Constitution on the Church in the Modern World* this sentence occurs: "Therefore from the moment of its conception life must be guarded with the greatest care, while abortion and infanticide are unspeakable crimes."[1] Springer comments on this direct statement and remarks: "Though no one would hold that animation at the moment of conception is here defined as a matter of faith, no one can deny that this teaching demands respect. It was discussed, phrased and approved by the Bishops with the greatest care and in view of the disregard for life in the world today."[2]

Is it not true that the crucial question is raised right here? Is it not possible for any participant in the dialogue to agree with everything that is being taught about the person's right to life and still to disagree on the fundamental issue—*when* does the human person begin his life? All other questions are subordinate to this question which goes to the very heart of the dialogue. Besides, I do not see how the problem of the beginning of human life can be avoided. Law speaks of it; medicine speaks of it; philosophy and theology cannot avoid grappling with the issue.

Before advancing to this crucial question, however, it might be well to summarize the theological and sociological perspective on the question of abortion. Father James T. McHugh, Director of the Family Life Bureau, did this with remarkable clarity in a conference of diocesan lawyers on April 24, 1967.[3] What he said contains a concise statement of Catholic teaching on abortion. His position can be summarized as follows.

In the first place, the issue of abortion is specifically different from contraception and from sterilization. Any theological evaluation or any moral analysis should maintain this distinction. In the matter of public policy the implications are also different and no generalization can be made from previous public policy stands. Second, there are questions bearing on the matter of abortion, or more precisely on the matter of conception and ensoulment, to which we do not have final answers. More

---

[1] *Pastoral Constitution on the Church in the Modern World*, par. 51, in *Documents of Vatican II* edited by Walter M. Abbott (New York: Guild, 1966), p. 256.

[2] Springer, "Moral Theology Notes," *Theological Studies* (June 1967), p. 334.

[3] James T. McHugh, News Release of National Catholic Welfare Conference, April 24, 1967, p. 197.

adequate scientific data are required and we should be cautious about overstating the case. Nevertheless, since we are dealing with human life, we must favor the course of action that assures the greatest safety to the fetus. This is the real reason for the opposition to a change in the abortion laws.

McHugh reminds the Catholic participant in the dialogue to state Catholic teaching clearly, avoiding emotional arguments or sensationalism and emphasizing a reasoned presentation that accurately presents the value a Christian places on human life. However, we should never forget that other persons share with us this fundamental cultural value of life. Differences arise, as Springer points out, over the relative evaluation of unborn life in conflict with the health and happiness of the already born, and in the implementation of respect for life in our cultural and legal norms.

A.   When Does Life Begin?

Let us return to the crucial question—*when* does the human person begin his life? It is true that in the public forum social arguments should be emphasized—the benefit that redounds to society from the principle of respect for life and the threat that follows from a growing trivialization of its presence in permissive abortion bills. Granted that the dialogue should proceed on the formulation of social arguments, it is still true that the gnawing question that always comes to the surface of responsible discussion is our crucial question—*when* does the human person begin his life?

It is with regard to this question that some of the more recent writing by Catholics on the subject of abortion has suggested that there may be grounds for an improvement in the quality of the dialogue with others. This writing has raised questions in ecumenical exchange which might serve to offer tentative answers that will, upon further analysis, become more and more acceptable. Let me summarize some of the writing to which reference is made.

Robert F. Drinan, S.J., suggests that the principle of the lesser of two evils might be applied in abortion reform. This permits this medical procedure only in the rare cases of rape, incest or a predictably defective infant.[4] It has always been true that a person's moral role is situationally different with regard to the lesser moral evil than it is with respect to the greater. Surely, the moral choice between permitting abortion only in rare cases and in permitting it in all situations is obvious. The principle is even more obvious when the discussion takes place with someone who

---

[4] Robert F. Drinan, *America* (February 4, 1967).

maintains the most extreme position of all, i.e., that a mother should have the right in law to terminate a pregnancy at any time during the pregnancy for any reason whatsoever. This extreme position, advanced by some who refer to the *"wanted child,"* has been alluded to in Lader's book on *Abortion* as an enlightened and progressive one.[5]

Some moralists might object to, or place reservations on, the adoption of a public policy of approval, or at least of toleration, regarding a law that works evil, if lesser evil, in the overall results. Springer believes that it is quite a step from the lesser-evil principle to its application to abortion laws.[6] Nevertheless, Drinan's article was praised by Professor George Williams of the Harvard Divinity School who considered that it advanced the dialogue in the ecumenical and political orders.[7]

An interesting letter by Joseph Donceel to *America*,[8] commenting on the clear choice of the lesser of two evils, added that there is "a slowly increasing number of Catholic thinkers who are returning to the position of St. Thomas Aquinas, who claimed that there is no human being at all during the first few weeks of pregnancy, when most of the abortions mentioned by Fr. Drinan might be performed." The implication in these words is that there is a growing respectability for the doctrine of *mediate animation* in place of *immediate animation* which is regarded in questions of practice as the safer of the two alternatives.

B. Mediate and Immediate Animation

Let me explain what is the meaning of *mediate* and *immediate animation*. The rational principle in man, his vital principle or entelechy is his soul and if this is considered to be present at the very moment of conception, it is regarded as animating or vivifying the somatic counterpart *immediately*. If the rational principle is not present at the very moment of conception, and this is the position of St. Thomas Aquinas to which Donceel refers in his quotation, the animation is called *mediate*. Donceel's position is that of St. Thomas, and he briefly touches upon the philosophical reasons for this attitude in his letter in *America*. In a short article in the Spring 1967 issue of *Continuum*[9] he expands more amply upon the reasons, adds others, but draws no conclusions from the philosophical respectability of *mediate animation* in theory to its adoption in practice. However, if the election between the two kinds of abortion

---

[5] Lader, *Abortion* (New York: Bobbs–Merrill, 1966).

[6] Springer, *art. cit.*, 330.

[7] George Williams, "The No. 2 Moral Issue of Today," *America*, March 25, 1967, p. 422.

[8] Joseph Donceel, *America* (March 25, 1967).

[9] Donceel, "Abortion: Mediate vs. Immediate Animation," *Continuum* (Spring 1967), pp. 167–171.

laws mentioned above does become clearer by an examination of the evidence for *mediate* animation, why was this inference not made? Is it reasonable to suggest that in certain cases a return to this position of St. Thomas might apply in practice? My intention is to review and evaluate the evidence, supplement it with other evidence and then suggest provisional applications for consideration and discussion.

What are the reasons for a return to the traditional doctrine of *mediate animation?* Donceel examines this position as well as the position of *immediate animation* historically and then identifies his own position *(mediate animation)* in this way: "With St. Thomas I teach that at the moment of conception there originates a vegetative organism that will slowly evolve into a sentient organism to become, at a moment I cannot determine, a rational organism, a real human being."[10]

The evidence for *mediate animation* is first of all that it is more compatible with the hylomorphic conception of man and that *immediate animation* is less compatible or even incompatible with this theory. St. Thomas, following Aristotle, considered the soul as the first or substantial act of a physical *organized* body which has the capacity of life. He insisted that the human embryo must have a certain degree of organization before it can become the seat of a rational principle. It should have at least the beginning of a human shape and the essential organs should be present. *St. Thomas never questioned the presence of life in the embryo from the very moment of conception. But this first life is vegetative and when the proper organization is attained, a sensitive principle replaces the vegetative. When there is adequate organization commensurate for the presence of the rational principle, God creates and infuses this rational soul.*

This theory of *mediate animation* was replaced by the *immediate animation* theory in the 17th century. Why has this position been acceptable for so long apart from the fact that it is the safer in practice to adopt? The Cartesian influence upon philosophy is the root reason for the appeal that *immediate animation* has for so many. In such a theory of Cartesian dualism the soul is present and operating more precisely as an *efficient* cause. The soul is no longer the *formal* cause of the body but only the efficient cause in the aggregate of cells and it raises the question why a rational principle is even required on this hypothesis. However, such a Cartesian view of man hardly agrees with the hylomorphic conception of man and the notion of the soul as a formal cause that was stated in the Council of Vienne (Denzinger-Schönmetzer, 902).

If the thory of *mediate animation* seems to be more compatible with this hylomorphic conception of man that considers the soul as the formal

---

[10] *Ibid.*

cause of a real human body with some degree of commensurate organization, the theory has not been favored by Church legislation. Canon 747 enjoins that all living embryos, of whatever age, must be baptized unconditionally. This legislation in itself raises the question whether each menstrual discharge should be baptized because it might contain a fertilized ovum. Research scientists hold that approximately one third of all conceptions result in natural abortions.

The scientific reasons that appealed to many philosophers of the 17th and 18th centuries and that led them to reject the *mediate animation* theory of St. Thomas have lost their value. St. Thomas would be a welcome guest with his notion of man in process of evolving into a human status. On the other hand, for those holding the *immediate animation* theory, there seems to be no problem in stating that the rational soul may be the substantial form of an unorganized embryo, even when it is composed of a few cells.

Another piece of evidence for *mediate animation* is the case of identical twins. This occurrence may take place several days after fertilization and some research men in reproduction maintain that it might happen even after the implantation on the wall of the uterus. On a theory of *immediate animation* this phenomenon provides the problem of explaining how one fertilized ovum can split into two or more parts which then develop of themselves. The spirituality of the rational principle seems to rule out this divisibility if the principle is *intrinsically* independent of matter. Besides, is it to be considered an impossibility that embryologists might succeed in splitting the fertilized human ovum, just as they have artificially divided the fertilized ova of lower organisms? Will this not once again raise problems for the *immediate animation* theory where the spirituality, the non-divisibility of the rational form would apparently be in conflict?

We referred above to the large number of conceptions that result in natural or unavoidable abortions. There are theological difficulties for the position of *immediate animation* if these abortions take place spontaneously in a menstrual discharge and no baptism takes place. One theologian remarked about this phenomenon with just a trace of irreverence—"if this is true that there are so many unknown unavoidable abortions, if the rational soul is present from the beginning and if intra-uterine baptism is impossible, then there are more souls in limbo than in heaven and hell together."

Such are the arguments for *mediate animation* and for its speculative respectability: compatibility with a genuine hylomorphic conception of man and a more satisfactory explanation for the phenomenon of identical twins. The question now is: why should not the theory of *mediate anima-*

tion be used in difficult moral cases where abortion is suggested by ethically responsible persons?

II. ABORTION AND MEDIATE ANIMATION

It is here where some hesitation sets in and the bewilderment of many serious Protestant ecumenists begins to mount. Catholic moralists have to satisfy Canon 747 mentioned above, of course. It is not this canon that the ecumenists stumble over. It is the argument as it proceeds philosophically. Traditional moralists insist that this problem of the moment of rational life in the fetus is a *doubt of fact* regarding *mediate* or *immediate animation*. In cases of *doubts of law*, probabilism may be used but never in situations involving *doubts of fact*, if the doubts involve considerations of life, justice or the validity of contracts. In these situations, probabilism may not be used but the safer course must be followed. Obviously, the safer course here is to act on the theory that rational life is present from the moment of conception. The safer course is not necessarily the true one. The reasoning behind this is that one who is willing to kill what may or may not be human is, by the very terms of the proposition, willing to kill what is human.

Just one word on the *principle of probabilism* that operates only in case of *doubts of law*. It amounts to this: In situations where there is a *doubt of law*, where there is a genuine conflict between freedom and law, if there is a solidly probable argument for the non-existence of the law, then freedom is in possession because *a doubtful law does not oblige*. After this explanation the traditional moralist would deny its application in cases of *doubts of fact* involving considerations of life as in the case of *when precisely* animation takes place.

Now, I would like to raise the crucial question. Are we always obliged to follow the safer course when we confront a *doubt of fact* regarding a question of life? Are we *never* permitted to follow the less safe course in such an ethical situation? I suggested elsewhere[11] that moralist have on occasion allowed this procedure of the less safe alternative. Of course, they have permitted this alternative only where there were other values situationally at stake, and where apparently the obligation to adopt the safer course ceased to be present. Let me summarize the two illustrations that were previously suggested:

1) Moralists such as McFadden and others will permit a woman to use a douche after rape as late as 10 hours after the assault. Conception has been known to take place within that length of time and the woman

---

[11] Thomas A. Wassmer, "Questions About Questions," *Commonweal* (June 30, 1967).

is given the benefit of the doubt. The precise existential moment of conception cannot be known for certain. In our case regarding *animation* the precise existential moment of animation and the quality of animation cannot be known for certain. Nevertheless in the assault situation, in the absence of certitude and in the presence of the doubt of fact, moralists will allow the woman to act without adopting the safer course, i.e., to act within the period of 10 hours. To follow the safer course would have meant that impregnation and conception took place at the earliest possible existential moment after the attack or even during the attack.

2) The second case involves a patient with a *terminal* illness and provision has been made for all *ordinary* means for the continuation of his life. If there is no probability of his returning to rational consciousness, most moralists will permit the family and the doctor to omit the *extraordinary* means to keep him alive. The *doubt of fact*, doubt whether rational consciousness will be restored, does not entail the obligation to follow the safer of the two alternatives which would have required the continuation of all possible means.

Let me conclude these observations with certain tentative propositions of my own, especially on this subject of abortion and the dialogue in the political order.

1) It seems that there are and have been situations in which in the presence of a *doubt of fact regarding life*, the safer course is not always of obligation, if other human values are situationally at stake. Is it conceivable then that if there is *philosophical, theological* and *scientific* respectability for the theory of *mediate* animation, then this theory, admittedly not the safer of the two alternatives, might in certain situations be applied? Would dialogue with others who are just as passionately concerned with the question of life and the *quality* of life be improved at least a millimeter? Is it temerarious to suggest that abortion in the rare case of rape, incest or a predictably defective infant during the first few weeks of pregnancy should not be regarded as foreclosed by moralists?

2) Where men of good will and ethical integrity disagree is it always prudential for Catholics to try to impose their "traditional" answers on other citizens by way of a general civil law? Is it not the best index of a man's love of freedom that he respects the freedom of others, ethically perceptive and morally sensitive of the freedom of Catholics? This responsibility is of course reciprocal.

3) The problem of abortion has been called the problem of hard-core ecumenism. Does the ecumenist improve the dialogue if he insists upon maintaining *philosophical, theological* and *scientific* respectability, for *mediate* animation, while refusing to admit its application in the rare cases of rape, incest and a predictably defective infant?

4) It seems that the absolutization and polarization of a value apart from its situational presence in a whole constellation of human values leads to moral embarrassment. It seems to me that we have not done this by so absolutizing and polarizing life that where there was a doubt of its presence (and now I would like to say, of its *rational* quality), other values have not situationally permitted its forfeiture.

5) It appears that if in case of *doubts of fact* regarding life the less safe course may be adopted where other human values are situationally at stake, then such abortions are not the lesser of two evils, but can be within the situation ethically and morally good.

6) Dr. Joseph Fletcher has referred to hard-core ecumenism as the period of ecumenical exchange when the blandness ceases and the "nitty-gritty," "nuts and bolts" operations take place. What I have submitted here is a set of proposals to improve the "nitty-gritty," "nuts and bolts" exchange in the ecumenical and political dialogue with persons as ethically and morally sensitive as ourselves.

CHAPTER TEN

BETWEEN LIFE AND DEATH:
ETHICAL AND MORAL ISSUES INVOLVED IN
RECENT MEDICAL ADVANCES

Philosophers have always been vitally interested in discussions on death and many of them have consumed most of their speculative attention and concern with death and its implications. Socrates and Karl Jaspers (2300 years after him) have maintained that the whole essence and function of philosophy is to prepare a man for death. Others have attempted to apply either magic or mysticism to considerations of death. Epicurus observed: "When I am, death is not. When death is, I am not. Therefore we can never have anything to do with death." Pascal mentions this same paradox of trying to put death out of one's thinking and the constant preoccupation that death plays in one's ordinary routine: "Since men have not succeeded in eliminating death, they have decided not to think of it."

In this chapter we shall be thinking of the phenomenon of death as it concerns the medical, legal, philosophical and theological professions. Medically, death may be constantly receding and dreams of indefinite life spans may be experienced more and more, but the inevitability of death sometime somewhere occupies the attention of Everyman. Much of the fear and mystery of death may have been dispelled and Christianity may look upon the conquest of death as its great enterprise: "O death, where is thy sting? O grave, where is thy victory?" But death still remains and lawyers, philosophers and theologians look to the medical profession for a reconsideration of the medical definition of death in the light of recent procedures in heart transplantation.[1]

I.   GOOD MEDICINE IS GOOD MORALITY

It was pointed out by one of the participants in a Villanova Law School symposium at a meeting of *The American College of Cardiology* in San Francisco on February 28, 1968 that the members found themselves unable to align traditional ethics of medical practice with the new technology of human transplant. Dr. William Likoff, the president of *The American College of Cardiology*, pointed out also that such questions are no longer the private concern of the individual doctor alone. Ruth K. Franklin in an editorial in *The New Republic* for March 16, 1968 welcomes the encounter between law and medicine and indicates its urgency: "by being forced to grapple with the nature of death and the nature of consent and related ethical problems, law and medicine, long at odds, may lay the groundwork for a concerted attack on the foreseeable challenges of technology that are less pressing but equally basic: problems of human experimentation, genetics and eugenics, in sum, the humane use of human beings."[2] The conflicts between medicine and law may seem to imply that there are conflicts that are inevitable between medicine and ethics, and this is our concern here. What can the moral philosopher possibly contribute to this discussion on death?

Some ethicians are not unwilling to discern some relationship between *good medicine* and *good ethics* and *good morality*. The terms might be considered at the outset to be loaded, and it will be the role of the ethician to make clear his meaning. As a beginning we might say that good medicine regards the patient always as a person and not as a mere object of experimentation. It respects the person's attitudes toward life and death; it is interested in the quality of life and not only in absolu-

---

[1] "Death as a Constant Companion," *Time*, Nov. 12, 1965, 52–53.

[2] Ruth K. Franklin, "The Question of Transplants," *The New Republic*, March 16, 1958, 7–8.

tizing mere vegetative survival. It considers the patient as a person whose life has philosophical and theological implications that cannot be ignored by the medical profession. The interpersonal dynamic that takes place in the relationship between doctor and patient is a constant concern of the responsible medical practitioner. This responsible attitude of the profession is such an evident fact that the proposition has become almost convertible that *good medicine is good morality*. Just recently the criteria were spelled out by the Board of Medicine of the National Academy of Sciences that the judgment of the Board should be followed in cardiac transplantation cases. To read these criteria is to find the possible objections of the ethicist disappear more and more. Good medicine spells out what the ethician would in all probability say in other words. It might be well to read the criteria that were laid down by the *National Academy of Sciences* in order to see in the concrete what its Board of Medicine considered to be good medicine:

1) The surgical team should have had extensive laboratory experience in cardiac transplantation, and should have demonstrated not only technical competence but a thorough understanding of the biological processes that threaten functional survival of the transplant, i.e., rejection and its control. Investigators skilled in immunology, including tissue typing and the management of immuno-suppressive procedures, should be readily available as collaborators in the transplantation effort.

2) As in any other scientific investigation, the overall plan of study should be carefully recorded in advance and arrangements made to continue the systematic observations throughout the whole lifetime of the recipient. The conduct of such studies should be within an organized framework of information exchange and analysis. This would permit prompt access by other investigators to the full positive and negative results. Thus the continued care of each recipient would be assured the continuing benefit of the most up-to-date information. Such an organized communication network would also permit the findings to be integrated with the work of others and assist in the planning of further investigative efforts. In this way, it would be possible to assure that progress will be deliberate, and that the experience from each individual case will make its full contribution to the planning of the next.

3) As the procedure is a scientific investigation and not as yet an accepted form of therapy, the primary justification for this activity in respect to both donor and the recipient is that from the study will come new knowledge of benefit to others in our society. *The ethical issues involved in the selection of donor and recipient are a part of the whole complex question of the ethics of human experimentation.* This extremely sensitive and complicated subject is now under intensive study by a number of well-qualified groups in this country and abroad. *Pending the further development of ethical guidelines, it behooves each institution in which a cardiac transplantation*

is to be conducted to assure itself that it has protected the interests of all parties involved to the fullest possible extent.

Rigid safeguards should be developed with respect to the selection of prospective donors and the selection of prospective recipients. An independent group of expert, mature physicians—none of whom is directly engaged in the transplantation effort—should examine the prospective donor. They should agree and record their unanimous judgment as to the donor's acceptability *on the basis of crucial and irreversible bodily damage and imminent death.* Similarly the prospective recipient should be examined by an independent group of competent physicians and clinical scientists including a cardiologist and an expert in immunology. In this instance the consulting group should also record their opinion as to the acceptability of the recipient for transplantation *on the basis of all the evidence including the presence of far-advanced, irreversible cardiac damage and the likelihood of benefit from the procedure.*

Enumeration of the above criteria is based on the conviction that in order to obtain the scientific information necessary for the next phase in this form of organ transplantation, only a relatively small number of careful investigations involving cardiac transplantation need be done at this time. *Therefore, the Board strongly urges that institutions, even though well equipped from the standpoint of surgical expertise and facilities but without specific capabilities to conduct the whole range of scientific observations involved in the total study, resist the temptation to approve the performance of the surgical procedure until there has been an opportunity for the total situation to be clarified by intensive and closely integrated study.* (The Board of Medicine, National Academy of Sciences).[3]

To show the plausibility of the proposition that *good medicine is good morality* we can approach the ethics of heart transplantation from the point of view of the ethician and discover how the analysis leads almost to the statement of the same criteria. In *America* for February 10, 1968, John J. Lynch raises the two questions about heart transplantation operations: Is there any objection to the heart transplantation operation? If not, are there any limitations on attempting the operation? The ethical criteria that Lynch lays down are the following: (1) The heart transplantation is a necessary measure of last resort. (2) There is reasonable hope of substantial benefit to the recipient. (3) Thre is medical and surgical competence on the part of the operating team.[4] His conclusion is that "it does not seem likely that any serious moral objection will be lodged against the procedure so long as the above cautions are observed."[5] Do not both the ethician and the responsible doctor find themselves in

[3] "On Heart Transplants," *Saturday Review,* April 16, 1968, 59.

[4] John J. Lynch, "Ethics of the Heart Transplant," *America,* February 10, 1968, 194–195.

[5] *Ibid.,* p. 195.

agreement especially if their presuppositions include a recognition of the *sacred* inviolability of human life? When there is so much agreement on the criteria of good medicine and the criteria of good morality, some more profound questions that are raised by Lynch may be clarified: "Is human life especially sacred not merely because of the essential dignity of human 'personality,' but because human life is itself removed from man's dominion and reserved to God's providence? If so, to what extent is control of human life exclusively of divine right?"[6] In other words, is it to be admitted that man's right to his own life is not commensurate with a right of ownership but is identified with a right of legitimate use, legitimate stewardship? Is it possible to demonstrate that man does not own his life in the strict sense of proprietary dominion over his life? This brings us to the heart of many of the ethical and moral issues involved in problems of human experimentation, problems of genetic engineering, problems which tax the limitations of legitimate use of one's body and closely approach the area of manifest ownership. Let us develop these considerations gradually.

II. The Extent of Our Right to Life

It seems to me that the problems of determining death are intertwined with the problems of determining life and that this is even more patent for anyone who considers that both life and death are processes. The latter point brings into focus discussions on abortion and the possibility of getting down to the nitty-gritty in ethical choices in a pluralistic society where opinions on ethics and morality are so diverse.[7] Our attention is focused not on the beginnings of life but on the process of death. We are asking the medical profession what are the criteria that should be recognized now in the light of the most recent transplantation procedures.

Whatever contribution the philosopher-ethician might make to this discussion with members of the medical and legal professions might proceed in this fashion. Each one of us in regard to one another has a juridical right to life permitting us to terminate the life of another only when necessary in the event of an unjustified attack upon our lives. The criterion is always the employment of commensurate force in order to tranquilize the assailant and not necessarily to pulverize him. This right, which everyone has to his own life with respect to another, is not commensurate with a right of ownership over our lives. It is here where the

---

[6] *Ibid.*, p. 195.

[7] Thomas A. Wassmer, S. J., "Questions about Questions," *Commonweal*, LXXXVI, 15, June 30, 1967, 416–418; "The Crucial Question about Abortion," *The Catholic World*, CCVI, 1232, Nov. 1967, 57–61.

embarrassing question of Albert Camus is submitted to anyone who considers that the evidence is demonstrable and probative for denying man's ownership over his life. In *The Myth of Sisyphus* Camus asserts that the one problem in philosophy is the problem of suicide, the problem of showing with a minimum of presuppositions that man does not own his life and that life has a value that must always be recognized. Camus saw the difficulty of demonstrating that life has a value in a society that has cheapened it so much through war and increasing depersonalization. Without the admission of a number of presuppositions, one of which would be the radical contingency of man's nature in relation to an Absolute, there seems to be no apodictic, probative, demonstrable evidence against suicide. If the arguments against suicide are not compelling unless the discussant admit the presuppositions that go along with the evidence, neither is the implicit proposition compelling that man has no right of ownership over his life. Nevertheless, the right each man has over his life is one of stewardship and this right is enormously wide. It can certainly include situations in which it might be said that man has the right to die.

III.   Ordinary Means for Preserving Life

What does this mean? It means that a man ought to keep his life going by using those means which in the judgment of the medical profession are ordinary means. While the term *ordinary* is a relative, situational term, historically conditioned, some formulation may be offered as to its general outlines. *Ordinary means*, it seems, would include those medicines, operations, and treatments which not only can be lawfully obtained and applied without excessive cost, pain or inconvenience but which also offer appreciable benefit to the patient insofar as they promote the interests of his life (temporal and spiritual) in the discharge of acts that are human acts and not only the acts of a vegetable or an animal.[8] The judgment of what in the concrete case constitutes ordinary means is not a mathematical one but the judgment of reasonable, responsible medical men. An illustration might help:

> In a case of extensive paralysis of the respiratory muscles, due to poliomyelitis, it is possible to keep the patient alive for months by performing a tracheotomy and applying artificial respiration through a tracheotomy tube. There is no possibility of recovery, or even, owing to irreparable damage to the brain, of a return to conscious life, and incessant attention will be required to keep the patient breathing. Is it allowable to omit or

---

[8] Gerald Kelly, S. J., *Medico-Moral Problems* (St. Louis: The Catholic Hospital Association, 1959), pp. 128–134.

discontinue this artificial respiration and allow the person to die by natural asphyxiation?

In the case proposed, the method used to keep the patient breathing seems to be clearly extraordinary. If, therefore, the doctor knows that patient had no desire to be kept alive artificially, once all hope of real recovery and even of conscious life has ceased, or if he can reasonably presume that this was his state of mind and will at the moment of losing consciousness for the last time, he would certainly seem to be at liberty to refrain from the tracheotomy or discontinue the artificial respiration. In doing so, he is not killing by direct and positive act, but merely acknowledging defeat. When Arthur Hugh Clough wrote, in his ironical version of the modern man's decalogue:

> Thou shalt not kill; but need'st not strive
> Officiously to keep alive,

he was unintentionally but accurately stating a principle which has a correct moral and ethical application. No man may lawfully hasten his own death or another's death by direct means, but he is not bound to resist the natural approach of death as though it were the supreme evil, and if, when ordinary means of resistance have failed, he chooses to yield, it appears unwarrantably officious on the part of the doctor to prolong the struggle, especially a futile struggle, by extraordinary means. It is therefore a question of determining the will of the patient and the chances of success. If the patient has indicated that he wants to cling on to life as long as possible, however painfully or precariously, the doctor must normally struggle to the end with all the means at his disposal. Many doctors, especially those who have a conscientious respect for the moral law and the Hippocratic oath, tend to assume that this is always their duty, except when they are instructed otherwise. It is, in general, a tendency to be encouraged, not only as a counterbalance to the tendency of other doctors to accelerate death by positive euthanasian methods, but also as a powerful contributory factor in the progress of therapy and surgery.

Nevertheless, it seems that the patient's expressed or presumed desire to cling to life can, as a rule, be reasonably interpreted to mean *human* life, not just any kind of vegetative or animal existence. When therefore, as in the case proposed, there is no further possibility of a return to *conscious* life, we consider that the doctor can conscientiously and even laudably abandon the struggle. Doctors are always expected to keep up the struggle against disease itself, but not to the extent of treating their patients as objects to be experimented upon. One moralist, in the course of his investigation into this problem, was informed by religious in charge of a hospital for incurable cancer patients that they *never* used artificial life-sustainers; they merely did their best to alleviate the pain and to prepare the sufferer for a happy death. He remarked that it was a respectable attitude toward death by those who were convinced that life had a theological dimension that had to be honestly faced.

The ethician, therefore, would admit that a person has the right to die if he has the right on occasion to refuse the use of extraordinary means to promote his life. For instance, this might be the case for a person who might be told that he must continue in an iron-lung for the rest of his life. To omit the extraordinary means might under the circumstances bring about death; but this is not morally the same as positing an affirmative act which is productive of death *per se*. Admittedly it is here where most examination must be done because it can plausibly be asked just where the difference lies in accelerating the dying process by acts of commission as well as by acts of omission.

Father Charles Curran is one moralist who has raised this question in a dialogue with Dr. Robert White, a neurosurgeon who directs the Brain Research Laboratories at Cleveland Metropolitan General Hospital. In elaborating on the concept of death as a process, Father Curran pointed out the hang-up that we run into concerning euthanasia: "If death is a process rather than an instantaneous event, then we can ask: What about the morality of hastening the dying process by acts of commission as well as by acts of omission? What, ultimately, is the difference between the two from an ethical standpoint?" Let us look to his additional remarks:

> Many times, acts of omission can be more reprehensible than acts of commission. On the other hand, if we eliminate the traditional distinction that Catholic moral theologians have always upheld, where will this lead us? All of a sudden, you see the myriad possibilities to which this could rise. In one sense, the theologian is always involved in drawing lines, and there are inevitably certain inconsistencies in where the lines are drawn. But if we erase the lines altogether, if we give the state or anyone else unlimited control over human life, this could have terrible consequences. We've seen enough of this in recent history to cringe instinctively at the thought of surrendering such power to the private judgment of individuals.[9]

The ethical problem of the difference between the commission of certain acts and the omission of extraordinary means to keep the patient alive becomes very acute when consideration is given of certain pain-killing drugs which have the concomitant effect of accelerating death. While traditionally the employment of such drugs might be justified

---

[9] Dr. Robert White and Charles Curran, "The Morality of Human Transplants," *Sign*, March 1968, 23–29.

on the principle of the double effect, it is hard to see at times how the effect of death is not involved in the very intentionality of the administrator. It seems somewhat unreasonable to assert that a patient who is given such drugs in order to eliminate pain, although the process of death is going to be accelerated, is always unaware of this combined intentionality in the minds of his physician and his family. In fact, it could be conceived that the patient—before he ever went into the final stages of his terminal illness—might advise both physician and relatives that he would prefer to have these pain-killing drugs administered to him which have the concomitant effect of accelerating his death. Many would look upon such intentionality with regard to death not as an object of indirect intention but as one of direct intentionality. The traditional justification for these drugs according to the principle of double effect seems to be strained here and to invite an explanation that might be defensible in theory but does not confront realistically a patient directly intending his death in this context. Moralists will have to face this problem more and more despite the fact that embarrassments follow in its wake.

We have been using the concept of death as if there were complete agreement on its meaning. The symposium at Villanova gave evidence of the difficulties confronting the medical profession in offering a definition of death to the legal profession. If the legal profession waits upon the medical profession for such a definition, so does the philosopher-ethician. For that reason, the philosopher-ethician must consider the general and specific meanings that have been given to death.

IV. DEFINING DEATH

Death is essentially defined as the cessation of the integrated life functions.[10] These vital functions include respiration, heart beat, and cerebral activity. When these are operating normally, the human organism is physiologically integrated and psychologically functional. The phenomena of dying can be considered a process which occurs gradually and which involves two main phases[11]: *clinical death* and *biological death*.[12] *Clinical or medical death* is taken to mean the diagnosis of death made on the basis of the following physical phenomena: "the final cessation of the

---

[10] Vincent J. Collins, M.S., M.D., *Principles of Anesthesiology* (New York: Lea and Febiger, 1966), p. 34.

[11] From the standpoint of religion, some refer to "theological death"—the withdrawal of the soul. Others use the terms: intellectual death, spiritual death, social death. Our concern is with the two mentioned.

[12] Vincent J. Collins, "Iatrogenic Cardiac Arrest," *New York State Journal of Medicine*, LXI (1961), 3107.

vital functions" (*Oxford Universal Dictionary*) and "the apparent extinction of life, as manifested by absence of heart beat and respiration" (*Dorland's Illustrated Medical Dictionary*). Clinical death is a deduction from perceptible signs. *Biological death* is the cessation of vital activities in cells and the loss of the capacity to return to a functional state. A notable differential exists between cells of the body with respect to the time of death. This is evidenced in the fact that thymic and lymphatic tissue begin to age, regress, and die during the first months of life whereas after clinical death has occurred, the hair and nails continue to grow for several days. Since today the characteristics of death, such as absence of pulse and lack of respiration, are produced and reversed by physicians, Dr. Vincent J. Collins recommends that clinical death should be considered as "the cessation of 'sustained and spontaneous' vital functions."

In the United Nations Vital Statistics, death is defined as the permanent disappearance of every sign of life. Dr. Jorgen Voigt of Copenhagen points out how according to this definition it cannot be accepted that an individual has died when the function of the brain only has ceased.[13] He is critical of this definition as not being sufficiently comprehensive and offers this one as his own: "Death has occurred when every *spontaneous vital* function has ceased permanently." He gives this reason for his revised definition: because "in the definitins of death and life respectively, more subtle biological expressions of life such as residual muscular contractility, cellular motility, etc., are ignored. It is physiological life and not vegetative life which is of significance."[14] Professor Dalgaard in Denmark recently distinguished three forms of death: in addition to (1) reversible asphyxia and (2) irreversible death, he also included (3) suspended death, i.e., a condition in which the brain is irreversibly dead but where the circulation and respiration are maintained by artificial means.[15] Professor Voigt takes exception to the last meaning of death: "for formal reasons, I hesitate to recognize the last expression because in the expression 'suspended death' there remains a suggestion that death has not yet occurred and this implies, for instance, that one would hesitate to remove organs in this phase. For the sake of clarity, the expressions of life and death should be retained as the only alternative and the rare states of asphyxia regarded as a form of life."[16]

Dr. Voigt refers to the clear statement made by Pope Pius XII in 1957 and how it applies to cases of cardiac transplantation:

---

[13] Jorgen Voigt, M.D., "The Criteria of Death, Particularly in Relation to Transplantation Surgery," *World Medical Journal*, XIV, 5, Sept.-Oct. 1967, 144.

[14] *Ibid.*, p. 144.

[15] *Ibid.*, p. 144.

[16] *Ibid.*, p. 144.

These deliberations bring us to the question of when measures such as mechanical artificial respiration and external cardiac massage can and may cease. This question was discussed by Pope Pius XII among others. As early as 1957, he issued a very clear statement which is included in the CIBA symposium. The Pope states that respirators and other mechanical aids are *extraordinary* systems for prolongation of life and that the physician is only under an obligation to institute *ordinary* and not extraordinary measures. If the physician is convinced that there is no hope of reviving a patient who is virtually dead, then he is under no obligation to continue with these measures.[17]

He continues by saying how he himself would apply these norms:

I believe that it is of primary importance not to get unawares into a situation in which it may be necessary to make a decision regarding the continuance of respirator treatment. Before institution of such treatment, as with every form of therapy, a decision must be taken as to whether it is *indicated*. If not, it should be refrained from just as the surgeon does not find indications for operation in hopeless (inoperable) cases of cancer. According to most recent opinions, even the indications for so-called palliative interventions in inoperable cancer patients are doubtful (Halkier and Skafte Jensen).

Technical progress has offered and will continue to offer the medical profession unsuspected possibilities.

The question of extent of therapy must be seen in relation to other patients' medical and nursing requirements. Even if there may soon be no limits to the technical possibilities, it is our duty to ensure that development does not run amok and cause damage. Nowhere do human and economic resources suffice to do *everything* in *every* case. We must attempt primarily to know the indications for certain treatments and then invariably adhere to them.[18]

Recent advances and extensive use of transplantation techniques have brought with them a specific detailed elaboration of the phenomena of death. It may be true that men in unrelated (non-medical) positions may wish to develop the definition of death, but it must be understood that "the diagnosis of death must be the task of the doctor and that no legal rules can be drawn up for it."[19] Dr. Voigt considers that in a particular case, if brain damage has caused brain function to cease and if spontaneous circulation and respiration have ceased as well, then in his judgment the patient is dead according to the definition we cited above.

If the question then arises of his being a donor in a transplantation procedure, it may be justified to continue or institute cardiac massage

---

[17] *Ibid.*, p. 145.
[18] *Ibid.*
[19] *Ibid.*, p. 146.

and artificial ventilation to maintain the circulation of the organ to be transplanted in the brief interval until it is removed. There will inevitably come a time, sooner or later, when it is in the interests both of the patient and his relatives to stop unrewarding treatment. No one can be interested in being doomed to a "technical life" which is not a life at all but a soulless vegetative dependence upon one or more machines.

Medical progress is accompanied by new ethical problems. Sometimes these problems must be solved radically and rationally so that they do not persist as barriers. I consider that in the long run the public will come to accept the above-mentioned points of view, although establishing the criteria of death is scarcely a problem suitable for public vote.[20]

Because of the dynamic state of research and the discovery and quantity of data flowing in from all fields of natural science, there has not been any universal, accepted, official delineated criteria upon which to base a valid definition of death. But there now is a comprehensive outline which very likely will serve as the foundation upon which will be organized a detailed set of norms serving as the standard to be followed by all physicians in all countries. In the CIBA symposium certain criteria were offered to determine when the vital functions have ceased definitely. Greater experience is necessary in order to act with complete certainty but these 5 criteria were proposed by Alexandre of Brussels:[21]

1. Complete bilateral mydriasis.
2. Complete abolition of the reflexes.
3. Complete cessation of respiration five minutes after cessation of mechanical respiration.
4. Falling blood pressure (maintenance of blood pressure demands increasing doses of vasopressure drugs) and
5. Flat EEG, for four hours.

Alexandre requires all 5 of these criteria to be fulfilled prior to removal of a kidney. A flat EEG for five minutes is not adequate proof that brain function is definitely abolished. In the CIBA symposium, it is mentioned that the EEG should be followed up four hours before there can be any certainty that no restoration will occur. During the discussion Revillard added two additional criteria: (1) cessation of cerebral circulation as determined by angiography and, of lesser importance, (2) cessation of reaction to atropine. Dr. Voigt considers that these seven criteria introduce nothing new and that the most important criterion is actually the classical observation that death has occurred when spontaneous circulation and spontaneous respiration have ceased. Further, he thinks that "the question of *cerebral death* is of significance in determining whether there are indications for continued artificial mainte-

---

[20] *Ibid.*, p. 145.
[21] *Ibid.*

nance of respiration and circulation, but is not in itself a criterion of death." If only one of the vital functions continues spontaeously, Dr. Voigt maintains that the indications are present for maintaining the others artificially to the greatest possible extent. Under such circumstances "the patient remains inaccessible to the transplantation surgeons. How long the action of the heart and the activity of the brain should be followed electrocardiographically and electroencephalographically in order to be certain that spontaneous functions have ceased—this is left to the clinical staff." On the basis of present experience Dr. Voigt does not consider that this question can be answered with complete certainty. The determination as to when death has occurred should be left to the medical team in charge of the donor patient and not to the surgical team. In this way it will not cause undue anxiety among patients and their relatives and possible suspicion that the diagnosis of death has not been established on completely objective grounds.

With almost all of these precautions taken, and with these criteria for death, almost all ethicians would agree. On this matter of life and death Dr. C. Frederick Kittle, professor of surgery and head of the section of thoracic and cardiovascular surgery at the University of Chicago, made a statement with which most moralists would be in agreement: ". . . there are many forms of death; there is no need to reiterate these. But I think one has to differentiate between life and death in the pure biological sense such as is used, say, for describing a live bacteria or a live lower animal and the life of a human being. After all, life to a human means that not only is he breathing, that his heart is beating, but that he also has a worthwhile and an appropriate relationship to his environment."[22]

V. CEREBRAL ACTIVITY AND DEATH

We referred before to the electroencephalogram and to its use in ascertaining the amount of brain damage. This is one of the more recent techniques developed for extended diagnosis of patients. It is an electronic instrument which measures and records the bioelectrical impulses of brain tissue and enables the examiner to evaluate comparatively the condition of health or disease in the brain. With this instrument at his disposal and with the recognition that the brain is the center of intellectual and emotional—therefore of human—life activity, this vital organ has been recognized as of equal importance in determining the phenomenon of death just as previously the heart and breathing apparatus (the

---

[22] This observation was made in a radio discussion concerning heart transplantations on April 21, 1968.

lungs) were. EEG response is one of the chief criteria in determining when a human organism has died. We saw this in the criteria set up by Alexandre, Revillard, and Voigt. Because of the importance of this criterion in determining human death, it might be helpful to elaborate on this aspect of death and the attitude of the ethician towards the use of this criterion. In a recent edition of the *Journal of the American Medical Association*, Dr. H. Hamlin stated the function of the EEG: "The bioelectric activity of the living brain is silenced by anoxia which soon produces cerebral death (Anoxia is the condition wherein due to the lack of oxygen—usually caused by insufficient blood supply—cellular metabolism is disrupted and becomes irreversibly damaged) . . . Respirators and heart stimulators can maintain the look of life on the face of death while agonizing and expensive prolongation of false hope continues for all concerned." Dr. Hamlin says that "when the brain is so compromised, the EEG can signal the point of no return, although the cardiovascular system continues to respond to supportive therapy that produces a respectable EEG." Furthermore he says that "supportive efforts should be continued only so long as the brain shares physiological response together with heart and lungs. Adequate experience has been analyzed to show that competent application and interpretation of the EEG should gain medical approval for legal pronouncement of human death."[23] The French Academy of Medicine has defined death on the basis of brain function. If the brain is damaged beyond repair, as demonstrated by certain medical tests, even if the other organs of the body are healthy and functioning, the patient may be declared dead by a special committee for such a purpose.[24]

The crux of the matter is therefore to frame a definition of irreversible cessation of central nervous activity. In Sweden a team of medical experts, of which a prominent member is Dr. Gunnar Biörck of the Karolinska Institute, has differentiated three stages in loss of brain functions:

(1) *"sopor,"* with reflex functions maintained; these are the cases where maintenance of medical care can lead to recovery even after months;
(2) *"coma,"* with loss of muscle tonus, poor brain reflexes and poor function of respiratory, vasomotor and temperature-regulating centres; here recovery is again possible;
(3) *"abolished brain function."*[25]

---

[23] H. Hamlin, M.D., "Life or Death by EEG," *Journal of the American Medical Association*, CXC, 2 (1964).

[24] J. A. Fabro, "Transplant Ethics," *Commonweal*, LXXXVIII, 4 (1968), 118.

[25] "The Moment of Death," *World Medical Journal*, XIV, 5, Sept.–Oct. 1967, 134.

The working group would base a definition of death on two findings—a knowledge of the irreversible nature of the brain injury, and "the presence of stage 3 unconsciousness for say up to one hour." In an editorial in *The World Medical Journal*, September-October 1967, the writer offers these sobering words:

> However, proof of abolition of all brain activity depends on the presence of experts and equipment. Many deaths will still be certified in traditional manner. We may therefore see "two moments of death" recorded, that of brain death and that of circulatory arrest. Whether a change in the law in this sense could be made is something which the working group wisely refuses to pronounce upon at this stage. It will need a lot of education of the public to introduce a change so radical and so likely to arouse misgivings in older citizens, unjustly suspicious of collaboration between certifiers of death and their surgical colleagues, whose needs will become even more urgent when heart transplantation becomes a practical procedure.[26]

That these concerns raised in the editorial are constantly experienced by others is evident from an announcement made on May 9, 1968 by The American Heart Association. It stated that an investigation will begin into the scientific, legal and ethical problems arising from heart transplantation. Dr. Lewis E. January, chairman of the association's committee for medical and community programs, said the study would seek to develop detailed guidelines for heart transplantations that could be used by the medical profession and the public. The areas to be investigated by committees of the association are the establishment of criteria for death and the rights of the heart donor; the setting of criteria for the selection of a heart recipient; the identification of potential donors, the setting up of organ registries, and establishment of legal safeguards for donor, recipient and physician.[27]

VI. "BRAIN DEATH" AND "HEART DEATH"

Irreversible brain damage or irreversible loss of brain function has been proposed as a substantial norm of human death by Cohn of Stanford University. In "World Medical News" for April 28, 1967, Cohn said that "Physicians would prefer the criterion of death to be the cessation of brain function for 48 hours as indicated by an absence of waves in the electroencephalogram, rather than cessation of the heart beat. It is possible for the heart to go on beating for days after the brain has passed beyond possible recovery." The philosopher-ethician would not

---

[26] *Ibid.*, p. 134.
[27] *New York Times*, May 9, 1968.

oppose this definition of human death if it were the consensus of responsible, prudent, and conscientious doctors. From the above it does seem evident that "brain damage" is the proper criterion to be used in assessing the death condition in human beings. Before the electrical nature of that, perhaps, most vital organ—the brain—was recognized, the heart, thought to be the center of integrating activity in the human structure, was regarded as the principal organ upon which to evaluate the life or death of an individual. Now science recognizes the brain as man's central physiological and psychological integrating faculty and so properly uses this information to assess the condition of his existence. Dr. Gunnar Biörck of Sweden, professor of medicine at the Karolinska Institute, head of the department of medicine at the Serafirmer Hospital in Stockholm and scientific counsellor to the Royal Board of Medicine, points out how before the development of modern techniques of resuscitation and intensive care, things were reasonably simple:

The mutual interdependence of brain activity, heart and circulation, and respiration invariably resulted in death if and when one of these was critically severed. Inasmuch as consciousness disappears within 10 seconds of the cessation of circulation, and complete and permanent loss of brain function occurs within 15 minutes thereof, the disappearance of heart action or of the pulse or the last gasping breath shortly thereafter, becomes a simple and mostly reliable sign of death in the sense of complete breakdown of all the vital functions. If one tries to analyze the ultimate determinant of the death concept, this seems to belong to the sphere of consciousness. Thus, it was natural for a long time also in our culture to believe that the heart was the seat of the soul. Later discoveries of the function of the brain have not changed our procedure in stating death, because up to very recently no other possibilities were available. As a consequence, to most people also the concept of death is by tradition linked to the heart rather than to the brain. There can, however, be little doubt that the thing that we are aiming at, when we attempt to resuscitate patients or keep them on life-supporting treatment, is not mainly to keep the heart going but to achieve immediately or sometimes in the future, however distant, some degree of at least partial consciousness in the patient, enabling recognition of persons nearby and mutual emotional contact. This is the reason for which in every country unconscious patients are treated for months and years with available techniques, and in a fraction of these cases the care is ultimately rewarded.[28]

Therefore, because of this interdependence of all man's "parts and organs" and their proper coordination to maintain a healthy organization, the role of man's heart cannot be overlooked. "If the heart stops beating, according to the Swedish working team, brain function stops almost

---

[28] Gunnar Biörck, "On the Definitions of Death," *World Medical Journal,* XIV, 5, Sept.–Oct. 1967, 138.

immediately. The cerebral cortical cells are most sensitive to arrest of circulation, beginning to die within 5 minutes. The whole brain may be considered dead within 15 minutes."[29] Neurologists today state that under proper hospital conditions "brain death" can be diagnosed with at least the same degree of reliability as "heart death." Dr. Biörck admits that it is not easy to say whether the concept of "brain death" is in its essence different from the concept of "heart death" otherwise than with regard to procedure. He cites two apparent features that might signify a real difference to the patient's relatives: "brain death in a patient on life-supporting techniques may precede heart death—whereas in most cases of 'spontaneous death' the reverse is true; and such a patient may be kept warm and rosy until circulation, despite intensive care measures, ultimately breaks down, and the patient arrives at the stage of 'heart death'."

Dr. Biörck knows that the introduction of alternative concepts and procedures in the definition of death will give rise to considerable complications with regard to the civil law.[30] This became evident very early in the symposium in the exchange between Dr. William H. Likoff and the attorney, Emile Zola Berman, when questions were raised whether the medical profession should come up with a clear and distinct definition of death. The ethician has the same set of difficulties as the civil attorney if the medical profession finds problems in offering to them both the results of his own research into the concept and procedure that will structure a definition of death in the light of contemporary scientific knowledge. Even with the indications of "heart death" that are employed at present there are difficulties with the available methods of resuscitation and intensive care. The physician frequently has to decide to use or refrain from using the facilities at hand and this decision must be made in a matter of seconds. However, if pacemakers and pulmonary respirators are used upon the pronouncement of "brain death," it is possible for the patient to live for another day or two until finally the heart fails and "heart death" is stated.

Dr. Biörck distinguishes the two cases of certifying clinical and medical death by "heart death" and "brain death" in this way: "This means that the time of death, which formerly depended mainly on factors *within* the patient, may now depend increasingly on factors outside the patient: the availability of facilities, the decision to resuscitate, the choice of alternative death concepts and the decision to discontinue treatment." He admits that it is hard to tell whether any new legislation will be

---

[29] *Ibid.*, p. 138.
[30] *Ibid.*, p. 139.

attempted in Sweden relating to the definition of death. What he says about his own country can be applied equally to the United States: "It is unlikely that the medical profession will avail itself of new concepts and new procedures, unless public opinion has cleared its mind and some kind of agreement has been reached concerning what is ethically and legally acceptable."[31]

Dr. Frank J. Ayd, in his *Medical-Moral Newsletter* for January 1968 cites the case of a team of surgeons headed by Professor Clarence Crafoord of Karolinska Institute in Stockholm who removed, with her husband's consent, a kidney from a dying woman with irreparable brain damage and transplanted it into a patient with kidney disease. When objections were raised against what had been done, Professor Crafoord defended the operation. He said: "Don't keep already dead people alive . . . A surgeon must feel that it is not his duty to give help to a person whose brain does not function. . . . *What I want is a modern moral, ethical, religious, medical, and legal definition of the death concept.* The basis for such a definition must be: you are dead when your brain doesn't function any more—not when your heart has stopped beating. When the electrical activity of one's brain stops—which can be measured—life is gone and what's left is only a surviving organism which can be used to save the lives of other people."[32]

VII. When Is a Person Dead?

More and more physicians are becoming concerned with this question—when is a person dead? Not every physician will be as determined and fixed in his attitude as Dr. Crafoord. As Dr. Ayd points out in his *Newsletter* the question of guidelines that are morally and legally acceptable should be the concern of everyone—philosophers, theologians, moralists, lawmakers and judges. There is no legal definition of death based on twentieth-century facts. In some way the moral and ethical consensus of society must become known before any law is framed which is intended to reflect that consensus. In the view of many doctors once the human brain has undergone irreversible damage, thereby producing a flat EEG reading over a certain period of time, even if the patient's other vital organs are alive and functioning (possibly by artificial means), the human being is dead because self-consciousness, emotion and understanding are to all reasonable empirical investigation terminated. Where there is extensive brain damage, we know that the dying nervous system dis-

---

[31] *Ibid.*
[32] Frank J. Ayd, Jr., M.D., "Is Brain Death Legal Death?" *The Medical-Moral Newsletter*, IV, 5, Jan. 1968, 18.

integrates by steps and the person dies in stages.[33] Dr. Ayd describes the process: "First there occurs 'clinical or medical death' at which moment spontaneous respiration and circulation cease. 'Biological death' or permanent extinction of life quickly follows unless reanimation procedures are started. If this is done, the brain may be stimulated to function for a time. Nevertheless, at this stage, the patient is immobile with atonic muscles. There are no reflexes. There is no reaction to pain. All vegetative regulations, such as body temperature, cease. Only the heart continues to function. An electroencephalogram (EEG) tracing is totally flat and this many physicians believe justifies the conclusion that the central nervous system is dead."[34]

It is the period of time over which a flat or negative reading is made that is the crucial point of controversy. No definite time has as yet been established and agreed upon by all. Dr. Hannibal Hamlin of the Harvard Medical School at the 1964 annual meeting of the American Medical Association encouraged physicians to use the EEG to establish when the brain has died and declared that this was the means of determining death. Then he recommended that, even though artificially sustained cardiopulmonary function goes on, the pacemaker and the respirator ought to be turned off. A flat EEG is indicative of the cessation of brain activity but the length of time ranges from one minute of EEG silence, three to five minutes, etc. to 48 hours set by the French Academy of Medicine in 1966. At the Ciba Foundation symposium in 1966 Professor Jean Hamburger of Paris attempted to show how unreliable these intervals were and how these difficulties are present if brain damage is considered the sole criterion of death by citing two patients who recovered from barbiturate coma after a "flat EEG for several hours."[35]

Despite this problem of time the French Academy has ruled that a person be declared legally dead when his brain has ceased to function, even though other organs may be kept alive by artificial means. It is precisely here where many physicians would be opposed to the harden-

---

[33] Once the brain has been irreversibly damaged, even if the heart and respiration continue of their own accord for a time, they eventually will cease functioning in a short period in view of the fact that the integrating mechanism (nervous system) of the body has been destroyed. If the brain is not irreversibly damaged, but only the heart or some other vital organ, then medical means can be taken to rectify the disturbance in functioning, i.e., a respirator, heart massage procedure, transplant, etc. can be employed. The case of artificially sustaining the vital organs when the brain is irreversibly beyond repair is an example of extraordinary means to promote the life of the patient.

[34] *Ibid.*, p. 19.

[35] "Is Brain Death Legal Death?" *The Medical-Moral Newsletter*, IV, 5, Jan. 1968, 19.

ing into law of a definition of death that would spell out the exact period of time in which the person is ruled to be dead. This judgment many physicians would prefer to be reserved to them and they would object vigorously against the intrusion of law which would take out of their hands lives that could possibly be restored. While appreciating the reluctance that the physicians have toward a legal definition of death that would hold them responsible before civil law for terminating life even by the omission of extraordinary means, we might begin to raise certain questions concerning the attitude of the unwilling doctors. Dedicated to a scrupulous consideration of the value of life and convinced at times that even the distinction between ordinary and extraordinary means by an ethician is an unfortunate one in application for doctors, the physicians themselves might reasonably begin to raise questions about some of the implicit presuppositions in their unwillingness to agree to any definition of legal death. Before going into the deeper issue that seems to underlie the dissatisfaction physicians have with establishing a suitable length of time for a silent or negative EEG, let us examine how some doctors are equally unwilling to accept at all times the distinction that the ethician makes between ordinary and extraordinary means to promote life.

A vigorous defense of what he called "aggressive or extraordinary means of treatment" to prolong life has come from Dr. David A. Karnofsky, of Sloan-Kettering Institute for Cancer Research.[36] As the patient continues in a seemingly inexorable decline, said Dr. Karnofsky, "the state of dying may be protracted by expensive and desperate supportive measures, and the patient is rescued from one life-threatening situation only to face another. Many objective observers, in contemplating this dismal scene, plead with the doctor to let the patient go quickly, with dignity and without pain." He is critical of the deliberate omission of extraordinary means when he says: "withholding of aggressive or extraordinary treatment can be urged and supported by state planners, efficiency experts, social workers, philosophers, theologians, economists and humanitarians. For here is one means of ensuring an efficient, productive, orderly and pain-free society, by sweeping out each day the inevitable debris of life." Roundly rejecting any such advice, Dr. Karnofsky said that life must be prolonged on the ground, among others, that there is always the hope during a temporary reprieve that science will find a more effective and longer-lasting treatment. Temporary relief can be stretched a long way. Dr. Karnofsky cited the case of a patient with cancer of the large bowel. A colostomy relieved an intestinal obstruc-

---

tion. A recurrence of cancer nearby was relieved by X-ray treatment. When the abdominal cavity began to fill with fluid, radioactive phosphorus checked the process. Bronchopneumonia was cured by an antibiotic. Cancer spread to the liver, and again X-rays were used. As liver function progressively declined, many medical measures supported the patient. If some of these treatments had been withheld, according to Dr. Karnofsky, the patient would have died within weeks or days. Successively, they kept him alive for ten months. Dr. Karnofsky puts the question this way: "When should the physician stop treating the patient?"—his answer is direct: "I think that he must carry on until the issue is taken out of his hands."

VIII. THE QUALITY OF LIFE: WHEN IS LIFE HUMAN?

It is obvious that not every one ethically responsible will answer the question in exactly the same way as Dr. Karnofsky and it is here in the diverse answers to the question that we discover diverse attitudes on the *quality* of life. Life is not something merely *quantitative* and *mathematically* measurable. Even the case cited by the doctor above brought ten months more of existence to the patient. What was the quality of that existence during the ten months? *Here is the crucial question which is fundamental and which operates as a dynamic in the thinking of different physicians.* The doctor who finds himself unable to admit to a definition of death established by irreversible brain damage measured by a certain period of time of a silent or negative EEG, however long and protracted that period might be, even the 48 hours of silence of the French Academy of Medicine, certainly displays a great respect for life, whatever the quality of life might be during the use of all means, ordinary and extraordinary. This attitude should be respected because it gives the widest berth to euthanasia; it completely avoids anything like defeatism; it is surely easiest on the conscience of the physician. There are disadvantages to such an attitude and they should be honestly confronted. The principal one is that it creates the impression that physical existence of whatever quality, even a prolonged vegetative life with no reasonable promise of a return to rational consciousness, is valued by everyone in exactly the same way. Death is looked upon as the greatest evil—a strange attitude to be adopted by patients who are convinced of an after-life.

The moderate position on professional standards strikes the ethician as the more reasonable one. By the moderate position we understand the acceptance by the person as obligated to use all ordinary medical procedures within his means to prolong his life but not necessarily extraordinary methods. What are the advantages or reasons for this moderate position on what ethical and moral claims may be placed upon the physician in his relation to the patient? In the first place, the moderate position is more in accord with the traditional policy of ethicians in interpreting duty and obligation according to a reasonable limit. Second, it seems to be in accord with a good religious attitude accepted by those patients who admit of an after-life. Thirdly, it appears that it is less likely to impose excessive burdens on the family and the relatives of the patient. The disadvantages of this position are the advantages of the more rigorous attitude toward professional standards. The admission of defeat may be made before it should be made and it might create difficulties in the minds and consciences of the attending physicians. Nevertheless, the moderate position with its admitted presuppositions and admitted disadvantages is to be preferred to the attitude that would prolong life at all times regardless of the quality of existence.

During the Villanova symposium discussion did not develop for too long a period on the *quality* of life and it was precisely here where the discussants were divided. To absolutize physical vegetative existence where there is little likelihood of a possible restoration of rational consciousness displays an attitude toward life and its meaning that invites discussion and reasonable dissent. But here we must be most honest. To appeal to the value of the *quality* of life and not only to the *mathematical quantity* of life as an important factor in the decision to withhold the use of extraordinary means in the case of irreversible brain damage is not the only situation where the *quality* of life ought to be considered. On the subject of abortions and the beginnings of existence, Roman Catholics might well listen to the appeal made by others who raise the point about the *quality* of life, the *quality* of life of the embryo, the *quality* of life of the fetus compared with the mother. It is somewhat inconsistent to advance the importance of the *quality* of life in cases where life is going and not to listen to appeals to the *quality* of life by others as life is beginning to develop and evolve. There is much truth in the observation that "Roman Catholics have a remarkable theology of death but a horrible theology of birth."

It appears true that it is always over presuppositions that people divide and on the application of these presuppositions that they come to diverse conclusions. At the CIBA symposium this became so very clear in the exchange between two doctors. Dr. Cortesini developed the attitude of Pius XII on the question of transplantation and reanimation. After he explained the position of the Pope there was an interesting conversation between Dr. Starzl and Dr. Schreiner. Let us first listen to Dr. Cortesini:

The Pope was asked in 1957 when a doctor should stop artificial respiration to a patient who is virtually dead and is being assisted by a respirator. The Pope replied that the respirator and other systems for aiding circulation were extraordinary systems of prolonging life, not ordinary systems. The physician can give ordinary treatment but is not obliged to give extraordinary treatment. If the family tells the physician to stop the respirator, and if the physician thinks that there is no hope of life being prolonged, he can stop the respirator with a clear conscience. The principle here is that of the double effect. Stopping the respirator does not cause death, because death results from another cause, the disease or injury. From the theological point of view it is very important to differentiate between the action and the effect.

The definition of death is a scientific definition, not a theological one, and theology is not concerned with this point, the Pope said. He says that when the vital functions finally stop then even if the organs are alive there is no longer life in the body. This is very important because it makes a clear distinction between vegetative life in the organs and superior life in the vital functions. The vegetative life is not considered by the Pope to be life in the spiritual sense.[37]

Dr. Starzl addresses himself to this point made by Dr. Cortesini and the difference in presuppositions becomes manifest as one reads his words:

I think all the members of this meeting would support the view that extraordinary measures to prolong vegetative life are not justified. In turning off a respirator, we are discontinuing a form of extraordinary care. However, when we talk about removing between that time and the time of circulatory arrest, our role is no longer passive. Positive action is taken which can further harm the patient—further shorten his declining curve of life, and if unimpaired organs such as the heart or the liver are removed, the physician would be the direct instrument by means of which that curve is terminated.[38]

Dr. Louisell agrees with Dr. Starzl that in the present state of the law life still continues in the conventional sense—e.g., if there is still a heart beat—and that a doctor would incur the danger of a possible charge of homicide if by removal of an organ he causes death, if life still continues in the conventional sense. For the law to be changed there apparently has to come a social and philosophical consensus on this point. Dr. Louisell advises the cooperation of theologians, philosophers and physicians in the formulation of a judgment of propriety before it is crystallized into a definite statutory rule. He considers that the five criteria of Dr. Alexandre, supplemented by the two of Dr. Revillard, might be the starting point for a legal evolution.

---

[37] David W. Louisell, "Transplantation: Existing Legal Constraints," in CIBA Foundation Symposium: Ethics in Medical Progress: With Special Reference to Transplantation (Boston: Little, Brown and Company, 1966), p. 97.
[28] Ibid., p. 98.

Dr. Schreiner points out the philosophical difficulty he has with accepting Dr. Starzl's description of a "declining curve of life":

> This description implies to me that life is quantitative and depends on some biological function. Does this mean that we progressively become less alive? In effect life can be described in terms of blood pressure or biological function, but this brings us right back to the original trap because then one is endowing each specific organ and cellular function with the definition of human life. Heart muscle is particularly viable: electrocardiograms on a dead person sometimes go on for a very long period of time, and long after the heart action has stopped hair growth continues, and so on. To push this to its ridiculous logical conclusion, the lady who gave the HeLa cells from her cervix for tissue culture is now living all over the world in glass bottles in every laboratory that grows tissue cultures. I can't accept a cellular or a quantitative definition of life. *Philosophically one has to have at least a concept that a co-ordinating vital principle exists which is either there or not there.* Our problem is how do we ascertain that the external manifestations of this co-ordinating principle (vital principle) are no longer expressing themselves in this individual? There has to be some medical definition and not a quantitative concept.[39]

Dr. Hamburger shows the difficulty in answering the question about the life or death status of the criminal whose head has been cut off by the guillotine but whose heart and lungs can be kept going for days. Dr. Pickering clarifies the several kinds of death and points out how some of his medical colleagues are concerned with *cytological* death when the concern ought to be *physiological* death and how best to establish this physiological death. He tells the story of a former Professor of Biology at Cambridge who went to the market and bought a piece of beef.

> He cultured the muscle cells in tissue culture in the laboratory and pointed out to his class that there are several kinds of death. Though this meat had apparently come from a dead animal, the cells were alive. He said the extreme form of death was *cytological* death. The next form is *physiological* death when the vital functions have ceased. Another stage is *intellectual* death, which to my mind is immortalized by Gracie Field's song: "He's dead but he won't lie down!" Then there is *spiritual* death, *theological* death and *social* death. What our medical colleagues want is cytological life, and what we are all concerned with in this instance is physiological death.[40]

Dr. Muller summarizes what he considers to be the duty of the doctor when this physiological death has been established from irreversible brain damage:

> Once he is certain that the nervous system is dead and no longer able to take over its controlling functions in the body, the doctor should give

---

[39] *Ibid.*, p. 100.
[40] *Ibid.*, p. 101.

up the struggle on his own responsibility. Clearly he cannot ask the opinions of the family or their permission to stop maintenance of vegetative life, but he must collect all the relevant clinical, biological and electroencephalographic information and maybe after consultation with others participating in the maintenance work draw up a statement justifying his decision to abandon his efforts. If his action is challenged by any authority, he will then have the means to defend his decision.[41]

If these procedures are followed, possibly the consensus will develop for the gradual acceptance by all concerned of the principal criterion of death to be irreversible brain damage testified to by an agreed time interval of a silent or negative EEG.

---

[41] P. H. Muller, "Legal Medicine and the Delimitation of Death," *World Medical Journal*, XIV, 5, Sept.–Oct. 1967, 142.

Also

D. Chauncey Leake, "Technical Triumphs and Moral Muddles," *Annals of Internal Medicine*, LVII, 1967, 44.

Thomas E. Starzl, "Ethical Problems in Organ Transplantation," *Annals of Internal Medicine*, LVII, 1967, 36.

Carl Wasmuth, "Legal Aspects of Organ Transplantation from Living and Cadaver Donors," *Journal of Anesthesia and Analgesia*, XLVI, 1967, 25.

CONCLUDING SUMMARY

My approach in this book arose out of the following observations. It seems to me that contemporary culture can be characterized in four ways: (1) by a sense of historical evolution; (2) by an awareness of subjectivity growing out of developments in contemporary psychology; (3) by a scientific attitude which is suspicious of any position that is not empirically verifiable; (4) by an appreciation of the human situation as described in existential theology and existential phenomenology. In April, 1968 at Princeton, one theologian at the *Fourth Edward F. Gallahue Conference on Theology Today* put it this way: "It is true that theology is no longer happy with the earlier Christian belief that man lives in an unchanging cosmos, possesses an immutable nature and is subject to fixed moral laws. . . . Theology is now caught up in the alluring possibility that history and the future are 'open,' that moral demands can be understood *situationally,* that God and reality may *both* be in process, that man and God may be together co-responsible for the future of man and nature, that truth is to be *created* more than *discovered* by man, that self-fulfillment rather than self-denial should be the mark of the Christian's relationship to his body and his world." A third way of characterizing contemporary culture is by the twin deflation—(1) the deflation of doctrinal absolutes and (2) the deflation of moral absolutes.

Contemporary situational morality has emphasized these points—especially the fact that there is a deflation of strict moral absolutes, that is, in the sense that a specific act is intrinsically evil, always wrong. This is taking place even within the Roman Church, and I find this most healthy. Let me develop this briefly.

Max Weber in *Politics As a Vocation* discriminates between two ethics: (1) *an Ethic of Conviction* is that ethic whose ultimate concern is principle with more or less indifference to empirical verifiable personal consequences; (2) *an Ethic of Responsibility* is that ethic whose ultimate concern is empirical, verifiable personal consequences that result from an act. It seems to me that to absolutize or to polarize the first, or the thrust toward absolutizing or polarizing the first, leads to juridicism, legalism and moralism. This is found in religious traditions and the Roman tradition is certainly involved in the indictment. It seems to me that to absolutize or to polarize the second, or the thrust toward absolutizing or polarizing the second, leads to an extreme form of situational morality, a kind of relativistic utilitarianism, a type of antinomianism. My own position is that we cannot live consistently, constantly, uniformly, just on one of these ethics; we have to live on both and it seems to me that the authentic genuine ethic is the resolution in conscience of the dialectical tension that exists constantly between these two ethics, the *ethic of conviction and the ethic of responsibility.* If this be plausible, then I find that the contributions of situational morality to ethics are the following: (1) it has pointed up the deflation of strict moral absolutes in the ethic of conviction, moral absolutes in the sense that specific acts are always wrong, are always intrinsically evil; (2) it has pointed up the priority in contemporary moral thinking of the ethic of responsibility over the ethic of conviction; (3) it has sharpened the tension that exists between these two ethics, the ethic of conviction and the ethic of responsibility, and made the personal resolution of this tension in personal moral decisions all the more necessary although very difficult. In all of this, conscience for the religious person is revealed as a response with evaluational knowledge and freedom of one person to the

Person of God (Christ) incarnate in other persons. It is the resolution of the dialectical tension that exists between the two ethics, the *ethic of conviction* and the *ethic of responsibility*. The person is the communicating existent who stands at the convergence of a series of relationships arising from his encounter with another person or persons.

It should seem obvious that the morality of *every* man is situational —it all depends on how influential the impact of the principles, or now the cautious generalizations, are in the ethical situation. With the priority now more toward the ethic of responsibility rather than the ethic of conviction, how do we introduce someone, especially the adolescent, into this ethic of responsibility who has not been pedagogically trained in an ethic of conviction? Is it not at least discussible that the finest situationalist, the person who can exercise the best discretion and prudence is the person who has been trained in an ethic of conviction and possibly one of unquestioning obedience to principle and law? One is reminded of Aristotle's conviction that no one should study theoretical moral philosophy, what we now like to call meta-ethics, until he has lived existentially, at least until he is about 40. The drama which represented the professor writing an ethics-text after the chemistry had been somewhat altered is a case in point.

Let's try to put the dilemma in sharpest focus. While it is true, it seems to me, that the priority in ethical decision-making is in the direction of responsibility rather than conviction, how can the adolescent come to terms with this ethic of responsibility when absolutes are eroding and he has not been disciplined to such searching awareness of all the concentric circles going out from his ethical behavior? (This dilemma is marvelously illustrated in that inexpensive production "Sundays and Cybele"!) In short, how do you introduce a genuine morality, a true morality, to one who is unprepared for it? Again, to put it in another way—If situationalism has theoretical and practical respectability, how can it be taught when its demands are so great? Have not some situationalists given the impression that situationalism is an easy ethic when really it is a most difficult one?

Let me take another approach. There is no doubt that situationalism has pointed up the peripheral nature of much of the older morality. Dr. Fletcher likes to put it this way—"it is more moral to go to bed with the woman next door to whom you are not married but whom you really love, than to have coital exercise with your wife whom you hate." How true it is that the superficiality of the older morality is exposed when we put the hypothetical situation into this form: "If the only reason for the morality of the one is the presence of juridical words, and the only reason for the immorality of the other is the absence of the same, then how profound is the older morality?" Now this is appreciated by the young who refer to the phoniness of so much of the older morality. But is there not some phoniness in some of the trivialization of the new morality? Canon Streeter made this point when he was critical of the application of the new morality to the whole question of marriage. He put it this way: "When passion is the arbiter, my own case is always recognized to be exceptional. There never were in history lovers like 'we two,' never were any kept apart by a fate as hard as ours. When Aphrodite whispers in my ear, a principle which admits no exception may nerve me to resist; but if any exception is admitted, *my* case is certain to be the one." In other words, is it not true that there is no greater deception than in situations in which the erotic is in control and the philiac and agapaic are given a back seat? It seems to me that the best situationalists are those who have been disciplined on an ethic of conviction, and those who are most likely to trivialize the ethic of responsibility are the ones who have not been so disciplined. An ethic of conviction in the past structured the character for situationalism. Will there be such structured character entering the situation now?

Let me put this general uneasiness I have with situational morality this way. Situational morality tends to place the emphasis on the ethic of responsibility, on agape, and on the empirical verifiable consequences upon persons. This is as it should be. But does it not tend, in the hands of many situationalists, to display not a neutrality toward principle and cautious generalization but possibly a minimization of principle in not recognizing that *not every* situation is a *crisis situation* for which principle and cautious generalization must be tailored? Dr. Graham B. Blaine seems to be saying this when he is critical of the role of the university with regard to a liberalization of the parietal regulations. In other words, is it not true that by minimizing principle, at least in the more complex ethical situations and contexts, we no longer have any means by which our selfishness (unrecognized, of course) is challenged again and again? The ethic of responsibility by minimizing law in these complex situations loses a good measuring rod for one's own unselfishness. It is difficult, if not impossible, to be selfless, agapaic, kenotic when the control of our selfishness by the constant presence of the principle or the cautious generalization is not consistently being exercised. It seems to me that without the presence of the principle and the likelihood that its application is relevant, without the floor of principle for my moral life but only the ceiling of agape open, the possibility for self-deception increases.

This has been pointed out by others. Peter Bertocci's *Sex, Love and the Person* (Sheed and Ward); Evelyn Millis Duvall's *Why Wait Until*

Marriage? (Methodist) and Wayne Anderson (Congregationalist) show how sexual intercourse out of context undermines the value system of human personality—values such as loyalty, service, and real love. Sexual intercourse is a totality of sharing, of persons, of value systems, etc. In addition, the value system of heterogeneous and socially outgoing sexuality according to Anderson is undermined by an overly permissive attitude towards masturbation. In other words, do not principle and cautious generalizations provide us with the best instrument for non-deception?

Here is one example that I find helpful. It seems to me that it is unquestionable that someone convinced of the immorality of the Vietnam war should not participate in it. However, would it not be some indication of the selflessness of this position if the person so convinced began to consider the empirically verifiable consequences upon others who are not equipped with the same sophisticated conscience? In other words, does it not seem appropriate (and here I begin to show embarrassment) that if situationalism is a genuine ethic, if the ethic of responsibility is now to be accentuated over the ethic of conviction, should not the first responsibility of the conscientious objector be a willingness to show the ethically naive that conscience is elaborate and that prismatic analysis is the prerogative of all free men? I find this to be one of the most healthy results of contemporary breathing for the unsophisticated—no one can escape the situational nature of the ethical enterprise and the discovery by some in my own church that conscience is not the simple imposition of law and principle from without but the agonization of the dialectical tension between the two ethics of conviction and responsibility—this discovery has been one of the most salutary results of the operation of ecclesiastical history.

Select Bibliography in Christian Ethics
(General Recommendation: Consult Bowker Paperback Catalogue)

Barnette, Henlee. *The New Theology and New Morality*. Philadelphia: Westminster, 1967.

Baum, Gregory; Dewart, Leslie, and others. *The New Morality*. New York: Herder & Herder, 1967.

Bennett, John C. *Christian Ethics and Social Policy*. New York: Scribner's, 1946. *Christians and the State*. Scribner's, 1958.

Böckle, Franz. *Law and Conscience*. New York: Sheed & Ward, 1966. (ed.) *Moral Problems and Christian Personalism* ("Concilium," vol. 5). Glen Rock, N. J.: Paulist Press, 1965. *War, Poverty, Freedom*. Paulist Press, 1966. *Understanding the Signs of the Times*. Paulist Press, 1967.

Bonhoeffer, Dietrich. *Ethics*. New York: Macmillan, 1965.

Bourke, Vernon J. *Ethics in Crisis*. Milwaukee: Bruce, 1967.

Brunner, Emil. *The Divine Imperative*. Philadelphia: Westminster Press, 1947.

Cox, Harvey (ed.). *Situation Ethics Debate*. Westminster, 1968.

Curran, Charles E. *Christian Morality Today*. Notre Dame, Indiana: Fides, 1966.

——, *A New Look at Christian Morality*. Notre Dame, Ind.: Fides, 1968.

Enslin, Morton S. *The Ethics of Paul*. New York: Abingdon Press, 1957.

Fletcher, Joseph. *Morals and Medicine*. Boston: Beacon Press, 1960. *Situation Ethics*. Philadelphia: Westminster Press, 1966. *Moral Responsibility*. Philadelphia: Westminster Press, 1967.

Gilleman, Gérard. *The Primacy of Charity in Moral Theology*. Westminster, Maryland: Newman, 1960.

Grossouw, W. *The Spirituality of the New Testament*. St Louis: Herder, 1961.

Gustefson, James. *Christ and the Moral Life*. New York: Harper & Row, 1968.

Häring, Bernard. *The Law of Christ*. 3 vols., Westminster, Maryland: Newman, 1961–66. *Christian Renewal in a Changing World*. New York: Desclée, 1964. *Toward a Christian Moral Theology*. Notre Dame, Indiana: University of Notre Dame Press, 1966.

Higgins, Thomas J. *Ethical Theories in Conflict*. Milwaukee: Bruce, 1967.

Kee, Howard C. *Making Ethical Decisions*. Philadelphia: Westminster Press, 1967.

Keeling, Michael. *Morals in a Free Society*. London: SCM Press, 1967.

Knox, John. *The Ethic of Jesus in the Teaching of the Church*. New York: Abingdon, 1961.

Lehmann, Paul. *Ethics in a Christian Context*. New York: Harper & Row, 1963.

Lepp, Ignace. *The Authentic Morality*. New York: Macmillan, 1965.

Lewis, Clive S. *Christian Behavior*. Macmillan, 1943.

Long, Edward. *A Survey of Christian Ethics.* New York: Oxford U. Press, 1967.

Lunn, Arnold and Lean, Garth. *The New Morality.* London: Blanford Press, 1964.

McDonough, Edna (ed.). *Moral Theology Renewed.* Dublin: Gill and Son; 1965.

McGlynn, James V. and Toner, Jules J. *Modern Ethical Theories.* Milwaukee: Bruce, 1961.

McQuarrie, John (ed.). *A Dictionary of Christian Ethics.* London: SCM Press, 1967.

Mann, Jesse and Kreyche, Gerald (eds.). *Approaches to Morality: Readings in Ethics.* New York: Harcourt, Brace & World, 1966.

Manson, T. W. *Ethics and the Gospel.* London: SCM Press, 1960.

Mersch, Emil. *Morality and the Mystical Body.* New York: Kenedy, 1955.

Michels, Florence. *Paul and the Law of Love.* Milwaukee: Bruce, 1967.

Monden, Louis. *Sin, Liberty and the Law.* New York: Sheed & Ward, 1965.

Morgan, Everett J. *The Social Conscience of a Catholic.* Milwaukee: Marquette University, 1964.

Mouroux, Jean. *The Christian Experience.* New York: Sheed & Ward, 1954. *The Meaning of Man.* New York: Doubleday Image Books, 1964.

Niebuhr, H. Richard. *The Responsible Self.* New York: Harper & Row, 1963.

Niebuhr, Reinhold. *Moral Man and Immoral Society.* New York: Scribner's, 1932. *An Interpretation of Christian Ethics.* New York: Harper & Row, 1935.

Pike, James A. *Doing the Truth.* 2nd ed.; New York: Macmillan, 1965.

Ramsey, Ian (ed.). *Christian Ethics and Contemporary Philosophy.* New York: Macmillan, 1966.

Ramsey, Paul. *Basic Christian Ethics.* New York: Scribner's, 1950. *Nine Modern Moralists.* Englewood Cliffs, N. J.: Prentice-Hall, 1962. *Deeds and Rules in Christian Ethics.* New York: Scribner's, 1967.

Robinson, John A. T. *Honest to God.* Philadelphia: Westminster Press, 1963. *Christian Morals Today.* Philadelphia: Westminster Press, 1964.

Salm, Luke (ed.). *Readings in Biblical Morality.* Englewood Cliffs, N. J.: Prentice-Hall, 1967.

Schnackenburg, Rudolf. *The Moral Teaching of the New Testament.* New York: Herder & Herder, 1965.

Sellers, James. *Theological Ethics.* New York: Macmillan, 1966.

Sloyan, Gerard S. *how do I know I'm doing right?* Dayton: Pflaum, 1967.

Spicq, Ceslaus. *The Trinity and Our Moral Life.* Westminster, Maryland: Newman, 1963.

Thielicke, Helmut. *Theological Ethics.* Philadelphia: Fortress Press, 1967.

Thomas, George. *Christian Ethics and Moral Philosophy.* New York: Scribner's, 1955.

Tillich, Paul. *Morality and Beyond.* New York: Harper & Row, 1963.

Tillmann, Fritz. *The Master Calls.* Baltimore: Helicon, 1960.

Todd, John (ed.). *The Springs of Morality.* New York: Macmillan, 1956.

Vann, Gerald. *Morals and Man.* New York: Sheed & Ward, 1960.

Von Hildebrand, Dietrich. *Christian Ethics.* New York: McKay, 1953.

Woods, G. F. *A Defense of Theological Ethics.* New York: Cambridge University Press, 1966.

INDEX